HAPPY HOUR IN PARADISE

Twelve Years on *Beachouse*

HAPPY HOUR IN PARADISE

Twelve Years on *Beachouse*

Coral Beach

To Susan Shannon —
May you live your
dreams too —
Coral Beach
12-15-09

iUniverse, Inc.
New York   Bloomington

Happy Hour in Paradise
Twelve Years on Beachouse

iUniverse books may be ordered through booksellers or by contacting:

iUniverse
1663 Liberty Drive
Bloomington, IN 47403
www.iuniverse.com
1-800-Authors (1-800-288-4677)

Maps by Creative Force, Inc., Tampa, Florida

ISBN: 978-1-4401-5795-0 (pbk)
ISBN: 978-1-4401-5797-4 (hc)
ISBN: 978-1-4401-5796-7 (ebk)

Printed in the United States of America

iUniverse rev. date: 10/16/2009

To Mom and Dad for providing worldwide adventures for me, Joe, Molly, and Matt and for teaching us the thrill of travel and love of the water. Since you would not write this book, it was left to me. It was done with an awe of your accomplishments, to provide documentation for future generations, and, most of all, as an expression of love.

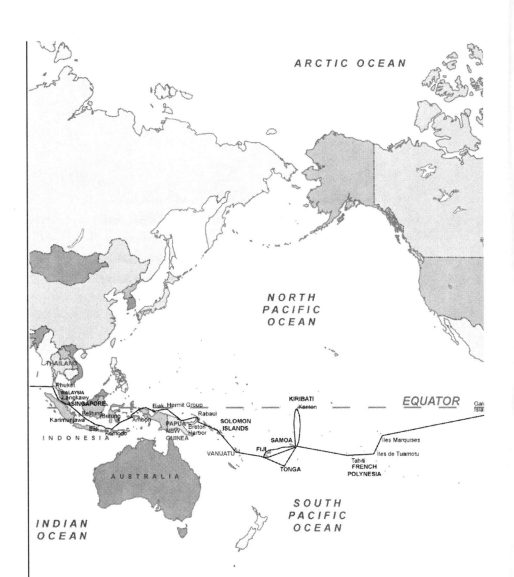

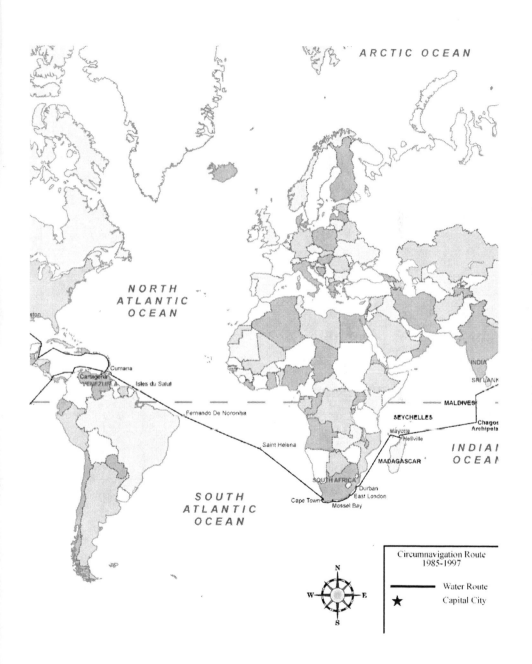

ARCTIC OCEAN

NORTH
ATLANTIC
OCEAN

SOUTH
ATLANTIC
OCEAN

INDIAN
OCEAN

Cumana
Cartagena
VENEZUELA
Isles du Salut
Fernando De Noronha
Saint Helena
SEYCHELLES
Mayotte
Nosy Be
MADAGASCAR
SOUTH AFRICA
Cape Town
Mossel Bay
Durban
East London
INDIA
SRI LANKA
MALDIVES
Chagos
Archipela

Circumnavigation Route
1985-1997

——— Water Route
★ Capital City

N
W   E
S

Contents

List of Letters

List of Maps and Illustrations

Preface

From 1985 to 1997, Buford and Jerry Beach sailed the oceans of the world on their yacht, *Beachouse*. There was no Internet, and satellite trans-ocean communication was expensive; cellular phones were nonexistent. VHF radio or written letters were yachts' only methods of communication.

Jerry Beach wrote letters to her family and friends during *Beachouse*'s twelve-year circumnavigation. The thirty-six letters are printed as written. Only minor grammatical errors and misspellings have been changed.

Between Jerry's letters is narrative describing happenings that are not detailed in her letters. Direct quotes from Jerry's daily diaries, which she kept beginning in 1981, are interspersed throughout. All diary quotes are in italics, beginning with the date of the entry.

Another source of material is Buford Beach's Navigator's Log Book, the captain's daily account of *Beachouse*'s location and movement. Lastly, firsthand accounts of visits to *Beachouse* by family and friends supplement the written documents.

All photographs were taken by the Beaches or visitors to *Beachouse*.

Introduction

An Excerpt from Letter 36

Duke of York Islands
Near Rabaul, Papua New Guinea
April 2, 1993

Dear Joe and Jan,

We're sitting in a beautiful anchorage in a group of islands about twenty miles from Rabaul. We're waiting for our new sail to arrive from New Zealand so we can move on through the Admiralty Islands to the north coast of P.N.G. at Madang. We are in fifteen feet of white sand, surrounded by palm trees and great reefs for snorkeling and diving—also lots of canoes with little boys in them who love to come and watch the white people. We seem like Martians to them, but they love the hard candies we pass out. They call them "lollies" here. Most of them have a working knowledge of English, as their village schools are taught in both English and Pidgin, the local patois.

Now to answer your questions about the cruising life—including probably more than you want to know. First—"it ain't all beer and skittles" out here for two big reasons. One is that anything that is on, around, or near saltwater immediately begins to rust, rot, corrode, smell, mildew, and rapidly deteriorate. Number two is that the things that must be done for day-to-day living are much more difficult here than at home, where everything is available and convenient. I once made a new burner for our gas grill out of a tuna fish can, and it lasted a year. Jerry does the laundry in a bucket, using her foot for a plunger. You have to improvise a lot.

Our longest crossing was from the Galapagos to the Marquesas. This is the longest leg to be made on a circumnavigation, three thousand miles. Or, to be exact, 2,980 nautical miles. We took just under twenty-two days for an average speed of 5.7 knots. A little slow, but not bad for on and near the equator, where the winds can be very light. This was a very easy crossing, with good weather all the way. Cindy and Roger were on board, so each of us had only one watch each night. Normally, Jerry and I sail the boat alone, and in eight years I have had to get out of the cockpit only twice. Roller furling is the only way to go.

We have never been in really bad weather. We've seen winds of over fifty knots, but in a squally that didn't last long. I call myself a 20-20 sailor. If you stay within twenty degrees of the equator and out of hurricane season, you will almost never be in bad storms.

We don't know how long we will continue sailing, but obviously, at least long enough to finish our circumnavigation. We are still enjoying it, and the old bodies are hanging in there.

Buford and Jerry

*****

Introduction

In a small town in the Rio Grande Valley where they'd grown up, Buford Curtis Beach and Mary Geraldine (Jerry) Radford were married on May 14, 1949, in Mission, Texas. Buford, twenty-six years old, was a crop duster, and Jerry, eighteen, was a bank bookkeeper.

Depression-era children, they came from broken homes with little money. Buford's father left when he was a small boy and was never a part of his life. His mother made a meager living as a clerk for the Hidalgo County Water Department. She shuffled Buford among his aunts while he attended various valley schools.

At sixteen, Buford worked for a crop duster after school and during summer vacations. He got free flying lessons on Sundays as a bonus for his labor. He dusted crops commercially, which exempted him from the World War II draft until 1943; dusting was considered an essential occupation. In 1946, after serving for three years in the Army Air Force, Buford was discharged and returned to crop dusting in Mission, Texas.

Jerry's parents divorced when she was a teenager. Her older brother died when he was nineteen and Jerry was seventeen. She was outgoing and popular—the cheerleader and Homecoming Queen—as well as smart, skipping two grades in elementary school. She had a quick wit, made friends easily, and could talk to anyone. Her creed was to always treat people nicely and they would return the favor.

In the 1940s, women commonly married and started families rather than attend college. So in June 1948, after one year at Texas Agricultural and Industrial College, Jerry moved back to Mission to be with her girlfriends. Buford and Jerry met, dated—somewhat scandalously since Buford was eight years her senior—and married within a year.

With a wife to support, Buford went to work as a pilot for Clint Murchison Sr., an oilman from Dallas, Texas. Buford and Jerry made their first trip together—they moved to Tampico, Mexico. Buford ferried passengers and supplies from Tampico to Murchison's privately owned island and ranch. It was an exciting two years for a boy and girl from Mission, Texas.

When Buford and Jerry married, they vowed to create a stable home life for their children, something neither of them had experienced as kids. In 1951 they moved to Dallas, where Buford worked as a pilot for a commercial airline. Their first daughter, Coral, was born in the same year, followed two and a half years later by their second daughter, Cindy.

After flying commercially for two years, Buford switched to corporate aviation, piloting jets for businesses for the remainder of his professional career. In 1983, after nineteen years of service, he retired as aviation manager from Southland Corporation.

The Southland Aviation Department flew many celebrities from all walks of life. Buford had Secret Service clearance and was authorized to fly all government officials up to and including the vice president. Henry Kissinger and John Connally, the Texas governor, were frequent passengers. Sports and show business personalities were often on board, among them Bob Hope, Jerry Lewis, and Darrel Royal. One of Buford's favorite passengers was the physicist Dr. Edward Teller, a very interesting person; among his least favorite were the Duke and Duchess of Windsor—too much luggage and not considerate to the help.

Buford was a very quiet man who spoke infrequently, but when he did speak, he often revealed an amusing dry wit. He did not possess the talent for small talk, believing that the less you said, the better—and whatever you said needed to be accurate and true.

With no formal mechanical or engineering education, Buford learned by watching the airplane mechanics who surrounded him at work. He had the patience to fix anything and would endlessly tinker with broken gadgets to find a way to repair them. He took up one new hobby after another that required him to grow or maintain things, such as large saltwater fish tanks and a greenhouse full of hydroponic tomatoes.

Once Buford committed to a project, he was determined to see it through to the end, no matter what happened. For example, he once decided to make a stained glass window for the dining room. He studied how such windows were made and drew an intricate design for his first attempt. It took him many hours to create the four-by-two-feet window. Once the window was installed, he declared that was enough and never made another one.

As one would expect of a crop duster, Buford was a risk taker, but a calculated one. He invested in numerous businesses over the years. His most successful endeavor was building and owning the first hand-operated carwash in Dallas, Texas. His craziest investment was part ownership of a chinchilla farm, which made little profit.

He also invested in real estate. His investment philosophy was like his temperament—patient. He bought early and sold late, which enabled him to hit a homerun on beachfront property on South Padre Island.

While Buford was traveling, often for two or three weeks at a time, Jerry was in charge. She jumped into mothering full force, joining the Parent Teacher Association, singing in the church choir, and leading Brownie troops. She was very creative and an expert seamstress.

Jerry was brilliant and inquisitive. She read copiously and consumed culture in the form of all types of music, from classical to country. Movies were her passion. If you wanted to know who starred in a particular movie, Jerry always knew the answer. She was the reigning lifelong champion of her favorite board game, Trivial Pursuit.

As intelligent and social as she was, Jerry worried constantly about everything; most nights, she got little sleep. In front of a crowd, however, none of this anxiety showed. Buford claimed she could get "a rock to talk." In contrast, Buford worried little. Jerry considered him a "steady rock" in her ocean of anxiety.

Once Coral left for college and Cindy was in high school, Jerry needed something to fill her time. Answering an advertisement in a Dallas newspaper, she became part-owner and manager of the company Purse Strings, which operated several mall kiosks selling women's handbags and accessories. She worked hard helping to expand the company. When she sold her interest in 1981, the company had grown to include several large stores in busy malls in Dallas and Austin.

Buford's flying career provided Jerry with travel opportunities when the corporate jets were not full. These trips sparked their desire to travel together—the more places they went, the more places they wanted to see.

For their twenty-fifth wedding anniversary in 1974, Buford, at the age of fifty-one, and Jerry, at forty-three, took up scuba diving.

Coral Beach

The hobby took them to islands throughout the Caribbean Sea. They chartered trimarans, very stable boats with three hulls, and decided they loved the independent lifestyle of cruising from island to island.

A dream began to grow. Could they live the carefree life as ocean cruisers fulltime? They began planning to do just that.

Setting Up House

October 1980–June 1985

Putting the Dream into Motion

The dream of living a cruiser's life solidified when Buford helped crew a ninety-five-feet trimaran on its maiden voyage from Canada to the British Virgin Islands in 1980. Duncan and Annie Muirhead, friends Buford and Jerry had met through scuba diving, built the sailing vessel (S/V) *Lammer Law* for chartering. Duncan needed help sailing the *Lammer Law* from a shipyard in Canada to its home in Totola, British Virgin Islands. (The *Lammer Law* and its sister ship, the *Cuan Law*, today remain the world's largest trimarans.) Though Buford was a professional airplane pilot and had flown since the age of sixteen as a crop duster, he'd never sailed a boat. The trip on the *Lammer Law* changed his life. Instantly, he decided to build a trimaran and start ocean cruising.

For most people, such a decision might seem rash; but Buford was not one to act impulsively. The trip on the *Lammer Law* employed all his life skills and abilities—navigation, engineering, and world travel. He had seen the world from the air as a professional pilot and now wanted to see it from the water. He'd never had a sailing lesson but thought sailing must be like flying, with the wing vertical instead of horizontal. These were the practical explanations he gave for such a life-changing decision. Deep down, however, he simply thought it would be a wonderful challenge.

Jerry, on the other hand, was not so sure. It was one thing to dream about ocean cruising and another thing to actually go and do it. She was used to her independence and wondered if she and Buford would enjoy being together every day in close quarters.

Most men who have the dream of sailing into the sunset can't convince their wives to join them. After all, while the man is living his life's dream, the wife on a sailboat usually winds up doing what she did at home: cooking, cleaning, and keeping house—except now she's doing it while standing in the water. But Jerry knew Buford was determined, so she figured she might as well hang on for the ride—and it did sound fun.

The search was on for a boat that would have all the comforts of home on the water. There was no need for sleekness or speed; only comfortable living was required. Not finding what they wanted, Buford contacted naval architect Edward B. Horstman, well-known for his Tri-Star multihull designs. Buford and Jerry spent many hours deep in consultation with Horstman, working and reworking the design as they sat around the kitchen table. Trimarans, especially sixty feet long, are rarely used in the cruising world; when *Beachouse* was built, it was the largest trimaran in the state of Texas. Even today, *Beachouse* is pictured on Ed Horstman's Tri-Star Web site as an example of a successful trimaran that circumnavigated the globe.

Jerry sold her interest in several ladies' accessories stores in Dallas to devote herself fulltime to the boat plans. She and Buford chose Galveston Island, Texas, as the building site since their daughter Coral lived there.

Buford was contacted by John Casanova, an experienced Horstman boat builder, and his wife, Joan, who were sailing their catamaran off the British territory of Gibraltar. Casanova had heard that Buford wanted to build another Horstman boat and was interested in the project. In March 1981, Buford sent one thousand dollars to the Casanovas as a retainer for their services. (Later, the Beaches marveled that Buford had sent money halfway around the world to someone he didn't even know to do something he had no idea how to do!) The Casanovas set sail for Galveston to supervise the building of *Beachouse*.

Building Begins

The Beaches created Beach Boat Builders, Inc., a Nevada corporation, to build two identical yachts. Impressed with the boat plans, a friend of Buford's decided to build an exact copy of the *Beachouse* design as a business investment. The Dallas real estate developer planned to take his yacht to the Virgin Islands, hire a crew, and make it available for vacation charters.

In June 1981, the Casanovas arrived in Galveston. For a boat-building location, Buford secured a place at Payco Marina, a small marina at the base of the Galveston Island Causeway. In August, while Jerry began fulltime work on the boat construction, Buford kept working in Dallas, traveling to Galveston on the weekends. For the remainder of 1981, hired workers molded fiberglass for the outer hulls of both boats.

Buford spent every weekend in 1982 going back and forth from his job as an executive pilot at Southland Corporation in Dallas to the Galveston boat construction site. He and Jerry purchased a small house on the beach, close to their daughter Coral and her husband, Joe Murphy, so Jerry could stay fulltime at the building site. It became a cozy refuge from the daily grind of boat construction.

By the end of 1982, the six individual hulls were nearly fiberglassed and almost fully formed.

March 17, 1982. The boat is beginning to shape up. Really big! BC is pleased with the progress. This is the first quote from Jerry's daily diaries. There would be many more boat-related entries in the months and years ahead.

The next step was to put the hulls together to form the boat frame, which required a much bigger construction space than Payco Marina. Buford leased a large tin building on Bolivar Peninsular, thirty miles from the marina, a round-trip ferry ride from Galveston Island across the Houston Ship Channel. The structure was used for building shrimp boats, making it ideal for constructing two sailing trimarans.

Moving the partially constructed hulls thirty miles through a busy urban area and across the heavily traveled channel was quite an ordeal. It required police escort and extra-wide-load trucks to pull the massive fiberglass hulls down the Galveston Seawall and across the ship channel on the Bolivar Ferry.

Building hulls on Bolivar Peninsula, March 1983

Buford retired from Southland Corporation in early 1983. The Beaches sold their house in Dallas and relocated to Galveston Island. This downsizing to a beach house was the first step toward downsizing again—onto a boat.

On August 2, 1983, after celebrating their thirty-fourth wedding anniversary, Buford and Jerry loaded up a trailer and their pet Chihuahua, Linda, and headed to Galveston to build their dream.

An Unpleasant Surprise

Hurricane Alicia passed directly over Galveston Island at 1:45 AM on August 18, 1983, with winds of one hundred miles per hour, only two weeks after Buford and Jerry had settled into their beach house. Their unpacked belongings, stored underneath their house, were washed away.

August 18, 1983. All our underneath (of the house) is gone—as is everyone's. Many houses destroyed.

August 19, 1983. We were in shock last evening. Woke up ready to do a little work. We cleaned and gathered junk all day. All our personal pictures gone—all scuba gear—luggage—tools, etc. Very traumatic.

For several weeks, the Galveston beach community scoured the fields around their hurricane-damaged homes, searching for belongings. Fortunately for the Beaches, the boat-building site, set in a protected marina, was not damaged, and the partially constructed boat hulls were left unharmed by the hurricane.

Learning to Sail

Though Jerry was heavily involved in building a sailboat and planned to cruise the oceans, she had no actual sailing experience. She and her daughter Cindy decided to take a five-day sailing course at a marina in Kemah, Texas, late in 1983.

Each day after the lessons, they returned home to the Galveston beach house with another hilarious story of their misadventures with their instructor, Mike Sweeney.

October 10, 1983. Cindy and I are the only ones in the class. Mike is our instructor. We are a circus. Cindy and I are not the world's finest sailors—but we're learning.

On the second day, after many displays of ineptitude, Sweeney said out loud, "At least I have still never had anyone fall overboard."

October 11, 1983. Another disastrous day at the sail place. Cindy and I are really klutzes. We hit docks and, for a grand finale, I fell overboard.

She and Cindy used the phrase "bombs away" when they turned the wheel away from the direction of the wind because they couldn't remember the official nautical phrase, "helms alee."

On the last day of the course, Jerry begged Sweeney not to send them out alone, which was a requirement for graduation. He denied her request. Jerry took the boat out from the dock only a few yards, panicked, and tried to make her way back to shore. She hadn't mastered the skill of moving the jib to set the boat's direction. Cindy took the helm but didn't fare any better. When they tacked, thinking they'd surely go toward the dock, they ended up pointed in the opposite direction. Jerry became semihysterical. They kept randomly maneuvering for what seemed like hours.

October 14, 1983. Cindy and I went to our last session. I really was a coward. I embarrassed myself. Cindy did all the work. I came home in a blue funk.

After the course, Jerry asked Sweeney if he'd ever had worse students. "No," he replied. "Once there was a couple worse than you, but then they took the two-day course."

Hard Work

Buford and Jerry spent all of 1984 building the boats. Ten- to twelve-hour days were routine. Jerry's duties included bookkeeping, payroll, filing, placing equipment and supply orders, and driving all over Houston to pick up parts—generally acting as a "go-fer." Jerry was soon promoted to painting and varnishing, while Buford's duties included designing and building the electrical, plumbing, and mechanical components. They were constantly tired, dirty, and discouraged with the slow progress of the detailed work of boat construction.

June 12, 1984. Woke up with a sore throat and virus. Off to work anyway—no shirking. We are all working as hard as possible.

June 22, 1984. Up and at 'em. Fatigue is cumulative. I am painting. BC is plumbing and wiring.

Jerry had surgery on a broken nose; she'd been in a car accident while driving home exhausted from a long day of boat building.

Progress on the interior of *Beachouse* began to slow down, and Buford wondered if he could speed up work by taking a more active role. John Casanova officially quit at the end of July, leaving Buford in charge of finishing the construction.

July 30, 1984. We are torn between relief and terror.

Beachouse's sister boat, the *My Way*, was launched, on her way to Florida to have her interior finished. Now, with only one boat in the construction shed, Jerry and Buford could devote all their energies to *Beachouse*. Jerry ran a daily shuttle service to take workers to and from Bolivar Peninsula. After hundreds of trips, her car finally gave out by the side of the road. She sold it for scrap for sixty dollars.

Carpentry work began on the main salon interior. Jerry varnished her life away, and the bottom was painted. Buford wired the cockpit panel and galley.

November 8, 1984. Up and over. All the days run together. Very discouraging.

November 9, 1984. Same old grind. We can't seem to get completely rested anymore. Taking our lunch to boat now.

In December 1984, Jerry wrote the first of many letters that would chronicle their journey around the world.

Letter 1

Galveston, Texas
December 1984

Dear Friends,

We are sitting on the deck facing the sea on Galveston Island. It is a beautiful, balmy Christmas Eve. The sun is shining, and it's seventy-five degrees. We got so many Christmas cards asking about us and the boat that I decided I'd best take pen in hand and write a progress report.

It has been quite a year—year and a half, actually—since we left Dallas; the hurricane, the killing freeze last Christmas, and the oil spill last summer. We've come through them all slightly "bloodied but unbowed."

The boat became much more of a project than we'd ever anticipated. We expected to be on the high seas by now—but here we are, still in a tin barn. Our builder left by mutual consent last July, and BC took on the massive job of finishing both boats. It has been quite an experience. The other boat was launched on September 6 and is now in a yard in Ft. Lauderdale being outfitted. We are finishing our interior ourselves. BC has done all the wiring, plumbing, and mechanical work alone. He did have some help from two of our good diving buddies, who are now living in Houston. They've been great moral support, too. We have two young men working with us fulltime. Ron has been with the project since the beginning and is planning to sail with us. Rick came aboard in October and is doing all the cabinetry. He is a phenomenon—a real craftsman. We were lucky to find him. My role is "go-fer," and a rotten job it is, too. I'm sent for parts and pieces I can't pronounce, much less describe. It is quite an operation.

We've had a lot of visitors in the last year, and those of you who haven't been to see us are missing a real opportunity to see mass confusion at work. We've stopped trying to estimate the finish with any accuracy, but hopefully we'll launch in the spring. It really is going to be a hell of a boat. We think it will be beautiful.

One big plus in the whole project has been the chance to live on the beach close to Coral and Joe. With Cindy in Houston, we've had a chance to be with our girls again on a fairly regular basis. It has been delightful. It's great when your children become your friends. We feel very fortunate. We've also met some lovely people here in our little beach community. We aren't here a lot, though. We leave at 6:45 AM and get home at 6:15 PM five days a week. The boat is in Port Bolivar, an hour's drive minimum each way.

BC and I are together almost every waking moment—great training for the boat. Haven't killed each other yet. Hope you all feel welcome to come visit at any time. My boss might give me a few days off to entertain. We would love to see each and every one of you.

Our love and sincere best wishes for a great New Year.

*****

Description of *Beachouse*

Beachouse was a sixty-feet-long, thirty-three-feet-wide trimaran, meaning it had three hulls made of fiberglass. She accommodated twelve people in four guest cabins, each with a queen-size berth (bed), the owner's stateroom with a queen-size berth, and the crew's cabin with two berths.

The outer hulls, called amas, each contained two guest quarters (staterooms), followed by a separate dressing room with stainless steel sinks. Furthest forward was the head (bathroom), with a toilet and shower.

The main hull (in the middle) contained the crew cabin forward, followed by the crew head with a toilet and shower. Next was an office/work area with a curved desk and storage, followed by the main salon (living area) and galley (kitchen).

Half of the main salon

Below the main salon was a separate pantry, which Jerry called her "root cellar," housing a large built-in refrigerator/freezer and shelves for dry goods storage. Opposite the galley was the navigation station.

Jerry's "root cellar" for food storage

Just outside the main salon was the large thirty-three-feet-by-six-feet cockpit, containing the helm station with a two-person raised helm seat. It was protected with a fiberglass hardtop and four large windshields. Molded fiberglass benches allowed for outside seating with solid teak flooring. The aft (back) part of the main hull contained the owner's stateroom with its own head.

The mast was seventy-five feet high, and the boat was rigged to be sailed from the cockpit and handled by two people. Two dinghies, called tenders, used for transporting crew and equipment to shore, were strapped to the deck during water crossings. They were appropriately named the *Outhouse* and the *Oarhouse*.

A schematic drawing of *Beachouse* is in Appendix A, and a detailed list of the equipment that was on board is in Appendix B.

Outside cockpit with navigation station

Launching the Boat

Buford and Jerry worked feverishly in hopes of launching the boat in March 1985. They planned to put the boat in the water and live on it while finishing the inside. Two of their scuba-diving friends, Dick Littleton and Zenas Clarkson, came daily to help with the plumbing, refrigeration, and electrical work. Again, ten-hour days were the norm.

Beachouse was finally launched at 11:30 AM on March 28, Jerry's fifty-fourth birthday.

March 28, 1985. Had fiasco in coastal canal. Many folks watched and came by for beer and champagne. It seems strange to be on the boat at last.

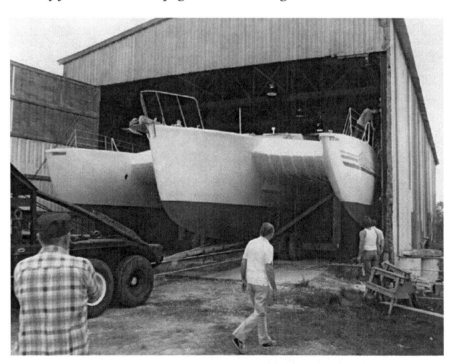

Buford watches the removal of *Beachouse*
from the building shed, in preparation for launching.

Jerry sits on *Beachouse* as it hits water for the first time.

Buford and Jerry spent April 1985 testing the mechanics and trouble-shooting problems. The hydraulic system leaked when it was initiated, covering everyone with hydraulic fluid. The heads (toilets) didn't work properly. The engines were fired up to motor the boat across a small basin, but they didn't work at full speed.

April 21, 1985. The propeller on the port side won't work. Big problems. I'm not sure we'll ever get this thing going.

At 11:00 AM on May 9, a gorgeous day with light winds, *Beachouse* went for its first sail. Everything worked according to plan, and there was a grand celebration afterward. The Beaches set a departure date of late June so their daughter Cindy and her husband, Roger, along with two hired crew, could accompany them on the first voyage.

The Beaches sold their Galveston house and moved the boat to the Galveston Yacht Basin. On June 15, a *bon voyage* party, or "open boat" party, as Jerry called it, was held on *Beachouse*. Friends from all over Texas came to wish them well.

Jerry stocked the boat with food and supplies, and she and Buford took *Beachouse* on cruises to identify any mechanical and electrical failures.

June 23, 1985. We went sailing—what a disaster. Large crowd here. Rigging was a mess, and propeller quit. BC was really down. Hopefully bad rehearsal/good show rule works.

Buford, who was extremely handy and a naturally good engineer, methodically worked through each problem. However, when one part was fixed, another one broke. His talents and perseverance were tested during the shake-out period, but eventually he resolved all the malfunctions. *Beachouse* was finally ready to set sail.

After three years of planning, three years of building, hirings and firings, sales of two houses and several beachfront lots, a hurricane, and a broken nose and car, *Beachouse* left Galveston on June 30, 1985, at 12:30 PM, never to return. Buford, at the young age of sixty-two; Jerry, fifty-four; and boat dog Linda, eleven, finally began their new life as cruisers.

Living on the Caribbean Sea

July 1985–December 1990

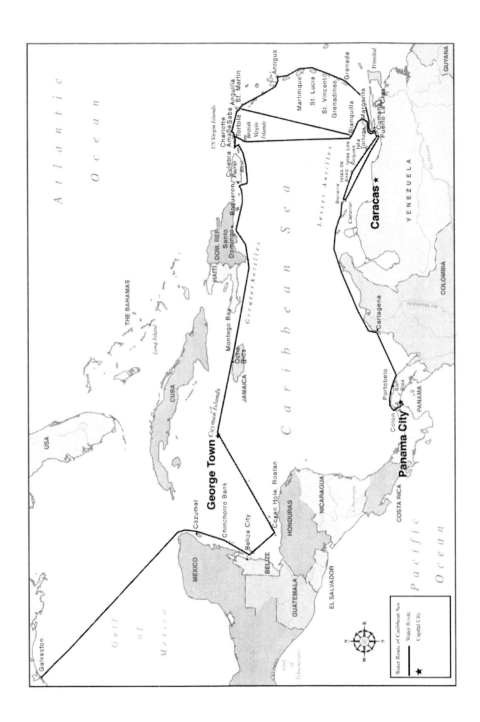

Letter 2

GREETINGS FROM MARGARITAVILLE!

Despite four years of advance notice, we left Port Bolivar on June 30 in such a mad rush that we neglected to say proper good-byes, not to mention a long list of things undone and unpurchased. We had set a goal of July 1, and after missing so many deadlines, we were determined to meet that one.

We pulled out at noon on Sunday and spent the next nine and a half days becalmed, storm-tossed, and all stages in between. Our crew of five sturdy young men, BC, and I (the cook) made it all in one piece—and still speaking to each other. We had quite a mixture. Matt and Mark (M & M), sailors and riggers; Steve, just back from one year of Army service in Korea; Ron, who had worked on the boat for years; and Ed, a physician.

We had two and a half days of no wind (very inconvenient for a sailboat). One night we broke out the deck table, wine glasses, and candles and had an Italian dinner al fresco. The guys caught enough fish for several meals. The big ones all got away, however. We had a mass of porpoises with us at one point—over twenty-four by count—riding in our bow wave. We also spotted a whale blowing. He tossed his flukes at us—a wonderful sight!

As on all shakedown cruises, we had a few problems but made it into Cozumel harbor on Tuesday, July 9 at midnight. We were all glad to see land.

Ed and Steve went home within a few days, Ron stayed until August 1, and M & M are still with us. We've had some rigging problems but hope to get them solved soon and be on our way.

M & M took the SCUBA certification course here and have taken to diving with a vengeance. We have moved up and down Palancar Reef and seen some beautiful sights. The water here is incredibly blue—from midnight blue to azure—and we have had very good visibility.

Linda, our boat dog, has adapted to the life with ease. Once we managed to convince her that a two-by-two-feet square of Astroturf was "THE spot," she settled right into the routine. She loves having people around all the time.

Having lived in Mexico years ago and on the border growing up, we were semiprepared for the shopping situation. It is a shock, after our U.S. supermarkets, to cope with open-air fruit and vegetable markets, rudimentary grocery stores, unrecognizable cuts of meat at semisanitary butcher shops, and bakeries where the sweet breads and cakes all taste the same. The abundance of fresh, wonderful pineapples, bananas, avocados, tomatoes, watermelons, limes, and cantaloupes almost compensates. I would give a great deal for a big, huge chef's salad, and BC is having withdrawal pains from Mario's Pizza. (By the way, having raised two girls, I was ill-prepared for the appetites of five guys between twenty-one and thirty-one. There were times when I felt Linda wasn't safe!)

Cozumel is a fairly small community if the cruise ships and diving tourists are discounted. We've become acquainted with a few people, but there aren't many boats here. Jim, who had his boat tied up next to us in Port Bolivar, is here. We've had a few highly charged games of Trivial Pursuit. Coral came for five days and Cindy and Roger for a long weekend.

Our major inconvenience is the lack of communications. We bought an SSB (single side band) radio, but the transmitter is not working—very frustrating! I only wish that all of you who feel Ma Bell is not treating you right could be here to cope with the Mexican phone system (Señora Bell?). Absolutely incredible! We called Coral to tell her of our safe arrival. Ten minutes—fifty-five dollars! Now we call collect or on our credit card. But they will only place these calls between 9:00 to 11:00 AM and 3:00 to 6:00 PM. Quite a challenge to get a message through to the States, especially with time differences.

> ## VIGNETTE TO DESCRIBE LIFE IN MEXICO
>
> I had my hair cut last week. The shop's plumbing was inoperative, and they shampooed my hair by dipping water out of a bucket. Both bucket and water were borrowed from the store next door. The hair, however, was fine.

We can see that isolation will be both a blessing and a curse. We know absolutely nothing of what is going on north of the Yucatan. That is good when the news is bad. Unfortunately, we miss out on the good news, too.

To quote Mac Davis, we are about ready to see Cozumel in our rearview mirror. We plan to slide down the coast to Belize, diving as we go. We're looking forward to exploring Turneffe and Glover Reefs. Tentatively, we are planning to head for the Caymans via Swan Island when Belize loses its charm, but we have no time frame. We have lots of space and issue an open invitation for any visitors. Let our booking agent (Coral) know. We try to stay in touch with her (an expert radio technician would be greeted with great fanfare and huzzahs, but ordinary klutzes like ourselves are more than welcome).

We think of all our friends often and do a lot of speculating on who is doing what to whom. As for us, we are well and having a hell of a good time. We hope to see you in the near future, somewhere, somehow.

Love & Kisses,
Jerry & Buf

*****

Letter 3

Georgetown, Grand Cayman, B.W.I.
November 4, 1985

We have reached Grand Cayman—a civilized society, at last! The crew of Beachouse *has been sloshing around in the backwaters of the Caribbean Sea since we pulled out of Cozumel on August 20.*

BC, Matt and Mark (our stalwart crew, a.k.a. M & M), and I sailed down the Mexican coast right into a real storm. We ducked behind Banco Chincarro and spent a few days waiting for calmer weather. The diving was good, and we loaded up on fish and lobster. So the time passed quickly. A Mexican gunboat pulled in beside us. BC turned a little paranoid—the way everyone does when they see a cop—but they were also looking for a safe anchorage. We moved down to Turneffe Reef and spent a night there before going into Belize.

The channel into Belize City itself is long, winding, and very shallow. It took us three and a half hours from the mouth to the anchorage. Trying to describe the mooring there without being indelicate is not possible. The Belize River is the sewer system for the city, and it empties directly into the anchorage. Just looking over the side every morning was an adventure. The depth was marginal—we were in nine feet of water, and that was about a half mile from shore. BC found "urgent" business to attend to in Houston and left M & M and me over the Labor Day weekend. It was not a popular decision. Our anchorages are scientifically divided into "attaboys" and "aw shits." This one put BC firmly in the latter category for a very long time.

The redeeming feature in Belize was the people. So friendly, helpful, and pleasant. We could buy most anything we needed. We were still without our SSB radio, however, and there was no one to repair it there. M & M said they were offered (but refused?) a wide variety of earthly pleasures when they went into town alone. However, no one propositioned me with anything—humpf!

We left for Lighthouse Reef on September 5. *The diving there was great. M & M have taken to diving with all the fervor of religious converts. It's fun for BC and me to watch their astonishment and enthusiasm for this new world they have discovered.*

We anchored next to a lovely fifty-four-feet ketch on Lighthouse. We had seen her off and on since arriving at Cozumel. After waving back and forth for a day or so, we went over in the dinghy and introduced ourselves. There was a family from Dallas living aboard, complete with a ten-year-old boy and a German Shepherd. George is an engineer on leave from Texas Instruments. Incredibly, his specialty is troubleshooting problems on high-tech equipment. We couldn't believe it! Ripley wouldn't have believed it! Here we were, parked next to the only person in a thousand-mile radius who could fix our radio—and he did. He claimed it was recreational therapy.

It took him six hours, and he spread it all over the saloon, but it worked when he got through.

If you want to contact us, you can do it by following these instructions:

1) Dial the AT&T high seas operator at 1-800-SEA-CALL between 5:30 and 6:00 AM, Dallas time (you'll see why below).

2) Tell them you want to leave a message for the yacht Beachouse—WSP 8874 *(pronounced "Whiskey Sierra Pappa 8874").*

3) Ask the operator to transmit the message from 0730 to 0900 Eastern Standard Time that morning. If they receive no response from the boat by 0900, then cancel the message.

We try to turn on the radio each morning at 7:30 AM to listen for messages as well as note the weather information they pass along. If we hear the message, we will call you back. Please do not be offended if we call you collect, as we do not feel that it is prudent to announce our telephone credit card number over the high seas radio for anyone to copy. If you do not hear from us, leave the message again the next morning (we only listen to the SSB early in the morning). This system isn't perfect, but we usually get the message and will call back as soon as we can.

We also solved our rigging problems while parked at Lighthouse Reef with the components BC brought back from Houston.

On September 15, we moved on to the Honduran Bay Islands and pulled into Coxen Hole, Roatan, at 5:00 PM on the sixteenth. Another "Aw s—!" The rickety dock had two boats anchored in nine feet of garbage-laden water—Beachouse and an incredibly rusted freighter unloading the ubiquitous Coca-Cola.

> ## VIGNETTE TO DESCRIBE COXEN HOLE
>
> *Boat dog Linda had not been ashore since we left Cozumel. After a night at the Coxen Hole dock, we found fleas on her. She had **not** been ashore. Coxen Hole is aptly named, and we hope that we never meet Mr. Coxen.*

If Coxen Hole was one of the worst ports we've found so far, we also found one of the best. Port Royal, at the opposite end of the island and accessible only by sea, is absolutely beautiful. It is clean, deep, and historically very interesting. It was home to as many as five thousand people during the buccaneer days, including pirate Henry Morgan. The current population is fewer than twenty-five, scattered around the perimeter. As a famous pirate refuge, there is a sunken galleon still there. M & M found it (with directions from the locals). Nothing much left but the wooden ribs, but it was exciting all the same. No gold doubloons, unfortunately. All the locals told us we couldn't sail to Grand Cayman from there. We would be sailing directly into the prevailing easterly winds. They suggested we go back through the Yucatan Passage, past Key West, and around Cuba from the east. You know BC. At that point he would have rowed all the way if that was what it took. We had two guys from Houston join us, John and David. We provisioned at the only grocery store on the island, which was in the aforementioned Coxen Hole. I bought what we had to have, ignoring both price and sanitary conditions. Even the fruit and veggies were bad here. I did institute a requisition for paper towels after paying the equivalent of three U.S. dollars per roll.

We left at dawn on October 6, prepared for a crossing of up to twelve days; we had a contingency plan to run back to Cozumel if necessary. Instead, we had incredibly good luck with our wind direction and pulled into Georgetown, Grand Cayman, at 5:00 PM on October 10—four and a half days later. The voyage itself was smooth and easy.

I did find out mid-voyage that crewman David is a master chef by profession. Very intimidating to an amateur cook. We enjoyed him tremendously; an English gentleman with a marvelous sense of humor and a blue-water sailor to boot. John left for Houston as soon as we landed, but David stayed with us for a week of good times. He prepared beautiful meals for us with fish and lobster but refused to sign on as permanent chef. Hopefully he will rejoin us for another sail.

The waters here are the best so far. Absolutely clear, and the diving is exceptional. We have made a couple of trips to the far north wall where the commercial dive boats seldom venture (it's too far from the hotels). We just anchor for a couple of days and get our fill.

Coral and Joe spent a long weekend with us, and Matt's father came for a week. Don and Judy Youngs are here with us now and are taking this letter home for the mail.

Our next scheduled stop is Jamaica, with an interim layover on Little Cayman—our favorite dive spot. Don't know exactly when we will sail, but sometime in the near future. We just hang loose and play each day as it comes.

Half of our M & M team had to leave for home. We really hated to see Mark go. Anybody want to sign on? We can promise low pay, long hours, but great working conditions. If we ever make any real plans, Coral, Cindy, and Don & Judy will probably know what they are.

We're looking forward to seeing some old friends soon.

Y'all Come Down!

We'd love to see you.

Love,

Jerry and Buford

P.S. Pizza is available here. BC considers that to be the primary criterion that separates us from the savages.

*****

At the dock in Coxen Hole, Roatan, Honduras, September 1985

Scuba diving, Grand Cayman

Crew Troubles

Additional crew members joined *Beachouse* in Roatan, Honduras, for the sail to Grand Cayman. Chef David from Houston was great; however, John was a fiasco. He was excited about crewing on *Beachouse* since he owned a sailboat and ocean sailing was his dream. He and his wife docked their boat at a marina in Kemah, Texas, and sailed on weekends in Galveston Bay.

Once *Beachouse* left the sight of land, however, John was sick the entire trip. He stayed in his cabin and didn't take night watches, which is what he signed up for! He also couldn't handle the lack of air conditioning. Once they reached Grand Cayman, John left the boat without looking back, and he never set foot on *Beachouse* again. That was the end of his cruising dreams.

Original crew member Mark also left in Grand Cayman. Annie Muirhead, their friend on the *Lammer Law*, sent a replacement. Matthew, not to be confused with Matt, the original crew member, was six feet five, nineteen, and not a real sailor. He lasted four days.

November 16, 1985. New crew is a disaster. BC told Matthew he was fired. He took it well. He's a nice boy but knows nothing about boats or sailing.

Another crew member, Albert, arrived and seemed to be just what they needed. It seems employee problems exist even in paradise!

Letter 4

Virgin Islands
March 11, 1986

Beachouse *finally made it to the Virgin Islands on Valentine's Day. There were times, washing around in the western Caribbean backwaters, when we began to doubt. This really is a yachting paradise. Unfortunately, it is not a well-kept secret. Two out of every three boats in the world seemed to be thrashing about these waters.*

After five weeks of dining and sailing on Grand Cayman, we pulled out—twice. On November 16, with a weather forecast of 10- to 15-knot winds and small swells, we turned the north corner of the island—directly into 35-knot winds and huge seas. Our captain (known as Chicken of the Sea) immediately turned back into port and threw down the anchor. The crew greeted these orders with enthusiasm. We tried again on the twentieth, hit a driving rainstorm, but got to Little Cayman in twenty-six hours. Albert Rodriguez from Houston joined us in Grand Cayman as new crew. Matthew is still with us, so we had A & M as resident expert sailors. The diving at Little Cayman was as great as we remembered. The anchorage was awful! There is a large sound on the island, but it is very shallow. A native passing in a fishing boat assured us we could anchor inside the reef. We did, but we spent the wee hours of the mornings listening to the hull bounce on the bottom. (Why do people ask any passing resident about local weather, geography, or navigation? It could be the village idiot giving you directions.) Three nights of thumping on the sand took the fun out of the spectacular diving, and we moved on for Jamaica on January 23.

All BC's experience with navigational aids has been in the aircraft industry, where the charts are updated weekly. Maritime charts are another matter entirely. A lot of their information is from the nineteenth century, and changes are made very rarely.

> ## *VIGNETTE TO DESCRIBE AVAILABLE NAVIGATIONAL AIDS*
>
> *As we sailed into Montego Bay, the chart advised us to use a tall palm tree and a church spire to find the entry channel. Unfortunately, the entire beachfront was covered with high rise hotels. The last chart revision had been made in 1957.*

Montego Bay was lovely. We stayed moored off the Yacht Club there after we arrived on the twenty-fifth. We even played bridge on their game night. Matt took up windsurfing, and we all did a lot of the tourist things. BC and I took a train across the interior of the island. It is really a beautiful land.

Everyone in Jamaica was very friendly and helpful. We moved down the coast to Ocho Rios and spent ten days. We were anchored in front of the Sheraton and Americana Hotels. We were used by all the jet-skiers and windsurfers as a pylon. It was sloshy but interesting. A & M met some guys on the beach and got involved with the local nightlife. Cindy and Roger came to visit for a long weekend. There were lovely places in the countryside here, including Dunn's River Falls—which you see in all of the tourist posters. We did it all! We went east down the coast to Port Antonio, where Matt flew home for Christmas. BC, Albert, and I had a Jamaican holiday and shared it with a very nice group of yachties who were anchored in a well-protected harbor. We all had a big Christmas dinner and partied a lot through the season. We did miss being with the girls on Christmas Day. It was the first time ever we had not all been together. Coral and Joe came on the twenty-ninth, though, so we had New Year's with them. We covered the east end of Jamaica together. There have been a number of movies made here, including Brooke Shields's Blue Lagoon *and a new one with Peter O'Toole. It is really a lush tropical island.*

Matt got back, and Jim Ford from Galveston joined us for our sail to the Dominican Republic on January 8. Jim was a great help to us. He was the best helmsman we've had on board. On the ninth, BC thought he spotted a U.S. Navy ship headed straight for us—and he was right. After following us for an hour or so, she ordered us to heave-to (nautical for "pull over"). We were boarded by a party of four Coast Guards. One Coast Guard and four Navy men stayed in the launch, which was beating the bejabbers out of the side of our boat at the time. They were looking for what they termed "unauthorized persons." Maybe being only fifty miles south of Haiti was a factor. Anyway, they searched with a great show of force. Shotguns, side arms, flak jackets, and the entire enchilada. Meantime, the destroyer's gun turret was rotated in our direction. We decided Linda, our resident watch dog, was outclassed. After half an hour or so of poking in holes, they gave us a safety inspection, and the officer in command promptly fell into the ocean while trying to negotiate the jump. We pulled him back on board while the Navy floundered around. All in all, it was a very trying afternoon for everybody.

We pulled into Boqueron, Puerto Rico, on January 22. We picked this harbor by chance, and it was great big, quiet, and smooth. There were a few American boats and tourists, but it was essentially used by locals. The city of Mayaquez was twenty miles or so up the coast. There is a large mall there—stateside style—Sears, Woolworth's, and all. I ran down the aisles shouting "Charge!" Eight months away from U.S. stores had left us short on a variety of items—from underwear to kitchen gadgets. We rented a car one day and drove across the middle of the island. It was beautiful up in the mountains. BC and A & M wanted to visit the radio telescope at Arecibo. It is the largest of its kind in the world. They found it very interesting.

We moved on around the southern coast of Puerto Rico to the island of Culebra off the east coast. I would recommend it as a great hideaway vacation spot. We stayed a few days and did a little diving. As we got closer to the Virgins, we began to see more and more boats and met a variety of boat people.

A & M and I made a dive on Sail Rock, which is in the middle of the Mona Passage between Puerto Rico and St. Thomas. It was spectacular. Lots of reef fish, plus many pelagic fish.

With typical Beachouse *luck, we sailed into Charlotte Amalie, St. Thomas, just in time for an oil spill. It did minimal damage, but it was messy. We found quite a group of boats and boat people here that we knew. Some were from the Houston-Galveston area and some from our Caribbean travels. It's nice to see a familiar face from time to time.*

Albert left us here and went back to Houston. It was just as well. BC, rabid University of Texas fan that he is, was having a hard time handling a crew called A & M. Matthew, BC's sailing expert and my great dive buddy, is still here.

Zenas and Marlene Clarkson and Dick and Judy Littleton from Houston joined us for a week. We had a great time diving and sailing into new harbors every night. Some were great, a few just good—no *"Oh shits,"* thank goodness. It's hard to find those in these waters. Zee and Matt had the experience of a lifetime. We spotted a pod of whales while sailing in Sir Francis Drake Channel. Zee and Matt suited up as fast as they could—Dick manned the dinghy—and dropped in right among the whales. The guys were overawed. Even on Beachouse, it was an experience to follow along and watch the whales blow and surface. A spectacular day!

We expect to stay in the Virgins until the first of April or so; then we'll move on south through the islands. Don Youngs is here for a long weekend, and Coral surprised us with a sneaky fly-in yesterday. The weather is great, the water is beautiful, and the sailing is a lot of fun. Come and join us.

Hope you are all well and happy. It's hard for BC and me to realize we launched Beachouse almost a year ago. We are still having a wonderful time, but we miss seeing you all. Please let us know how you are.

Love,
Jerry and BC

*****

U.S. Coast Guard boarding *Beachouse*, Dominican Republic

In Port Antonio, Jamaica, *Beachouse* was docked next to the one-hundred-feet yacht owned by Doris Duke. It made *Beachouse* look like a tug boat. The crew were friendly, especially the Turkish captain, who was fluent in English. He laughingly told a story about a stormy crossing where he had a crewman on top of the mast, making repairs. The yacht was tossing and turning and the crewman was working feverishly when one of Mrs. Duke's guests approached the captain to ask where the olives were. She could not find the olives in the galley. The captain claimed this was a typical guest who had no clue or interest in the crew's dangerous chores.

Enjoying a guided float down the Rio Grande in
Port Antonio, Jamaica, December 1985

Sailing against easterly winds, the trip from Jamaica through the Dominican Republic to Culebra, Puerto Rico, was rough.

January 8, 1986. Left Pt. Antonio. Was stormy all night. We all got sick—even me. Very rolly. Didn't have to cook anyway.

Buford also was not feeling well, with cramps and diarrhea. While sailing from Boqueron to Culebra, Jerry wrote:

February 7, 1986. Another long sailing day. Very rough beat. Seems worse than some of our other crossings.

Jerry was sore from spraining her back. Even boat dog Linda had to be taken to a veterinarian for worms, ear fungus, and cataracts.

Buford fired Albert, the newest crew member, who returned to the States. He and Jerry, now comfortable sailing *Beachouse,* didn't need a second crewman. Matt, who had been a *Beachouse* crewman since leaving Galveston, was still on board.

In St. Thomas, Buford and Jerry saw the *My Way,* the sister ship to *Beachouse,* for the first time since it left Galveston for Florida. It was a gorgeous boat for charter in the Virgin Islands. The *Lammer Law,* the trimaran Buford helped sail from Canada that was responsible for his desire to cruise, anchored next to them.

Letter 5

Nelson's Harbour, Antigua, B.W.I.
May 25, 1986

Here we sit in English Harbour, Antigua, among the ruins of Lord Nelson's eighteenth-century anchorage and dockyard. It's a beautiful protected harbor surrounded by stone ruins of the old fortifications. Our big news comes from Galveston, however, where Coral and Joe are awaiting the birth of our first grandchild in November. Very exciting for all of us.

We spent two and a half months in the Virgin Islands, both U.S. and British. We did lots of diving and visiting with Annie and Duncan Muirhead, who have a trimaran chartering company in Tortola, B.V.I. In fact, our chartering with them on numerous occasions is what started this whole madcap existence. We had a boat from Corpus Christi anchor by us in Charlotte's Armpit (yachties' slang for Charlotte Amalie, St. Thomas). They came over for a visit, and we found they had chartered with the Muirheads and had gotten the fever, same as us. He's a drop-out dentist from Corpus, and she is a semipro belly dancer. Boaters are an endless variety—fascinating! We have found flying our Texas flag is a sure way to meet a lot of fellow expatriates. There's a little (or a lot) of Texas pride even down here. Most all the boats with Texans aboard have a Lone Star flag right alongside the Stars & Stripes.

BC ran into Bob Stanford of 7-11 commercial fame at The Moorings in Tortola. We had a great time with him and Shirley. Went for a day sail and laughed about the old Southland days.

Ro and Jon Dee Lawrence and their kids—Craig and Kathy—visited over my birthday. We had a wonderful week. Matt caught us fish and lobster for dinners extraordinaire, including one ten-pound lobster giganticus. It was four feet two inches from tip of antennae to end of succulent tail. He was inordinately proud of himself—with reason.

Matt, much to our regret, has gone back to real life in Houston. We

36

really miss him, BC as a sailing person and me as a dive partner without peer. I'll have to galvanize BC back into action. He's been hanging out on the boat, waiting to eat our hand-fought catches.

Before we left the Virgin Islands, we had managed to sail through two of the big yacht races held each year. We nearly were run down in St. Thomas—had to maneuver violently and got our MPS (large, colorful, multipurpose sail) tangled up. I'm sure all the locals now know who we are.

Lesley Fidler and Johnny Evans, a British couple from London via Los Angeles, have joined us for the sail south to Venezuela. They are working their way to Brazil. It's wonderful to have another lady on board to help with the same old boring domestic chores that go on forever, whether you live in a house, castle, cave, tent, or boat. The dishes are always with us. Lesley is an art director, and Johnny is an ex-foreign exchange broker. Lots of fun and great Trivial Pursuit players.

We sailed out of the Virgins for St. Maarten on April 24. It's an interesting island that is half French and half Dutch. It has two good points—Philipsburg and Marigot. We had Pat and Goodwin Powell from Lubbock visit us here for a day. They were on a cruise aboard the Sun Princess. *We finally got to see a real ocean-type liner—it was great fun. We toured the island and ate a real French lunch. The food on the French side is marvelous—and expensive.*

We pulled out one flawless day for Saba—our favorite island. It's a volcanic cone that rises straight up out of the sea—no beaches and no harbors. It requires perfect weather. We had to motor a lot of the distance because it was so calm. We tied up to the rudimentary pier that is the only place for a boat on the island. Very few boats even visit Saba for an overnight stay and at about 9:30 PM we found out why. The wind came up, the swells began rolling in, and we pounded against the pier all night long. We had all our fenders out plus many extra spring lines, and we paced the cockpit most of the wee hours. We sustained no damage except to our nerves. As BC put it, we spent a month in Saba that night. We went back to Philipsburg the next day and anchored at dusk, just ten minutes before a storm hit. We clocked forty-seven-knot winds on our gauge, and all the boats in the harbor were pitching and turning violently. One empty charter boat broke loose and barely missed us. We fended her off. As the storm abated, Johnny took the dinghy, ran her down, boarded, started her, found a spare anchor, and reset her. Our resident hero. The charter company was *properly grateful (a check $). We had a private ceremony, complete with medal and champagne. It was quite a couple of days. Sure got the old blood going. And people wonder why sailors drink!*

We moved on to a succession of beautiful islands that have limited anchoring facilities. Each is very unique and has its own character and interesting features.

May 14—St. Barts. We spent our thirty-seventh wedding anniversary here. Johnny and Lesley took BC and me to dinner. Another French island with food to die for. Even in the grocery stores, we found pâtés and cheeses that were superb. Our idea of a civilized lunch is fresh French bread, pâté, cheese, garden tomatoes, and a nice little wine. Food is the redeeming feature of the French race. St. Barts is also where BC tried to maim me on a moped. We decided autos are more appropriate from now on.

May 16—St. Eustatius (Statia). This is a Dutch island, where the United States was first recognized as an independent nation by a foreign power. The first commander saluted a U.S. ship during the Revolutionary War, for which Statia was promptly sacked by the British. There is a low waterfront community that has been built on the ruins of the old docks and warehouses. The fort is on a cliff overlooking the area.

May 17—St. Kitts. We anchored in the commercial dock area and ate ashore at a fisherman's wharf. Delicious lobster and fish.

May 18—Nevis. We visited several sugar plantations that have been converted to inns and hotels. Most have a fabulous view.

May 19—Montserrat. We found a very nice small harboring area here, so we spent a couple of days. We took a hike up to a waterfall through a rainforest—beautiful. We also hiked to a live volcano center. It was reminiscent of Dante's Inferno, with bubbling mud, boiling water, sulfur fumes, and abundant steam. It was a nice place to visit, but I wouldn't want to live there.

May 22—Antigua. We sailed south from the V.I. toward Antigua at the time of the big race week here, so we weren't able to find charts of the island—sold out. We navigated in using the proverbial Natural Geographic Map. We hit English Harbour dead on. Don and Judy Youngs arrived on the twenty-third, and Cindy and Roger are coming today. It's great to have company.

We will be moving on soon and expect to be in Grenada by mid-July. Please sit down today, take pen in hand, and drop us a line.

> ### *VIGNETTE TO DESCRIBE*
> ### *CARIBBEAN MAIL SERVICE*
>
> *BC and I bought new glasses in St. Thomas. We expected to sail shortly so asked they be sent to St. Maarten, an hour's flight away. They were mailed Air Express on April fourteenth. They were delivered on May thirteenth. Bureaucracy is alive and well and living in paradise.*

Love and kisses,
Jerry and BC

*****

Buford looking over "Charlotte's Armpit," St. Thomas, U.S. Virgin Islands

Buford and Jerry's favorite Caribbean island, Saba, May 1986

Letter 6

Puerto La Cruz, Venezuela
Christmas 1986

Hello Everybody, and Happy New Year from Grandma and Grandpa Beach.

Molly Beach Murphy (Molly B.) arrived on November 29—the most beautiful and brilliant baby ever born—naturally! We have spent three weeks getting acquainted and are heading back to Venezuela and Beachouse *December 29.*

The French islands are a painful paradox for Buf. He loves the scenery, wine, and topless girls. He hates the French. They are not known as the "Nasty Frogs" without reason. He worked his way down the Windward Islands looking at boobs, buns, and hardware stores. Guadaloupe was our first French stop. We anchored in three places, including Cousteau National Underwater Park. It was a spectacular dive site on Pigeon Island. We made some inland trips by alternating with Johnny and Leslie, the English crew on board.

Dominica is the most beautiful island in the chain, but desperately poor. The anchorages are very bad, so we weren't able to stay but a few days. Again we alternated inland trips so that two of us were always on the boat. Two days after we sailed out, there was a storm that drove five boats up on the beach—spooky!

We anchored in Anse Mitan on Martinique. It is across a huge bay from Fort de France, the capital. Fort de France is a very large and sophisticated city. Anse Mitan is smaller and more manageable, with lots of cruising boats. We began to meet more and more people humming along like we are.

We got to St. Lucia two weeks before the pope. The best anchorages in the Windwards are here—Rodney Bay and Marigot Bay are the two we used. Absolutely lovely!

We only stayed one night in St. Vincent before sailing on to Bequia, which is the northernmost island in the Grenadines. By the time we got here, most of the charter boats were farther north, and everybody we met was cruising. The variety of people on these boats is fascinating. Among the group we now count as our real friends and cruising companions: a former producer of the NBC Today show, the former assistant librarian of Congress, innumerable teachers and professors, doctors, a dentist (he cleaned our teeth in a completely modern chair on his boat), plus many plain old folks like ourselves. It's kind of neat to find out that we aren't the only nuts in the world. The guys have a pirate network on the single side band radios. They are as bad as a group of old maids on a small-town party line. Every morning at seven thirty or so, they crank up and talk and gossip all over the area. It's actually quite helpful info about anchorages, shopping, weather, etc.

We had a big Fourth of July party on the boat and then left Bequia to spend a couple of weeks cruising from spot to spot in the Grenadines. The water is incredible here, and there are many lovely islands and bays. We especially enjoyed the Tobago Keys. It is a network of very small islands and underwater reefs. We anchored looking east with nothing but ocean between us and Africa. It was great! We woke up every day with sand blown from the Sahara all over the boat. We didn't believe it, either, but I swear it's true. Linda, the boat dog, now runs for the helm seat whenever she hears the anchor chain coming up. She loves to ride up there where the action is. It's also a good place to get lots of attention and tidbits.

We stayed in an anchoring area in St. Georges, Grenada, which is affectionately dubbed "the cesspool." There are lots of cruisers moving in and out of these waters in the late summer. It is far enough south for hurricanes to be a real rarity. The weather is constantly a factor when you are on a boat.

Coral visited us here for the last time before the aforesaid wonder baby, Molly, was born. We did some land exploring and a lot of lazy gossiping and partying with the gang in the harbor.

DIGRESSION

Explaining the West Indies English vernacular—If you've traveled in the islands, you know the language patterns are unique.

Examples:
On a dilapidated pier in Grenada, "THIS DOCK HAS A DISCONDITION"

Public announcement at the airport, "Flight #307 will arrive approximately immediately."

A holiday notice in the newspaper, "FREE COKES, FREE HOT DOGS, FREE VASECTOMIES."

We pulled out for Venezuela on August 4 and spent a few nights in the Testigas on the way. We thought we had died and gone to heaven when we hit the island of Margarita. It's the resort area for Venezuela and a free port. All the things we had not been able to find in the islands were available here, and the money exchange was loaded in our favor. I have hardly cooked a meal since we got to this part of the world. The restaurants are marvelous and so cheap for we Americans. Twelve to fifteen dollars a couple is a first-class, fancy café. It's wonderful! We stayed on the island for a month and then moved to Cumana on the mainland. We took the boat out of the water for a bottom job and various and assorted repairs.

Imagine running a trailer under your house, dragging it halfway up a sand dune, and then leaving it at a thirty-degree angle while a dozen men wearing boots and carrying hammers run around banging on the walls. That was us in the boatyard. It took us five and a half hours to get pulled out on the rail. We had a lot of work done, including painting and some mechanical refit. BC had lots of projects to do while we were high and dry. It was incredibly dirty and noisy, so we lived in an AIR CONDITIONED hotel for the twenty-three days we were on the hill. We had to sneak Linda past the desk in a bag every night. She finally began to jump in by herself and loved being carried with her head sticking out, watching the world pass by.

Johnny and Leslie had left us when we reached Margarita. They babysat a couple of boats when their owners went home for a while but are now working their way overland to Brazil.

After Cindy's visit, we sailed on down the coast to Puerto La Cruz with a couple of overnights in secluded bays. BC and I are really enjoying being alone on the boat. So far we've had no situations we couldn't handle. Hopefully we never will. BC has been able to fix or "southern engineer" any problems we've had so far and is constantly upgrading equipment and systems. A boat is the perfect place for a born tinkerer.

We left the boat and boat dog in the care of friends in the marina in Puerto La Cruz and flew home on December 8. It has been great to visit with the family and spend Christmas in the U.S.A., but we are on our way back on Monday, December 29.

Hopefully it won't be as long between visits home from now on. We are still looking for company and are planning to hang out in the southern end of the Caribbean through hurricane season 1987. BC loves the docile weather down here. We plan to make a side trip or two to Bonaire and other close-by islands. Please drop us a note at Galveston and it will get down with the next tourist.

HAPPY NEW YEAR to you all!

Love,
Jerry & Buford

*****

First Haul Out in Venezuela

The haul out in Cumana, Venezuela, in 1986 was a dusty, dirty mess, with setbacks and mistakes made by the local workers. Jerry was an "absolute wreck" when the boat came out of the water. Once it was on land, they discovered new problems, including a crack in the hull by the root cellar and a bad crack in the rigging. Boat dog Linda fell into the engine room but, luckily for her, didn't break any bones.

Jerry expressed frustration:

September 26, 1986. They painted today and what a disaster! They didn't cover the teak cockpit floor and didn't get the dirt off it. The deck was white, and the paint is full of dirt. BC told off everybody. We left very down.

September 27, 1986. I didn't sleep well at all. Too many disappointments. Hoped we were all through with this when we left Port Bolivar.

September 29, 1986. Still going so slow. They do everything in half motion.

September 30, 1986. Still moving along at a snail's pace. More sanding and putting down paper. It blows off, and they put it back. Day after day. Sure getting tired of eating out of an ice chest.

October 2, 1986. I can't believe our bad luck! They were finally painting the entire top of the boat—then it rained and ruined a lot of it, and they have to do it over. BC and I were sick.

October 8, 1986. I never thought they would get us out today, but they had everybody working hard. Great to be back in the water. The boat is filthy.

With *Beachouse* back in the water, Buford spent an entire day loading three hundred gallons of fuel into the gas tanks by emptying barrels with a small pump.

Out of water for repairs in Cumana, Venezuela, September 1986

During Cindy and Roger's visit to Venezuela in October 1986, the four made a land trip to Angel Falls. At 3,212 feet, with an uninterrupted drop of 2,648 feet, it is the world's highest free-falling, freshwater waterfall. It is located in the Canaima National Park and named after Jimmy Angel, an American bush pilot and gold-hunting adventurer, who discovered it in 1937. They ventured from Caracas to the city of Canaima, where a plane flew them directly over the falls. The next day, Jerry and Buford had a six-hour round-trip canoe ride up the Churun River to Isla Orchedea, with a full view of the falls. Their guides cooked chicken over an open pit. While returning through Caracas, they toured the capital area, including Simon Bolivar's house.

Happy Hour

Buford and Jerry enjoyed happy hour each day around 5:00 PM. They established this rule to diminish the temptation of over-imbibing on warm, lazy days with beautiful sunsets, which occurred almost every day when sailing. Several times a week, Buford and Jerry had fifteen to thirty-five people join them for the ritual drinks and snacks. Everyone had drinks with ice from Jerry's root cellar, a luxury for most yachties. Usually the revelers consumed their second drink while watching the gorgeous sun set over some exotic locale.

One happy-hour participant explained that Buford and Jerry kept to their rule pretty well. He found that cocktails didn't happen around five—they happened at exactly five—within minutes. They didn't have a "couple of drinks"; they had exactly two—no more, and, to quote Jerry, "for damned sure no less."

In Puerto La Cruz, like everywhere she went, *Beachouse* was the center of the social scene for cruisers. Because of its size and large amount of deck space, parties were common on board. "Let's have a party!" was Jerry's mantra. If a party was anywhere in sight and she wasn't invited, someone needed to explain why. When she attended or gave parties, she was the best guest or hostess imaginable.

Because of their hospitality, Buford and Jerry were elected to have the New Year's Eve party for all the boats on the Puerto La Cruz dock. Jerry ended her 1986 diary:

December 31, 1986. Thirty people on board. It has been a spectacular year. Hope the next one is as interesting.

Beachouse spent so much time in Venezuela in 1986 and 1987 that it was featured on the front of the official Puerto La Cruz city map.

Letter 7

Bonaire, Netherlands Antilles
May 1, 1987

Dear Friends:

We had such a whirlwind tour at Christmas. We got back to Venezuela and couldn't believe we had spent three weeks in the U.S.A. We had a great time babysitting "Marvelous Molly" and visiting with quite a few of you. We were only sorry we didn't get to see everyone.

Linda, the boat dog, was glad to see us, although she had gotten fatter and more spoiled by the yachties in the marina, who all felt sorry for her because she was left behind. We arrived in Puerto La Cruz at noon on December 30 and found that a big New Year's Eve bash had been planned for Beachouse. Actually, it was the easiest party ever, as the group furnished everything, including napkins and garbage sacks. We had thirty-two on board, but only a few of us lasted until midnight. In Venezuela, New Year's Eve is a quiet family holiday, with the real festivities saved for January 1.

We left the marina on January 7 and hung around the coastline until the seventeenth, cleaning the bottom and catching up on all the little chores.

VIGNETTE DESCRIBING THE CAREFREE CRUISING LIFE

7:00 a.m.	Radio on	Buf is communications officer
8:00 a.m.	Breakfast	Jerry is galley slave
9:30 a.m.	Head stops up	Buf is plumber
11:00 a.m.	Hand wash clothes	Jerry is laundress
12:30 p.m.	Lunch	Jerry is galley slave
1:45 p.m.	Hydraulic leak	Buf is engineer
2:00 p.m.	Polish stainless steel	Jerry is boat grunt
3:00 p.m.	Tighten rigging	Buf is deck hand
3:30 p.m.	Make canvas gear	Jerry is sailmaker
5:00 p.m.	Tend Happy Hour	Buf is bartender
7:00 p.m.	Dinner	Jerry is g.s.
8:00 p.m.	Lights flicker	Buf is electrician
10:00 p.m.	Bed	Buf and Jerry are exhausted!

My cousin Jeanne and her husband, Stan, arrived in Puerto La Cruz on January 21. BC took us cruising to the local high spots, including our favorite hideaway, where he promised we would feel we were the only four people on earth. We were settling down at 5:00 PM to watch the sunset and enjoy happy hour when a 138-feet motor sailor named Christina B. *pulled in and dropped her hook right beside us. She ran her generator and halogen lights all night long. I took pictures of us together, and now, when BC gets a little full of himself and his sixty-feet vessel, I can pull them out and bring him down. The* Christina B. *was truly magnificent. We had the last laugh, however, when they moved on to Puerto La Cruz and used our slip at the marina. Since we were prepaid, they had to move out when we returned—ha!*

Gene and Grace Smith came for too short a visit on February 10. We did our island tour again. We were really getting slick at it by then. After they had to leave on the fifteenth, BC and I got serious about provisioning to leave for the outer Venezuelan islands.

It is really fun to go to the stores when everything is so inexpensive. With canned drinks at 12¢, beer and tonic at 15¢, flour for 50¢ a five-pound bag, and canned veggies at 25¢ or so, the pain of shopping is minimized. BC and I went to the fresh vegetable market the morning before we left, spent seventeen dollars, and bought enough to last us six weeks. Incredible!

We sailed to Tortuga on February 20. It took eleven hours, and we anchored on the northwest corner along with a couple of other boats we knew. It is a pretty place, but we were anxious to move on to Los Roques. We left at 9:00 PM on February 25 in order to make the Roques in full daylight, since the entrances through the reefs are a little tricky. There was an English catamaran there under emergency repair; it had gone up on the reef six weeks earlier in the middle of the night. We didn't wish to follow her example. It took them ten days just to get her pulled off the rocks. There are several good-sized cargo ships sitting high and dry that aren't worth the expense of salvage.

The same reefs that make the area treacherous also make it incredibly beautiful. The water is translucent and every shade of blue. The fish life is abundant, and there is plenty of lobster available.

There were quite a few boats there, as it was carnival season; a lot of Venezuelan power boats had made the run from Caracas. We had prearranged a meeting with the Avanti, *a boat from Puerto La Cruz, and spent a week gunkholing with them. The area is very large, two hundred square miles, so there are a lot of places to get lost. There is a very small fishing village—and nothing else. It's really wonderful. The* Avanti *went back and we stayed on, meeting other American boats, making new friends, and cruising the area.*

It probably reads as though it would be rather lonely, but actually, BC and I only spent five nights without the company of other cruisers. It was almost the opposite of lonesome.

BC showed his shrewd business acumen by trading eight of our 15¢ beers for four pounds of turtle meat and two big lobsters. The local fishermen were happy to get ice-cold beer, and, heaven knows, we were happy with our end of the bargain.

We moved on to Aves on March 21. They are two small reefs about twelve miles apart, halfway between the Roques and Bonaire. They are very isolated and seldom visited. We had a lovely time. Aves means "birds" in Spanish, and the islands are a giant aviary—thousands and thousands of blue- and pink-footed boobies, pelicans, frigate birds, and many other varieties.

They are unaccustomed to people and weren't the least bit apprehensive of us. We could sit in the dinghy and drift within three or four feet of their nesting places in the mangrove swamps. We looked at them, and they looked at us. I presume it was mutually satisfying. I know BC and I enjoyed it thoroughly.

We sailed on into Bonaire on March 28 and got ready to enjoy some wonderful diving while we waited for much-needed parts from the U.S.A. The mail system is far superior to most other Caribbean islands. We spent one day flying to Curacao, seeing the sights and getting a hydraulic hose repaired. At the airport, while awaiting our flight back to Bonaire, we met a local who had seen our boat and was organizing filming for a TV program called Lifestyles of the Rich and Famous. In September you may be able to see Beachouse in full color with a young girl featured on the deck—you sure won't see BC and me. They were careful to shoot around the "crew," of whom they had never heard, and who sure as hell don't have any money. Don and Judy Youngs came for the week, and we all had a blast taking the TV group for a sunset sail. We got a free meal out of it at one of the local tourist traps. The girl's name is Ari something, and she plays one of the teenagers on Kate & Allie. I guess it was our fifteen minutes of fame that Andy Warhol talked about.

Don and Judy leave this Saturday, April 18, and Coral, Joe, and Molly arrive that same day. We are ecstatic that we will have Molly on board for a whole week. Thank God that at five months, she is still too young to crawl off. We'll probably have her completely spoiled by the time she leaves. That's what grandparents are for, isn't it?

We are hoping Coral brings us some letters telling us news of you all and your families. We can only repeat our open invitation for a visit any time we can coordinate. We will be leaving around the middle of May for Venezuelan waters to wait out the hurricane season. That will take us through next November. We haven't made any plans beyond that.

We think of all of you often and spend lots of sunset happy hours wondering how you are.

Love,
Jerry & Buf

*****

Cycles

In May 1987 *Beachouse* completed her first cycle through the Caribbean. Eventually, she would make three cycles, spanning four and a half years. Each cycle began in the Virgin Islands of the northern Caribbean in late fall. November through April was spent cruising down the island chain to the southern Caribbean. The hurricane season, May through September, was spent off the coast of Venezuela and in the Netherlands Antilles, both of which are approximately 720 miles north of the equator and outside the hurricane belt. They have the same stable climate all year round, with little variance in temperature—around eighty-five degrees Fahrenheit.

Buford claimed to be a 20/20 sailor—he sailed between twenty degrees north and twenty degrees south latitude. He thought as long as the Lord made warm water and cold water, it seemed to him that the good Lord meant for anyone with any common sense to sail in the warm water and to leave the rest for the fish and people with no good sense.

Daily Projects

When Jerry wrote about getting away from the marina and catching up on "all the little chores," she did not reflect the true amount of work and skills that were required to keep a large boat maintained. Work was virtually nonstop, with daily "projects," as Jerry referred to them. Here is a sample of what Buford and Jerry were really doing:

BUFORD	JERRY
Clean propeller	Scrape bottom using scuba tanks
Put ventilators in amas	Varnish all hatches
Make a yoke for foredeck and a yoke for outboard motor	Varnish windshields, saloon door, control panel
Work in engine room to find leak	Shampoo carpets
Fix radio antennae	Clean all heads
Fix speed log	Clean all stainless
Grease winches	Sew cover for dingy & sewing machine
Clear engine intake	Sew shorts and tops
Fix hot water heater and salt water pump	Wash boat
Fix plumbing for faucets in amas	Wash clothes using a bucket
Go up mast to replace deck light and fix TV antennae	Wipe down all teak with vinegar oil

The Aves and Roques Islands, Venezuela

The sail from Isla la Tortuga to the Roques required either Jerry or Buford to be on watch at all times.

February 26, 1987. We took turns on watch and dozing all night. Wind was steady at 18 to 22K most of the night. It finally began to calm down just after dawn to 15 or so. It was a very long night but not too rough. We got very little water in the cockpit. We sighted the island about 7:30 AM and anchored into calm water off a small mangrove island at 9:30 AM. It is absolutely gorgeous here. The colors of the water are incredible.

Even though *Beachouse* anchored in remote places—the Aves Islands are uninhabited except for the Guardia Civil to control the visiting yachts and fishermen—life was not dull. A typical day included Buford talking on the radio for an hour every morning; dinghy rides; walks on the beach; snorkeling and diving; cleaning the fish, conch, and lobster caught during the dives; cooking; chores; happy hour at 5:30 PM with guests from boats anchored nearby; dinner; and sitting out watching the stars.

Living off the sea provided Jerry and Buford with daily menus that we can only dream about: conch ceviche, conch stew, lobster omelets, lobster salad, lobster thermador, fresh grilled fish, and turtle steak.

The nightly entertainment was eating popcorn while watching a movie (or half a movie before falling asleep) from an extensive video collection. Jerry loved movies, often exclaiming "Thank God for the VHS," and was an expert at movie trivia. *Beachouse* had around four hundred movies on board, numbered and catalogued so other cruisers could check them out to view. Jerry and Buford often had matinees on board *Beachouse*, inviting a few couples over around 3:00 PM for popcorn and a movie. Jerry constantly borrowed movies from other cruisers so she could make copies for her collection. Whenever they were in port, one of her first stops was to a video rental store. It was heaven when the port had a movie theater running semicurrent movies, but the Beaches learned to be careful about the social customs. At one movie theater in Cumana, Venezuela, several people in their party were turned away for wearing shorts.

The Social Hub

Each time *Beachouse* encountered a new boat, Buford and Jerry immediately motored over in their dinghy, introduced themselves, and invited the owners for happy hour. Jerry's diaries are full of hundreds of boat names and the names of their crews, which she underlined in order to easily refer to them later. She remembered the boat name more often than the names of the boat owners.

As much as Buford and Jerry loved to be settled in anchorages away from land, which is when most of the work got done on the boat, they also loved to be in a marina with all the cruisers. Little work got done there, as the social scene took over. Sightseers as well as fellow cruisers were constantly dropping by.

June 16, 1988. Hard to get things done with all the company. Everybody loves our cockpit.

On one approach to the marina in Bonaire, Jerry wrote:

August 31, 1988. Crowds of people here we know. Lots of fun we'll have.

September 29, 1988. I don't know what we do all day, but we are in constant motion.

Daily happy hours, dinners out with fellow cruisers, and impromptu parties for twenty-five to thirty were the norm.

Dinghy "raft up" for a party on *Beachouse*

Potluck dinners, which Buford hated, were almost always held on *Beachouse* because of the large deck space. Lentils and pasta—neither of which Buford ate—are easily stored on a boat and so were always prominent dinner offerings. Where was the meat?

Book swapping was also popular. Impromptu book exchanges, held on the dock, were open to all cruisers who wanted to bring books they had read and were willing to swap for others. Romance novels were the most common choice.

Whether in an anchorage or in port, cruisers kept the barter system alive and well. *Beachouse* received a big lobster for some gasoline and rum for a hand blender; Jerry described both trades as "a great deal for us." Eating and drinking were clearly priorities for them! They also traded with fishermen while they were away from ports—one day a sea bass, the next a big grouper. However, now spoiled, all they craved was lobster!

The only way for Buford and Jerry to communicate with family and friends in the States was by telephone, so they could call only while in port. Making a call involved going to town, finding a public telephone service, waiting in line, and attempting to get the call to go through on a usually undependable phone service. When no one answered, they had to start the process all over again. It was extremely frustrating, and each attempt took several hours.

After spending time in a marina, Buford and Jerry longed for solitude. Once boats left and projects were slow, Jerry wrote:

November 2, 1987. I'm a wreck. This is so boring. I'm ready to get out to an anchorage.

The circle began again—from solitude to the social hub for cruisers.

Letter 8

I'm sure it's common knowledge by now that I hate to write letters. However, after checking our mailbox (figuratively speaking), I've decided I'll have to send one to get one. I am working on a computer that was donated to this cause by Cindy and her husband, Roger. The only "C" I ever made in my life was in high school typing class, so I start this project with a definite handicap.

We thoroughly enjoyed the past eighteen months or so in the southern part of the Caribbean. We were in Venezuela, its offshore islands, and Bonaire. We did a lot of diving, fishing, lobstering, and lying around. It was a very relaxing time for us. We got so tired that we took a three-week vacation to Ecuador, flying from Bonaire. It was a lovely change being among many snow-capped volcanoes and making a jungle trek. The people were friendly, and the prices were low for food and lodging. We highly recommend it.

We sailed north to St. Maarten on November 1 for a one-month stay. Cindy and Roger met us there for a twelve-day visit over Thanksgiving.

We sailed on to the Virgin Islands to meet Coral; Joe; Molly, three; and Matthew, one, for the holidays. They were here for twelve days, and we had a wonderful Christmas. It was hectic but fun to be with the children. Linda (the boat dog) loved it. There were crumbs everywhere. We spent almost every night in a different anchorage, snorkeling, swimming, and admiring the scenery. We saw very little evidence of Hurricane Hugo; however, we have many friends and acquaintances who either lost their boats or sustained damage. The anchorages seem less crowded than they were two years ago.

We belong to the SSCA (Seven Seas Cruising Association), which is an informal organization for people like us who live on boats. At 11:00 AM on

New Year's Eve, we counted about thirty-six people anchored around us, so we invited one and all to Beachouse *for a party that night. Boats kept rolling in, and we wound up with forty-four aboard. A great time was had by all, and the boat held together. Linda especially enjoyed it. She nearly foundered on snacks and tidbits and managed to get stepped on only once. At fifteen plus, she is going downhill fast but still loves a party. Some of us decided to meet again for a potluck beach picnic the next afternoon, New Year's Day.*

BC has a wonderful opportunity coming up the end of January. Duncan and Annie Muirhead, our friends in the B.V.I., are moving the Lammer Law, *their ninety-five-feet trimaran, to the Galapagos. They are going to charter there. Duncan has asked Buf to crew down with him. He'll be gone most, or all, of February. I'll be staying with* Beachouse *in Roadtown, Tortola, resting and relaxing. No cooking and minimum cleaning. It will be heavenly. Buf is looking forward to the experience, especially since he is seriously talking about the South Pacific for 1991. We have to go soon or not at all before I get too old to lift the anchor. Cindy and Roger are considering a two-year or so sabbatical to go along. It would be great for us. We get a crew, and they get an adventure.*

Anyway, this delivery will give BC a chance to change his mind. I am just along for the ride (sail?). I can cook and clean anywhere.

I'm enclosing a new card. Please note the change of address. After five years and two kids, we decided to give Coral a break, and Cindy is now our mailperson and reservation clerk. Please let us know what's happening in your world.

We send love to all.

*****

61

Second Cycle

Besides Coral and Cindy, the Beaches had many other visitors from the States during their second cycle through the Caribbean. One island they enjoyed was Anguilla. Jerry wrote about an encounter she and Cindy had while walking along looking for a cab. A lady from Boston who lived on the island for half of the year stopped to offer a ride; she then promptly took them on a tour of the island and of her condominium, ending at a restaurant on the beach for lunch with some of her friends. Whoever said Jerry was shy or couldn't talk to a stranger?

April 14, 1988. The island is more settled and prosperous than we expected. The beaches are gorgeous. It's a good place to come back to someday.

While in St. Maarten, Jerry and Buford had great fun taking every group of guests to the nude beach and resort in Green Cay.

May 6, 1988. BC took Barbara, Joe, and Stacy to the nude beach—and they didn't know. They were all very surprised. The nude beach has been a source of fun for us all.

Jerry also repeatedly described the beauty of the Venezuelan Isla La Blanquilla, which they bypassed their first time in the southern Caribbean. It was a wonderful cruising spot with numerous easy anchorages and practically no people. *Street's Cruising Guide to the Eastern Caribbean Volume IV—Venezuela* describes the cove on the western side of the island as the most spectacular cove in the Caribbean.

May 18, 1988. Absolutely spectacular; really a gorgeous place.

At one end of the island is a narrow cove surrounded by cliffs. The interior is semidesert and desolate, with wild donkeys but not much else. They anchored next to boats of fishermen, trading fresh fish for rum or a homemade chocolate cake.

A beautiful cove on Isla La Blanquilla, Venezuela, May 1988

Other than the goal of avoiding hurricanes, two major reasons kept *Beachouse* in Venezuela for half of the year. First, unlike today, the government was stable and had a favorable exchange rate for Americans—usually thirty to thirty-two bolivars to one U.S. dollar. It was cheap at that time! Second, Cumana, Venezuela, had a well-known and reputable boatyard for hauling out boats and doing repairs.

Beachouse hauled out twice during this period, in November 1987 and December 1988. Jerry was always a nervous wreck and could barely watch as the boat was lifted out of the water. During the eight or nine days that *Beachouse* was "up in the yard," Jerry and Buford stayed in a hotel at night and went to the yard during the day. They completed small odd jobs on the boat while the workers sanded and painted the bottom or inside; they usually ate lunch on board. The yard was a dirty, noisy place, but at the end of the day, they had a nice, long, hot shower at their hotel—a wonderful luxury.

Jerry flew to Texas for three weeks in the summer of 1988 to visit family and friends in Galveston, Houston, and Dallas and attend a high school reunion in Mission. After being away from the States for a year and a half, she had to adjust to things like driving a car and shopping at Wal-Mart. She also couldn't get used to daylight savings time, when darkness fell at 9:00 PM.

June 21, 1988. Sure seems strange to be out in the traffic. It's not as scary as I thought it might be. I'm amazed at all the good stuff in the stores. It looks miraculous to me.

An Accident

Beachouse had her first accident while trying to leave Bonaire, a Dutch island off the coast of Venezuela.

October 3, 1988. It was pretty windy, so we vacillated about leaving. Finally decided to go and got way at 5:30 PM. We had a problem with the stowaway main so decided to come back in. We were just past the salt works. It was pitch black, and we ran upon Klein Bonaire. Got off with the help of the crowd in the marina and a dive boat. What a frightening experience. And so stupid. We were too busy watching the wrong side of the boat.

Jerry did not sleep that night. First thing in the morning, they looked for the anchor that was left, but they couldn't find it.

October 4, 1988. BC went under the boat to look at the damage. Miracles—the propeller was undamaged, and the drive didn't seem hurt at all. The hulls themselves are scratched up a little—nothing much. Also, the sail mechanism began working again, so it was all for nothing.

Hurricanes

The 1988 hurricane season brought two storms close to Bonaire.

September 10, 1988. Boats pouring into the marina. Hurricane Gilbert is passing two hundred miles or so to our north, causing large swells and some wind.

Gilbert passed over Jamaica and Grand Cayman on September 13 and was the main topic of conversation in the marina. The next month, Hurricane Joan hit.

October 14, 1988. It is moving in our direction. Everyone in the anchorage is putting down extra anchors and battening down for the storm. Hope the forecasters are wrong. We had a "hurricane watch" party.

October 15, 1988. I woke at 12:30 AM as the wind began to rise. The storm hit about 2:00 AM with winds 25 to 30K. The eye passed at 3:15 AM with twenty-five minutes of calm—then 35 to 40K steady, gusts to 48K. It was all over by 7:00 AM.

Through the dark night, booby birds kept flying into the rigging. Buford threw ten back in the air from the cockpit. By the afternoon, it had turned into a clear, beautiful day.

September 1989 brought Hurricane Hugo to the northern Caribbean.

September 20, 1989. The news from the Virgin Islands is very bad—80 percent destruction of the fleet in Red Hook and the armpit, as well as St. Croix. We heard Culebra has 136 boats on the beach and that Roosevelt Roads has an 80 percent loss. Incredible! We'll know a lot of the boats, I'm sure.

October 4, 1989. They have a list of the yacht status in the hurricane belt. We know a lot of the lost and damaged boats.

Civil Unrest

Buford and Jerry witnessed political demonstrations while in Cumana, Venezuela:

February 29, 1989. BC and I headed for the mercado (market) at 9:30. The buses and por puestos (taxis) weren't on the streets. We walked all the way and had just got inside when all hell broke loose. People were screaming and banging on the walls outside. They slammed the big metal doors shut, and we were inside. We kept buying stuff while the vendors were trying to close. We got as much as we could carry and started home. The mob had moved on, and we had no problems.

March 1, 1989. The country is under martial law. I went to the market early—had no problem. There's no trouble on the streets today. They looted all four Cadas in town yesterday. There is a curfew from 6 AM to 6 PM—it will last for two weeks. Luckily, we are all stocked up and ready to go.

The cause of the violence, which killed at least 130 people and wounded 800 in Caracas alone, was the government's decision to impose price increases on fuel and other goods as well as public transportation as part of a broad program of free market reforms. When the measures took effect, street violence that began in Caracas quickly spread civil unrest, known as the Caracazco, throughout the country. The government responded with force and implemented a state of emergency. Most of Venezuela went back to work by March 3.

After provisioning in Cumana, *Beachouse* moved on to Puerto La Cruz to finish loading the shelves before heading to remote islands again. Provisioning for long periods away from civilization was a time-consuming and labor-intensive task; Jerry became a master at it. She began her work by making lists of menus and necessary ingredients, then visited different stores to gather them. The stores were often low on items such as paper products, sugar, rice, flour, and oil.

While *Beachouse* was in remote sites, Jerry took a complete inventory of their foodstuff, except frozen items, to see how many weeks of food remained. With fresh lettuce and vegetables scarce, she resorted to growing sprouts and making sour dough bread starter and yogurt. After two months, food and supplies ran short.

May 10, 1989. It's just like a farm around here.

June 6, 1989. We are just about to run out of lots of things. We could still eat for a long time—but the meals might be a little strange.

A guest on *Beachouse* in Islas de Aves (bird islands), March 1987

Beachouse spent April, May, June, and September of 1989 in Aves de Barlovento, the eastern of the two Venezuelan islands that make up Islas de Aves. You would think such a long time away from civilization would cause boredom. That was not the case for *Beachouse*; in fact, the opposite was true.

April 27, 1989. It's amazing how busy we stay out here. I haven't had time to do any of the sewing projects I brought.

They were traveling with seven other boats: *Inshallah, Honeybucket, Rebecca, Fortuna, China Cloud, Pulsar,* and *Prelude*. Jerry referred to the activity as "quite a little beehive." Daily diving, searching for lobster and conch, and visiting the other boats took up most of the time. Everyone enjoyed board games and card games, including Rummikub, hearts, Pictionary, bridge, and, Jerry's favorite, Trivial Pursuit—which the women usually won.

Repairs Begin

By August 1989, Buford and Jerry had lived on *Beachouse* for four years. Many of the boat's mechanical parts were beginning to cause problems. Buford was constantly working to repair or replace systems, including the refrigeration, water maker, rigging, compressors, lights, cables, satellite navigation, hot water heater, freezer, gas tank, busted hoes in the engine, water pump, and spear guns. Repairs like these made for some of the worst days in a cruiser's life.

October 8, 1989. Well—another disastrous day. The fridge blew up again. Up to our hips in hydraulic fluid. We spent the whole day cleaning up again. What a mess. We had heavy rain all afternoon. BC started the fridge up with the Venezuelan-repaired pump. It promptly quit after ten minutes. More fluid. Very discouraging. We went to bed at 8:30 PM.

Even so, Buford began to think about sailing to the Pacific Ocean. He bought 179 nautical charts for the Pacific from a friend. Cindy and Roger began discussing the possibility of sailing with them.

October 7, 1989. They are serious about wanting to go to the Pacific with us. I hope it all works out. BC and I would have been too chicken to quit our jobs.

Third Cycle

Beachouse sailed back to the Virgin Islands in November 1989 to begin her third and last cycle through the Caribbean. Here Jerry described one of the best days of a cruiser:

December 11, 1989. Another wonderful day in paradise. The weather is lovely, and it's almost a full moon. It was a spectacular night. We watched the moon come up during the cocktail hour.

While in Hurricane Hole, St. John, Virgin Islands, Jerry unexpectedly spied Mike Sweeney, the sailing instructor who'd given her and Cindy sailing lessons in Kemah, Texas. He was captain on a boat anchored next to *Beachouse*. They visited and laughed about the fiascos they'd experienced during Jerry's attempt to master sailing. She was able to prove that, despite being one of his worst students ever, she was now a bona fide sailor!

In the British Virgin Islands, Buford and Jerry joined their good friends Duncan and Annie Muirhead on the *Lammer Law*. Duncan asked Buford, who'd accompanied him on the *Lammer Law's* initial trek from Canada, to sail through the Panama Canal to the Galapagos, where the boat would remain for chartering. Buford, seeing this as a practice run for his own passage through the canal, left Jerry in Tortola and joined the *Lammer Law* for a second time.

Buford's First Panama Canal Experience

Buford chronicled his trip through the Panama Canal with the *Lammer Law*, a ninety-five-feet trimaran, in a document titled *BC's Trip to Pacific Ecuadorian Coast, February 23–March 16, 1990.*

February 23, 1990. Fourteen people are on boat. Watches are two people, two hours with a new person on every hour, so twelve hours between watches. Neither of my watch mates can steer, so if steering is hard I have to steer the whole two hours.

The journey began from Norman Island in the British Virgin Islands and continued south across the Caribbean. On the second day, a small humpback whale followed the boat and, for a short time, swam right beside it. On the sixth day, they anchored outside the Panama Canal entrance. On March 1, Buford described the trip across Gatun Lake, inside the canal, as "really beautiful with many islands."

On the Pacific side of the canal, they docked at the Balboa Yacht Club. After several days of loading a large cargo, including two 450-pound jet skis, the *Lammer Law* sailed south through the Pacific, at one point accompanied by a large group of porpoises and pilot whales. They also experienced a "green flash," the famous but seldom-seen phenomenon that occurs just before the last part of the sun disappears from view over the water at sunset, when part of the sun suddenly changes from red or orange to green. The word "flash" refers to the sudden appearance and brief duration of this green color, which usually lasts only a second or two at moderate latitudes. (Happy hour on *Beachouse* usually included staring at the horizon for a green flash at sunset.)

The *Lammer Law* arrived at Isla De Malpelo, 315 miles off the Colombian Pacific Coast. It is uninhabited except for a small military post established in 1986. It is manned by the Colombian Army. A Colombian from a military ship radioed, asking who they were. After they identified themselves and expressed an interest in diving, they were told that there were sharks around. That was an understatement—Malpelo is a vast marine park, home to a unique shark population. Swarms of hundreds of hammerhead and silky sharks are frequently seen by diving expeditions, making it a popular shark-diving location. It is recognized as one of the top diving sites in the world because of its steep walls and beautiful caves that support the large "reservoir" of predators. In 2006 it was declared a natural World Heritage Site by the United Nations Educational, Scientific, and Cultural Organization (UNESCO), indicating that it is considered to be of outstanding value to humanity.

Site of Buford's fantastic dive off the *Lammer Law*,
Isla De Malpelo, Colombia, March 1990

Buford described an unbelievable day of diving at Malpelo.

March 5, 1990. I drove the dingy for Les and Bill to make a dive on one of the pinnacles off the main island. They saw many hammerheads. Duncan and I went for a dive and saw more than we could take in: many eels and large grouper, angels, etc. that I had never seen before. We found lobsters, and Duncan caught one. We sent Les and Bill back with a snare we made. They caught two Pacific lobsters, which aren't as large as Caribbean but are more colorful. There was a huge jack fish, the largest I have ever seen, which kept circling Duncan and me extremely closely. Duncan was peering in a hole, and I saw a large eel that looked like it was attacking him—but it swam right by his face and disappeared into the hole he was looking in.

There was no place to anchor around this sheer rock; the bottom was three hundred feet right up to the island. I suggested to Duncan that we tie off to the rocks, never dreaming he would do it. But we found a V-shaped inlet and tied off to the rocks, sheer cliffs with 280-feet lines fore and aft. What a day!! Wish Jerry was here. She would have made three dives by now.

The *Lammer Law* sailed further south in the Pacific Ocean to Esmeraldas, the largest port in northern Ecuador. Boats wanting to go to the Galapagos must wait here for permission to enter. After waiting for a week, with no permission in sight, Buford returned to Jerry and *Beachouse* in Roadtown, Tortola, without ever making it to the Galapagos Islands. He'd have to wait for the trip on *Beachouse*.

Visiting South America

Buford and Jerry took three trips to South America during their stays in the southern Caribbean. In July 1987, they flew to Caracas and then Barinas, the city closest to the Andes, taking the boat dog Linda in her knapsack. Now thirteen years old, she moved slowly and made little noise.

July 8, 1987. The stewardess spotted Linda and had a fit. No place to put us out—ha!

They rented a car and drove the highway to Merida, passing Santo Domingo and the Pico Aguila at 13,325 feet on the way. Clouds often obscured their view, and they were cold for the first time in years! They spent one night in the spectacular San Janier Valley. Upon arriving in Merida, they immediately took off for the mountains and rode the Telefinico, which is similar to a ski lift, up to the mountain peaks.

July 12, 1987. It was wonderful. The views were unbelievable. We went up in four stages. It was snowy and icy at the top—15,500 feet high. Really cold.

The Andes Mountains at the top of the Telefinico, July 1987

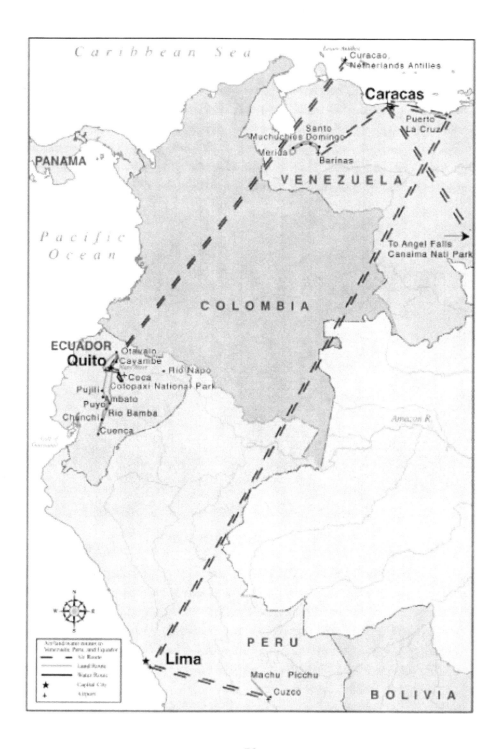

Whenever Jerry navigated, she insisted on exploring the smaller roads. Even though it meant driving extremely slowly, the spectacular scenery made it worthwhile. Buford complained that his "eyeballs hurt from sightseeing."

July 13, 1987. Our driving plans were a total fiasco. We took a road that was supposed to be good. It turned into a dirt road and then a rock trail. Left highway at Santa Cruz and got back on 36 kilometers later. Took us three and a half hours. We had to get some young men at a ranch to help us at one place. Five of them actually lifted the back of the car up—what an experience. They wouldn't take beer money.

Incan mother and son outside Cuzco, Peru, 1987

Two months later they flew from Caracas, Venezuela, to Lima, Peru, where prices were comparable to the United States but quite a shock from the low prices in Venezuela. After several days of sightseeing, they flew to Cuzco, Peru, altitude 11,155 feet, where they toured Incan ruins; then they left for Machu Picchu, a three-and-a-half-hour train ride.

August 19, 1987. The ride was gorgeous through the Andes Mountains and the river valleys. Then we took a bus to the top of the mountains to see the city. It was an awe-inspiring sight. Quite large and surrounded by sharp peaks. The ruins were quite well preserved and much more extensive than we had figured. Our guide was a dud. He spoke broken English and had too large a group to handle. We finally broke off and climbed to the top alone. It was gorgeous. The view of the city was fantastic. It was well worth the trip.

Incan Ruins at Machu Picchu, Peru, 1987

After touring more Incan ruins and returning to Lima, Buford and Jerry witnessed a public demonstration.

August 21, 1987. The square outside our hotel filled up after we had dinner. It really was interesting. Speeches for liberty, etc., protesting the nationalization of the banks. Must have been one hundred thousand people or more.

Peruvian banks at the time were in the hands of a few family empires. The president of Peru announced in a July 28, 1987, speech that the nationalization of Peru's ten privately owned banks, seventeen insurance companies, and six bank-owned finance companies would occur in mid-October. Demonstrations immediately followed for several months.

In July 1989 they traveled to Ecuador, a country that is one-fourth Pacific coastline, one-fourth Andes Mountains, and one-half Amazon jungle. Buford and Jerry, along with Terry and Laurie Tittle from the yacht *Inshallah*, left Bonaire and flew to Quito, Ecuador, where they rented a car. Buford had his pocket picked in a church in the old section of the city.

July 5, 1989. BC and I were disappointed in the place—too many people, and the buildings were junked up. BC was depressed over his billfold. Me, too!

While driving the car in the countryside and the Andes Mountains, they had three flat tires in twenty-four hours. For over two weeks they drove slowly, on marginal roads. The scenery encompassed the volcanoes Cotopaxi and Cayambe, as well as towns and villages, including Cayambe, Otavalo, Ambato, Banos, Puyo, Riobamba, and Cuenca.

July 9, 1989. The views were spectacular. The Indians were beautifully dressed and very friendly.

Otavalo man at market

78

In the third week, after leaving their bags and the Tittles in Quito, they flew to Coca, "a real scurvy-looking jungle town," in the Amazon jungle. They boarded a Flotel to take them deeper into the jungle via the Rio Napo.

They rode canoes, trekked the jungle, visited Indian missions, bird-watched, and took an excursion to see woolly monkeys on a small, remote island. After reuniting with the Tittles in Quito and having their "stupefying pizza and ice cream lunch," they returned to *Beachouse* in Bonaire.

Flotel Arellana on the Rio Napo, Ecuador, 1989

Linda the Boat Dog Dies

Linda the boat dog adapted easily to life on board. She learned to "do her business" on a two-feet-by-two-feet square of green Astroturf tied to the boat deck by rope. Jerry washed it by simply tossing it overboard and dragging it through the water. When *Beachouse* was near land, Linda was illegally smuggled to shore for walks, breaking all animal control laws.

Old age finally caught up with Linda. Soon after Buford's return from his trip to the Panama Canal on the *Lammer Law*, she died at the age of sixteen.

April 2, 1990. I was up all night with Linda, and she died while I was holding her at 5:00 AM. Poor thing really was suffering, so it was for the best. BC sewed her in canvas, weighted her, and took her to sea. So sad!

Buford carrying Linda in her bag, 1987

Throughout their marriage, Buford and Jerry had adopted a succession of dogs, usually two at a time, always Chihuahuas. Linda the boat dog was their last.

Last Caribbean Trek

Beachouse completed her third trek down the chain of Caribbean islands during May and June 1990. Their stops included St. Eustatius, St. Kitts, Montserrat, Guadaloupe, Dominica, Martinique, St. Lucia, and several islands in the Grenadines, such as Bequia, Cannouan, Mayero Union Island, and Carriacou. The only major islands they hadn't visited by now were Barbuda, Barbados, and Cuba.

The boat had its annual haul out in Cumana in July, while Jerry visited the States again.

After "stuffing the boat to the top" with provisions, including several palm trees, they sailed in August 1990 to Barlovento in the Aves, one of their favorite places, along with the yachts *Rebecca* and *The End*. Buford and Jerry, with lots of help from the other cruisers, went ashore and planted the palm trees, then took turns watering "the orchard" throughout their stay. They caught plenty of fish, lobster, and conch, filling the freezer to capacity—it would be the last fresh fish for months.

Living on the Pacific Ocean

January 1991–June 1993

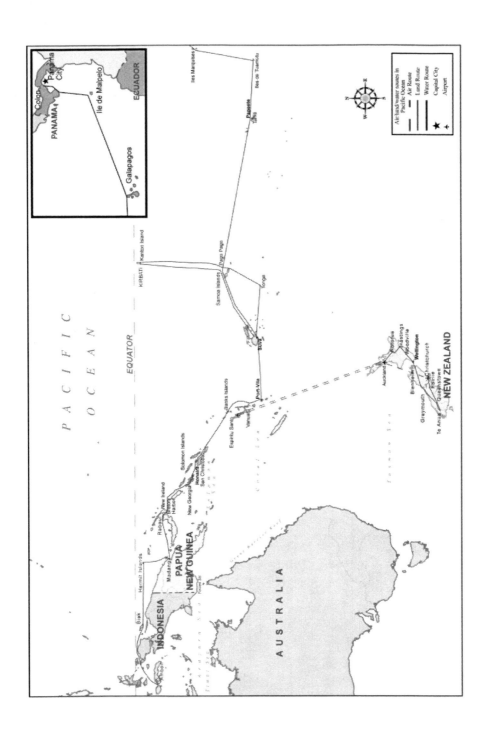

Letter 9

Tahiti, French Polynesia
June 1991

Tahiti, French Polynesia
June 1991

After six years of Caribbean cruising, moving the "house" frequently as the mood struck, both of us are healthy and fit and still enjoying the lifestyle. We have made every country in and around the Caribbean except Nicaragua, Haiti, and Cuba, and every island except Barbuda. It has been wonderful, but we decided to fulfill our original dream of a circumnavigation before we get too old. We headed west from Venezuela last August after a haul out, did some provisioning in Bonaire and Curacao, and spent Thanksgiving in Cartagena, Colombia. It is a unique city, with a beautifully restored historical section that is still in everyday use as a commercial center and residential area. Errol Flynn and his fellow buccaneers would still feel right at home in the narrow cobblestone streets.

We had our Christmas turkey in the San Blas Islands of Panama with the Kuna Indians. They are still mostly in native dress—at least, the women are. The men lean toward T-shirts and Adidas. I bought a ton of "molas," their appliquéd needlework.

We transited the canal in January, a really exciting experience. BC was cool and collected, as he had been through before on a friend's boat. I was a wreck, but it was quite easy. The port captain in Colon was from Houston and assigned us a good-ole-boy pilot to take us through. We spent one night in Gatun Lake, making the transit a two-day affair.

The Yacht Club in Balboa on the Pacific side has been dubbed the "world's worst yacht club," and it lived up to its reputation. We elected to anchor out a few miles away, within sight of two small islands. One had an estate of Noriega on it, and the other was a prison site—a sort of Panamanian Alcatraz. Just before we left, there was a prison break; everyone escaped, including the guards, on a large power boat that had

85

been anchored close to us. It seems the inmates from the drug industry were paying more and offering a new life in Colombia.

Cindy and Roger joined us on March 5, and we sailed for the Galapagos on March 8, down the water line, stuffed full of provisions and fuel but high in spirits. We made it in seven days on smooth seas and with moderate winds. Ecuador had promised us a cruising permit for a year, but it never came through. We had only six days, all on one island. A friend of the bartender at El Boobie Café took the four of us on a tour in the back of his pickup. We were determined to see giant turtles in the wild. A friend of a friend of his cousin (!) rented us horses. They were scrawny and tired-looking, with homemade wooden saddles and rope stirrups. We rode for two hours, looking in vain (gosh, there were hundreds here last week!). But before we left the Galapagos, we saw much of the famous wildlife: birds, iguanas, seals, and porpoises. We even found turtles—at the Darwin Wildlife Center.

With the sea lions escorting us out, we left on March 19 for the longest single sailing leg necessary for a circumnavigation, three thousand miles of ocean that is seldom traveled. We made 410 miles the first two days—a new record for Beachouse—*and thought we would be there in no time at all. Then the wind quit, and we didn't have enough to blow your hat off for the rest of the trip. We were exactly twenty-two days to the hour. It sounds like a long time, but we stayed busy reading, playing games, teaching Cindy and Roger bridge, cooking, making small repairs, etc. The most surprising occurrence was a U.S. Navy destroyer, requiring us to stand by for a Coast Guard boarding in the middle of the Pacific. (An Aggie drug raid? Smuggling drugs from Panama and away from the United States?) It turned out to be your tax dollars at work; they were conducting a routine inspection four thousand miles from the U.S.A., during which we received a citation for outdated flares.*

We had the customary King Neptune costume party when we crossed the equator and broke our dry ship routine with a bottle of champagne.

Landfall at Fatu Hiva in the Marquesas was exciting. BC was on watch at daybreak and got everybody up to see this huge mountain right where it was supposed to be. It was truly awe-inspiring, watching as the sun lit it up. The anchorage was spectacular. BC walked on deck every morning and declared that it looked like a fake movie set. Towering green mountains, palm trees, blue water—it was absolutely gorgeous. The locals provided us with fruit, fish, and local crafts. They didn't want money but were anxious to trade for makeup, perfume, and fishing gear. They enjoyed coming aboard to attempt conversations in English, French, and their Marquesan language. It was all very unspoiled but is changing rapidly. They installed electricity recently, and, while we were there, the phone booth was delivered for installation. They have had television for two months now, so they will soon be as Western as the rest of us.

We visited two other islands in this high, mountainous group and sailed for the Tuamotus on April 26. They are low atolls, all sandy beaches, reefs, palm trees, and lovely lagoons. Makemo was our first anchorage. The locals were shy at first, but after ten days, we were attending local dances and family picnics, and Cindy and Roger were learning the native arts with a group—Cindy was taught the hula by a thirteen-year-old and Roger was playing a log drum. We had a wonderful time and hated to leave. The diving was a disappointment. The reefs were not lush. The fish have ciguatera, a neurotoxin that, when eaten by humans, causes seafood poisoning. There are sharks everywhere. BC was completely frustrated by the sight of groupers of all sizes. The small reef fish are beautiful, and the colorations are completely different from those in the Caribbean. On our first dive, we saw four sharks; one whitetip kept circling quite close to me, and I stuck to BC like glue since he had the spear gun to jab at them if necessary. The locals described their fishing technique as three men in the water, one with a spear gun and two with clubs to keep sharks from the fish on the way to the boat. No, thanks; I'll eat chicken.

We celebrated our forty-second wedding anniversary on May 14, while underway to Tahanea, another atoll in the Tuamotus. It is uninhabited and quite lovely. We spent ten days enjoying the solitude.

Cindy and Roger are delightful companions, and we are having a lot of fun. We expect to be in Tahiti through July, but our plans are seminonexistent after that. We'll just go where the wind takes us—as long as it is out of the hurricane belt next winter. We would love to hear what's happening in your world. Roger's brother is forwarding our mail.

We trust you are well and happy.

*****

Circumnavigation Begins

Beachouse officially began her circumnavigation on August 16, 1990, from Cumana, Venezuela. After provisioning stops on the Dutch islands of Bonaire and Curacao, *Beachouse*, accompanied by another yacht, the *Rebecca*, for the first time sailed west instead of returning to the northern Caribbean.

Both yachts spent a month docked at the Yacht Club in Cartagena, Colombia, much of the time waiting for mechanical parts to arrive. In the Bonaire marina they'd been struck by lightning, ruining the radar and wind machines. Parts were sent to Houston, which meant a long wait for their return. It would take six weeks for the parts to arrive in Cartagena.

October 4, 1990. That lightning is costing us thousands of dollars—and time, too.

October 14, 1990. What a day—gloom and doom. BC started to put up the wind machine, and it is defective. So disgusting. We really got a terrible blow from that lightning strike. We are very low.

November 20, 1990. BC sat in the bar from 9 AM to 11:30 AM, waiting for phone calls that never came. He is really getting pissed. I'm sorry because it is ruining our stay here, and it's such a wonderful place.

Cartagena, founded in 1533, endured sackings and invasions for several hundred years. Twenty-nine stone forts guard the old harbor, and a high wall of coral encircles the city.

October 30, 1990. It is quite beautiful. The streets are very narrow—room for one car (or two horses, ha!)—and the balconies overhang with beautiful flowers and plants. Most of the buildings have been restored.

November 6, 1990. This is really an interesting city. The old forts are everywhere.

Jerry and Buford experienced the two-day Colombian national holiday called "Independence of Cartagena City." On November 11,

1811, Cartagena was the first city in either Colombia or Venezuela to declare its independence from Spain.

November 8, 1990. We went to the parade at 3:30 with Norman (a worker at the marina). We went across the bay in his big dinghy and walked two blocks to the beach. What an experience. People were crazy. We got pelted with flour and water, and firecrackers were going off under our feet. It was fun but a little nerve-wracking.

November 9, 1990. We watched the boat parade from our deck—what madness! There must have been one hundred boats of all sizes. We rocked and rolled around because they really roiled up the waters.

San Blas Islands

Jerry and Shar O'Donahoe, from the yacht *Raffles*, came aboard *Beachouse* in Cartagena to sail with Jerry and Buford to San Blas, Panama. San Blas, also known as Kuna Yala, is an autonomous Panamanian reservation formed by 360 islands and a small strip of the Caribbean Panamanian coastline.

Buford and Jerry's definition of the "perfect desert island,"
San Blas Islands, Panama, 1990

Only about fifty of the San Blas islands are permanently inhabited by about fifty thousand Kuna Indians; the others are used for fishing, coconut plantations, and tourism. The Kunas are one of the last full-blooded Carib strains that inhabited the Caribbean before the Spanish Conquest; they're said to be the shortest people in the world after the Pygmies.

The San Blas people are friendly to strangers since sailing and trading vessels have visited their islands for many years.

December 4, 1990. It is very pretty here. Lots of mola cayucas, local handmade canoes full of women selling their needlework, came to visit—and we bought several things. Candy for the kids is a big hit. One cayuca has two girls, Linda and Dina; they are adorable. Really cute and giggly. They came twice—and Dina's husband, Juan, came in a new cayuca he had built.

A Kuna woman selling molas from her cayuca

The ability to shape a tree trunk into the graceful form of a seagoing dugout called a cayuca is a rare skill of high prestige among Kuna men. Sam, an eighty-year-old Kuna man, visited *Beachouse* to show off his own cayuca.

December 12, 1990. He was a real kick. We gave him six books to read. His English was good.

At an early age, a Kuna girl starts acquiring the patience and skill she'll need to make molas, brightly colored cloth panels stitched in many layers of appliqué, which are indigenous to the Kuna Indian women. She sews the mola panels into her blouses to express her own identity. Before the 1900s, the molas' subject matter drew from the women's daily life, including palm trees, birds, fish, and mountains. Since the opening of the Panama Canal in 1914, the subject matter has become progressively more tailored to the tourists on cruise ships— everything from sporting events to Mickey Mouse. Jerry bought more than her fair share as souvenirs.

Rio Diablo, Panama

On a visit to Rio Diablo, a typical Kuna village, several kids immediately took to Buford, holding his hands and walking with him through town.

Just a 10-mile sail up the coast from San Blas is Portobelo, a city with a storied past.

January 5, 1991. Beautiful scenery again. The anchorage is big and lovely. Old forts are on both sides of the bay. This was the loading port for Spanish gold and goods from the Pacific. The boats left here and formed convoys in Cartagena that went on to Spain. The old treasure house is still standing in ruins.

January 6, 1991. It is so green here—it hurts the eyes. The largest rainfall in the hemisphere, 240 inches a year.

Then they went on to Colon, the second-largest city in Panama, near the Atlantic entrance to the Panama Canal.

January 7, 1991. It was a thrill for me to come through the breakwater and into the canal zone. Lots of big ships anchored all around.

January 8, 1991. The town looks like a disaster area. It is filthy. Some of the buildings are full of bullet holes and burned. A real mess—and not safe to walk around even if you wanted to.

January 9 was a holiday in Panama, National Martyr's Day, so Buford and Jerry stayed on the boat to keep a low profile. The holiday is a memorial day for a 1964 uprising between Panamanian students and Canal Zone police officers over the right of the Panamanian flag to be flown alongside the U.S. flag. The incident is considered to be a significant factor in the United States's decision to transfer control of the Canal Zone to Panama.

In the Panama Canal, January 1991

Crossing the Equator

Beachouse crossed the equator with the customary King Neptune costume party on March 14. The purpose of the well-known equator-crossing ceremony is to garner the blessing of King Neptune, the mythical ruler of the oceans. During the ceremony, sailors typically dress oddly or cover themselves with a variety of unpleasant materials (for example, old food or marine mud) in an effort to appease King Neptune and get his blessing to cross the equator and sail on safely. A watered-down version of the ceremony, typically featuring King Neptune, is often carried out for passengers' entertainment on ocean liners and cruise ships.

Buford crossing the equator as King Neptune, with daughter Cindy

Buford and Jerry designated this anchorage in
Fatu Hiva, Marquesas, as the most beautiful of their circumnavigation.

Ten years later, Jerry remembered this gorgeous spot in an email she sent to her daughter Cindy:

April 21, 2001. Your dad and I were reminiscing at lunch today. Sometime when you and Roger are blue and depressed, think of that morning after twenty-one days at sea when Buf got us all up at daybreak and we watched Fatu Hiva come into view. And watched and watched. It must have been at least six hours before we dropped anchor. But we still say it was the single most beautiful anchorage we ever saw. It was a glorious day.

Letter 10

Dear Coral and Joe,

It was great being able to talk to you yesterday from such a remote place. It was lonesome around here for a while after you left, and we often mention things the children did—thanks for bringing them.

January 1992 finds Beachouse *on Kanton Island in the Kiribati— formerly the Gilberts. It's two degrees south of the equator, 172 west, and an ideal place to spend the South Pacific hurricane season—no storms! It's extremely remote and has a population of forty-one: twenty-five children and sixteen adults. They are supplied from Tarawa by boat four times annually and are really isolated from the world. Their welcome for us was almost overwhelming. We arrived with the S/V* Rebecca *(Dave and Linda, cruising friends from the Caribbean) on November 28, Thanksgiving Day. We were invited to a feast the following night—it lasted six hours and included a printed program of singing, dancing, and speeches. BC had to give speeches in reply. It was great. The local men are all government employees, caretaking the island. It was a U.S. airbase in the '40s and then a NASA tracking station in the '60s. The United States left in the '70s, and it is now a giant junkyard. BC and Dave have found all kinds of usable crap, even though it has been scavenged for years. The lagoon is a very safe harbor, and BC has made us a great mooring out of a massive old ship's anchor.*

Some of the people speak good English; others just smile a lot. They have nothing, and, consequently, they share everything. There is no electricity or running water and very rudimentary food supplies—fish and coconuts, flour, sugar, and rice about covers it. We took a TV set, VCR, and generator ashore, set them up in an abandoned building, and show all-night movies once a week—they love it! Believe it or not, BC takes them fishing. They have no outboard motor. In a couple of hours they catch 100 to 150 pounds of fish—wahoo and yellow fin tuna outside the pass and grouper and red snapper inside the lagoon. The fish life is phenomenal. We have a school of fifty or so tame fish living under the boat, just waiting for our garbage. I feel guilty when I have no leftovers.

We plan to stay here till April resting, repairing, playing, and just hanging out. Then we'll head back to American Samoa. Pago Pago is a wonderful place to reprovision and get mail. You can write us c/o General Delivery, Pago Pago, American Samoa 96799. Please write. If you mail us a letter by mid-March, it will be there waiting for us.

Pago Pago, despite its romantic reputation, is a filthy harbor—all manmade pollution. Three tuna canning factories emptying all their waste and a large rusty fleet of fishing boats have turned the best natural harbor in the South Pacific into a cesspool. The island itself is lovely, and the people are great, but the stench can be overwhelming. It's hard to believe some of our diehard environmentalists haven't picked up on it.

We were in the Kingdom of Tonga for only ten days last August. The Vava'u group in the north is a cruiser's paradise. In fact, one of the reasons we are backtracking is to spend more time there this year. There are a lot of good anchorages and lovely beaches, similar to the Virgin Islands. Believe it or not, Roger found an old high school buddy from Heavener, Oklahoma (pop. one thousand) working as a fishing consultant for the United Nations. He's married to a Tongan girl, and they have a lovely family. They showed us all the sights and took the guys fishing.

We were in Suva, Fiji, for the month of September, waiting for a haul out. It was an ideal time to do some land-based sightseeing. We did river running in the Highlands and toured the island by car. The population is 50 percent indigenous Fijians and 50 percent Indian. The Indians were brought by the British to work the sugar plantations. They have preserved their culture, including language, dress, food, and religion. The Fijians are friendly and gregarious. They have made the transition from cannibalism to modern civilization in one hundred years. Suva is a sophisticated city. One of tourists' favorite souvenirs is a cannibal fork. It was used for human flesh only, and most were quite elaborately carved—the fork, not the flesh. They have preserved many customs and are very protective of their chief system. There are over three hundred islands in the archipelago, with fifteen hundred chiefs. They pulverize the dried root of a particular pepper plant into a powder and make a drink called kava. It isn't a narcotic, but it has a tranquilizing effect. It makes your mouth feel like you've just been to the dentist. Anytime you visit an island or new village, kava must be presented to the chief as an offering (bribe?). An elaborate ceremony of chanting, clapping, and other rigmarole accompanies this procedure. You can imagine how BC took to all this hogwash. Incidentally, that's kinda what the kava looks and tastes like!

Cindy and Roger left us here in October and went to Australia on a freighter. They planned to buy a world air pass and make their way through Asia and Europe and back to the States next spring. We hated to see them leave—they were a big help and a lot of fun. Coral; Molly, four; and Matt, two, came to Fiji for a month, and we had a great time. We went to Astrolabe Reef, fifty miles south of Suva, and swam, dived, lazed around, and played with the kids.

Our tentative plans are to be in American Samoa in April; Tonga in May, June, and July; and the west coast of Fiji in August and September. Anyone who wants a diving and sailing vacation can come on down. Check with Coral—our booking agent. All schedules are subject to RADICAL change, of course, but we'd love to see you.

We don't know how long this letter will take to arrive in the United States—or if it ever will. We thought you'd get a kick out of postage from one of the most remote places left in the world. The mail boat arrives in mid-January and stays for twenty-four hours. The last one was here in October.

Joe, BC kept referring to a local man as the "old man" until he found out the local is twelve years his junior. Damn!

The diving in the Pacific has been a great disappointment to us, and the number of sharks is appalling, but they say it is better in Tonga. No place can have more fish than here, though. On the days we want fish, I jump in and spear a small grouper (and I'm a lousy snorkler), or I troll and turn them loose until I get exactly the one we want to cook.

How do you like my form letter with a personal paragraph top and bottom? Computering is not easy for me—even my typing is pitiful.

We went to another welcome party this weekend. A new boat had come in. It started at 11:00 AM and lasted all day and into the night. Cindy and Roger left their video camera, so BC has been taping the singing and dancing. It really is fantastic. The women are all pretty hefty, but they really have some moves. The men drink a fermented coconut toddy and sing at the top of their lungs—but it sounds great. They jump up and dance when the spirit moves them.

The little kids have gotten over their shyness and are very friendly. They have a lot of minor infections and sores—they have no fresh food except coconut, a few papayas, and even fewer bananas. I'm sure they are vitamin deficient. Very sad!

I lost my glasses overboard on the trip up here—then one of my caps broke off. I'm falling apart! BC fixed my tooth—he put the piece back on with epoxy—and I dragged out my old glasses.

It's nice having Dave and Linda on the Rebecca here with us. We cook together a couple of times a week. We gave the locals a turkey to cook at Christmas. None of them had ever tasted it before. I make chocolate cake when we feast with them. They go crazy over it. They have very few sweets.

Their culture calls for gift giving, and I am up to my hips in shell necklaces. I found, at last, one of the big glass floats and have it hanging.

We'll talk to you soon again.

Love,
Mom and Dad

*****

The South Pacific

July 1991 in Bora Bora started a frustrating few months of repairs.

July 24, 1991. Today was a disaster! Cindy found water under the floor in the aft cabin of the south ama. The leak is around the drive shaft, and the whole hydraulic pump was covered with water. We got it emptied out and found where it is coming in, but we couldn't find anything wrong on the outside. We were all sick (at least, BC and I were). We will now run for American Samoa and a haul out. I just hate it!

They left immediately for Pago Pago, the capital city of American Samoa—a seven-day, eight-night sail. There the boatyard manager refused to haul out *Beachouse* due to its size and suggested they try Vava'u in Tonga. When Buford called Vava'u, he was again told no and given a suggestion of South Tonga. He and Jerry's disappointment was increasing daily; the harbormaster in Pago Pago had run out of suggestions.

August 7, 1991. I hate this place! BC is still trying to get phone calls through. It is so frustrating.

After several days of attempting to make phone calls to Suva, Fiji, Buford finally got a yes—they could haul out. They set Suva, by way of Tonga, as their next destination.

In Pago Pago, many of the yachties arriving from Suvarov, a coral atoll in the Cook Islands, had dengue fever, an infectious disease transmitted to humans by mosquitoes, which feed during the day. Symptoms include fever with severe headache, muscle and joint pains, and a bright red rash that usually appears first on the lower limbs and chest and may eventually cover most of the body. There may also be some combination of abdominal pain, nausea, vomiting, or diarrhea. Most of the yachties had mild cases, but a few required a stay in the Pago Pago hospital or a flight to Honolulu. Cindy came down with a fever and diarrhea, but a fellow yachtie who was a doctor conducted an examination and declared her free of dengue fever.

While sailing to Tonga, *Beachouse* encountered high winds of thirty-five to forty knots, with gusts of over fifty knots. Buford and Jerry could not reel in the genoa sail; it slipped and damaged the boat before they got it under control. As they started to motor later in the day, the sail got caught in the propeller. So now they had no propeller—the second propeller was still bad—and no sail. They crossed the International Date Line, losing a day, then "limped" into Vava'u, an island chain consisting of one large island and forty smaller ones, part of Tonga, where they spent days trying to get *Beachouse* repaired.

Buford and Jerry's first Sunday in Tonga was memorable.

August 25, 1991. Sunday is a very special day in Tonga. Everything is closed, and nothing goes on. The dress code (skirts or long pants for women—long pants for men preferred) is even stricter. I went to a Methodist service (with some other yachties). It was very interesting. The singing was great, all a cappella.

Fiji Islands

Its repairs completed, *Beachouse* sailed on to the Republic of the Fiji Islands, a South Pacific nation occupying an archipelago of 322 islands, 106 of which are permanently inhabited. Fiji's main island, known as Viti Levu, is home to nearly three quarters of the population. It hosts the capital city of Suva, as well as Nadi, the location of the international airport. When Coral, Molly, and Matt visited Fiji in October 1991, *Beachouse* cruised south of the main island, through an island group that contains Kandavu, the fourth-largest island of Fiji; it's surrounded by Astrolabe Reef.

The remoteness afforded them the opportunity to interact with the friendly local Fijians. One evening, the Beach clan went ashore on a small island for a feast with a local family. Seated on individual woven mats under a palm canopy were Saiasi, the head of the household; his wife, Susana, and daughter, Diana, five years old; his mother and two brothers; and a friend with his wife. Jerry contributed a cooked chicken and chocolate cake, while the local family provided lots of wahoo fish and unfamiliar local vegetables. Molly and Matt, typical American children, wouldn't touch them.

While swimming and snorkeling on another small island, a local man invited the cruisers on *Beachouse* to visit his home. As they sailed around the island by dinghy, they were surprised to discover a big village. Buford presented kava roots as a sign of friendship and peace. They received the formal kava ceremony, a social gathering conducted to welcome honored guests, but without the traditional drinking of the intoxicating liquid—not in front of the children.

Halloween in Fiji, 1991

Beachouse celebrated Halloween boat-style for Molly, seven, and Matt, five. Jerry and Coral made them costumes—a South Seas hula princess costume for Molly and a Tongan warrior knight costume for Matt, made of an egg crate. After a party on board, Buford motored the kids by dinghy to trick-or-treat for candy on nearby yachts.

After Coral and the kids left, *Beachouse* returned to Pago Pago, Samoa, crossing the International Date Line a second time, to prepare for a four-month stay in the remote Phoenix Islands. Buford made repairs while Jerry provisioned, planning the food and supplies they'd need for the long stay away from civilization on Kanton Island.

Life on Kanton Island

Kanton Island (also known as Canton Island or Abariringa Island), is the largest, northernmost, and, in 1991, the sole inhabited island of the Phoenix Islands, Republic of Kiribati. Roughly halfway between Hawaii and Fiji, the sole village on Kanton is called Tebaronga. Kanton receives supplies from Tarawa, an atoll containing the capital of the Republic of Kiribati; it was the site of the Battle of Tarawa during World War II.

Buford and Jerry, along with Dave Eliason and Linda Ward of the *Rebecca*, became part of the village for four months, and it proved to be one of the happiest times of their circumnavigation. On December 6, 1991, everyone on the island attended the elaborate welcome party for the four cruisers. The party had a typed agenda:

WELCOME PARTY

1. Opening ceremony—3 songs to be sung by Kanton people.
2. Welcome speech—Betero Ioane.
3. Three songs by Kanton people.
4. Meal time—Honorable guests first, followed by Kanton people.
5. Kanton choir—(string band) entertain guests and others while having a meal.
6. School choir to sing/dance etc … for honorable guests.
7. Five minutes break.
8. Floor is open for anyone to have a talk/speech or to sing.
9. Twisting and dancing—Kanton choir to supply music.
10. Honorable guests to have a talk/speech or to sing.
11. Song from Kanton choir.
12. Closing speech by Tabora Teseki.
13. Song from Kanton people all stand up.
14. The end.

While Buford and Jerry were in Kanton, a replica of a Christopher Columbus ship, manned by four Spaniards, arrived after struggling through eleven days of bad weather. The sailors were from the Canary Islands and were making a documentary they hoped to sell. During their stay, Jerry invited the crew to *Beachouse* for parties, and Buford took them scuba diving so they could take underwater photos.

Spending Christmas of 1991 in Kanton was fun and unique. Jerry and Linda wrapped presents for all the children, including balloons, jump ropes, fish hooks, and hair ornaments left by their daughter Cindy, plus fabric for the women.

December 25, 1991. What a great day! Christmas in Kanton was a real experience. We went snorkeling this morning in front of the village, south of the pass. It was fantastic. Really beautiful. Not much coral variety, but fish by the thousands. I saw a five-feet blacktip shark, but he was just cruising by. Bakeua picked us up at 1:30 PM, and we joined the celebration in the village. It was great. The singing is unbelievable. They treat us like royalty. It's rather embarrassing. They had cooked the turkey I gave them and many other things. I made two big chocolate cakes that went over as usual. The people are very, very generous. It was a great evening.

Ionne, best dancer on Kanton, December 1991

Nakua, Buford's fishing buddy, with the day's catch

Jerry documented all forty-one residents of Kanton (listed in Appendix D) as well as the English translation of a few words in their language, where *Ti* is pronounced *s*:

Mauri	Hello
Tiabo	Good-bye
Kouara	How are you?
I marurung	I am fine.
Taiaoka	Please
Ko Raba	Thank you
Te Raoi	You are welcome.
Te ika	Fish
Te ben	Coconut
I Matang	White man
Iraua am ririki	How old are you?

Letter 11

Dear Coral and Joe,

It was great to talk to you Sunday. We had been trying to get through on the radio for ten days or so but had no luck. We gave up and went to the Rebecca. Dave's antenna always seems to work better than ours. It makes BC crazy. Anyway, since you got the last letter, I thought I'd try again. The supply boat has been to Christmas Island and some of the other outer islands and is coming through here tomorrow on the way back to Tarawa.

We loved hearing the news about the kids. Molly must be very proud of her ribbon for racing. I hope you both did well in the next one. It'll be long over by the time you get this letter. Matt is off probation by now, I'm sure. I've never heard of a three-year-old getting expelled. We always knew our grandchildren would be exceptional.

Another boat came in last month. English registry, with an English captain and a New Zealand girlfriend. The boat is very small—twenty-seven feet—and would fit in our cockpit. They are quite nice. So there are now six yachties on the island. The local name for us is I Matang—white people from the clouds.

This is really a strange place. We feel kinda like we are in the Twilight Zone. The supply boat was delayed last month because one of the passengers jumped overboard—a suicide—and they spent a day searching for him. BC went aboard the ship when it was here and said he would have jumped, too. It was packed with humanity, dogs, pigs, and all sorts of cargo, including hundreds of barrels of fuel lashed to the decks. People camped outside on the decks for the whole voyage to the outer islands—as long as two weeks.

Two ships have sunk in the vicinity since December. One of them drifted by here with only the tip of the stern above water. We watched it all day, but it never got close enough to try to board.

Last week we had big excitement in the village. The headman's wife went missing for two days. They came to us for help to find her, so BC organized a search with the dinghy and a big boat they use for fishing (it has our 25 HP motor on it because they don't own one—on the island—go figure). There were about twenty of us searching, using the boats and a truck. Finally found her and got her back to the village. We decided it must be a domestic problem, and it was—a slight case of incest with a fifteen-year-old daughter. They seem to have gotten that all sorted out, and the girl is leaving on the supply boat to live with relatives in Tarawa. The husband and wife had a big party! He made a public apology, and life goes on. There was the usual singing, except this time family groups performed. BC and I got up and sang "For We Love Our Valley Home." We were a big hit. They barbecued a pig. It was delicious. Is all that weird, or what? This ain't Kansas, Toto.

There is a NOAA ship arriving on March 8. One of the locals runs a small weather station for them. He says they will be here only twenty-four hours or so. Hopefully long enough for me to con them out of some fresh tomatoes and an ice cream cone. Four months without going to a store is the pits. I have a few pitiful carrots left, and onions and potatoes that are dying a slow, agonizing death. BC planted some lettuce in a tub. It took a long time to get started, but we now can have a salad two or three times a week, supplemented with sprouts. Anyway, I hope to obtain some goodies by hook or crook, or, at the last resort, money.

By the way, not only did I lose my glasses, but my front tooth fell out. Remember that happened two years ago? Well, this is the other one. BC has super glued it back in for me—four or five times. He's a lousy dentist. Sure hope there is a better one in Samoa.

The fishing here is great but no challenge. BC goes out, drops a line and hook out of the dinghy, watches through the bucket, and dangles it in front of the fish he wants. I swear this is true.

We have a turkey left in the freezer, so we're going to have a March 2 Independence Day party for the yachties. I don't remember if I told you, but we took a turkey to the big Christmas dinner here. None of the locals had ever tasted it. On the other hand, they eat things here we've never tasted and hopefully never will. Like hermit crabs. They pen them up, feed them coconut for a while to fatten them, and pop them in the pot—ugh!

I seem to be making the locals sound like terrible people, but I don't mean to. They are very gentle, very generous, and very loving. The men have really taken to BC. I think they are astounded by his age and vigor. They are not healthy people, and their life span is much shorter than ours. Enough about this island paradise.

We talked to Glen after we talked to you. He said Cindy and Roger are still in Australia, so they must be enjoying it. I hope we do.

I really appreciate your checking on my glasses for me. The old ones I'm using are scratched and are making me crazy.

Tell everyone hello for us. We'll call again before we leave here—and, of course, from Samoa. We trust you are all staying well. Take care of each other.

Love,
Mom & Dad
Am enclosing our March 2 invitation—I'm getting better on the computer—but still s-l-o-w.

*****

More Parties

At the party Buford and Jerry gave on March 2, 1992, they celebrated Texas Independence Day with the other yachties. Buford delivered the party invitations the day before:

Ode to March 2

We invite you all to *Beachouse*
for a day of great celebration.
It may not seem much to you guys,
but for us, it's wild jubilation.

Our school days are over
but dates stick like glue
like Ten Sixty-Six
and Fourteen Ninety-Two.

Eighteen Thirty-Six
looms large in our lives.
If you guess what it is,
we'll give you a prize.

We welcome a Pom and a Kiwi
and one from Chicago, too.
We'll even go so far
as to have one from Kalamazoo.

So all you turkeys at Kanton
we are stuffing one of your fellows.
Please join us for our festivities.
It beats varnishing, cleaning stainless steel,

scraping the bottom, changing the oil, repairing the
sails, fixing the dinghy, watering the batteries,
cleaning soap out of the bilge, repairing generators,
fiberglassing, changing impellors/wiring/refrigerator
dryers, the laundry, galley slaving, general
cleaning, and all the other endless chores that
aren't mentioned in the yachting magazines.

Beachouse put out all of its flags, and Jerry and Buford dressed in their State of Texas T-shirts and cowboy boots. They were a big hit, and everyone had a marvelous time.

Teakai, Taati, and Teveve dancing and feasting, Kanton

Early one morning, Bakeua arrived at *Beachouse* to invite Buford and Jerry on an island tour. A pickup truck and fire truck, the only vehicles on the island, carried the whole village.

January 3, 1992. It was quite a ride. We bogged down in sand several times and had to work our way out. The boys on the fire truck pushed like crazy. They all thought it was hilarious. We went all the way around (twenty miles or so) to the old village. The boys netted fish and cooked them on a fire of coconut husks. They killed them by biting their heads! The ladies made us plates by weaving palm leaves. It took three hours going and two back. It was quite a day.

Jerry and Kanton women on island tour

Two months later, Buford and Jerry were invited to another party given by the locals.

March 7, 1992. We went to town at 7:45 PM in the fire truck! The party turned out to be a PTA meeting! The school committee. Interesting.

Dave and Linda on the *Rebecca* left Kanton in mid-March; *Beachouse* followed two weeks later. Several days before leaving, Jerry wrapped gifts and prepared sacks of goodies for everyone in the village. Buford and Jerry went from house to house handing out their gifts—mostly T-shirts, cards, some foodstuff, and cookies for the kids.

On Jerry's birthday, March 28, 1992, the village had a farewell party which, just like the welcome party, had an agenda.

FAREWELL PARTY
For *Beachouse*

1.   Opening of the event (By M/C Ruka). 7:30 PM
2.   Three songs by Kanton people. 7:35 PM
3.   Opening speech by Nateri Maunga. 1945 hrs.
4.   Songs from the school. 1955 hrs.
5.   Meal. 2000 hrs.
6.   A show conducted by the school. 2100 hrs.
7.   Songs by Kanton people (string band). 2130 hrs.
8.   Presentation of gift from people of Kanton (Nakau will make a speech for the whole people). 2145 hrs.
9.   Songs by Kanton people. 2150 hrs.
10. Someone to give a talk. 2210 hrs.
11. Songs by Kanton people. 2235 hrs.
12. A talk by guest. 2250 hrs.
13. Farewell song ("Now Comes the Time"). 2215 hrs.
14. End of the Farewell Party, and continue with video. 2230 hrs.

Thank you, good-bye, and good luck.
B/K
28/3/92

The next day, Jerry recounted the event:

March 29, 1992. All the village was there. The people here are genuinely sorry to see us go. A couple of the men cried. It was very touching. We had a great meal—lobster and tuna, and I got a lot of gifts—eleven new necklaces! A lovely evening.

Buford, Bureniti, Jerry (in Kanton T-shirt and shell necklace), and Bakeua

Bakeua and his wife, Veronika, gave Jerry an elaborate woven grass mat for her birthday. It was the couple's "wedding mat," crafted by Veronika's mother for their wedding night. In return, the Beaches gave Bakeua a two-person hammock he had eyed on board the boat. Hammock's large enough for Kanton men were hard to find.

The next day, Buford picked up the 25 HP boat engine, TV, VCR, and generator that had given the locals such enjoyment during their stay. They'd watched about thirty movies in the last week!

Beachouse sailed out of the Kanton pass for Pago Pago, American Samoa, on March 30. Buford and Jerry left with fond memories of a most extraordinary four months with the wonderful village people of Kanton. It was an experience they would never forget.

Letter 12

Years after leaving Kanton Island, the Beaches received letters from their Kanton friends. This letter was sent from Bakeua, the police chief.

Police Station
Banaba, Republic of Kiribati, Central Pacific
7 August 1994

Dearest Friends Jerry and Buford.
Hello Hello…

You don't expect this handwriting to be received again or to receive any mails from poor friends like us. Do not look down to the very end; you have to guess who.

But as you guess who, we would like to say "Mauri." Yes, it has been too far and too long time to miss communication again. We would like to apologise because we had lost and our writing communication was in a difficult problem. You have to say why…Because my dear Veronika left my address book somewhere in Kanton and maybe the kids took it away. We were very sorry, and we know that our link would be gone.

We left Kanton to Tarawa and Tarawa to Banaba with our memory with you always. It was a lucky turn when Veronika found paper junks in our chest. She cried to me when she found your address in one piece of paper. We shaked our hands because we can see you again in our writing communication. I hope you understand what was the problem.

Now, we have to tell news from Kanton before we left there. When you sailed away we felt unhappy or sad because we missed watching videos and other good fun. We talked about you mostly in our home and also on every Sunday at lunch time. We never forgot the "turkey" during the Christmas and New Year Eve followed with whisky. Thank you so very much. As I'm writing now, Veronika tells the story of you with the beautiful lights that sparkled from Buford's T-shirt. She likes that kind of shirt. Veronika is laughing again.

Few weeks gone when you left away and we could not imagine big parcels received. All the community people had a share in the parcel including items for the school. We were very sorry to inform you that all the school kids had nothing from items you sent for the school. The teacher Nateri took all those things. He told Veronika that his name "teacher" was written on the box, so he said those items belonged to him. As you know Nateri has no kid with him on Kanton so he kept most of those gifts as his personal issue. It's funny but we did not count it.

For us, we give you our sincere thanks for everything we received in our parcel. Veronika received good material paints, and she used it in pillow cases and lavalava. Myself received a pair of good shoe and some other fantastic items for the children including Eruma, my teenage boy. Thank you very much.

We like to inform you that we are living on another different island. We left Kanton in February, 1994, to Tarawa. We stayed working for a few months in Tarawa, and we moved again in November, 1994, to this island. It is Banaba, in English—Ocean Island. This island is in the Kiribati group. In those years in the past it was under the British Phosphate Company. They operated the phosphate mining on this island. Ocean Island is situated 150 miles or more southwest of Tarawa. So, if you want to write, our address is in the front page.

Anyway, I think it's very long now for you to read, so I have to stop here. But before I end up here, may I request you Beau. If you don't mind a spare perfume. It's for me to go for a dance in the hall. We get used with the smell of the cologne. It's boring.

We always love you Beachouse.
Your poor friends Veronika & Bakeua.

*****

Letter 13

The following was written by Tabora, the male nurse on Kanton during the Beaches' stay.

Mr. Tabora Teoelei
Aramari Dispensary
Fanning Island, Line and Phoenix Group,
Kiribati Islands
1 December 1996

Dear Jerry and Buford,

Mauri! Merry Xmas and Happy New Year.

For a long time from the time we met on a small islet of Kanton Island, Teakai and I, we cannot forget it.

We released or left Kanton in 1995 to this island Fanning Island to do the same job as in Kanton. This island, it looks the same as Kanton, with the population of more than a thousand people.

There were two dispensaries and one health centre. We have no doctor, but we use to contact the doctors at Christmas Island by VHF if there is any problem with sick person.

The load of my work here is not the same to compare with Kanton number of outpatients attendant at about five to ten per month.

How are you there. We hope that you are in good health. How is the yacht "Beach House?"

A sad story for our friend Police Bureniti is that he was dead. He left Kanton for his home island Tarawa for his retirement in 1994, and one day when he was not awake from his sleep.

We are very sad and say sorry in our hearts to remember our kindly friend who left his wife, Ioanna, and their children.

Before I'm going off with my pen Teakai and I will say Tiabo and hope to receive your letter soon.

Coral Beach

> *Your Kanton friends,*
> *Tabora and Teakai.*
>
> *See you later = ti a bo rimsoi.*

*****

Letter 14

Suva, Fiji
May 1992

Dear Gene & Grace,

We motored out of Pago Pago and motored all day on a flat sea with no wind. So after dark we turned our anchor light on and everything else off and went to bed. The next morning we got wind and had a fast but rough passage to Suva, Fiji.

Soggy Suva is living up to its reputation. We are getting light rain most of the time but are enjoying the city after being isolated for months.

Our departure from Kanton was very sad, like leaving family. Several of our native friends were crying, and so were we, knowing we would never see them again. That is the worst part of cruising—having to say good-bye to friends.

Gene, I really appreciate your getting me the drill. My old one had built the boat and lasted until six months ago. I need one often and could not find one. When I opened the box, I yelled to Jerry, "I gotta find something to screw!" She wasn't amused.

We will be here for about three weeks. I have some work to do on the boat, and we will be visiting other boats we have met along the way that are arriving from New Zealand. They went south when we went north to Kanton.

From here we go to Vanuatu for around a month, then a long 1,200 nautical mile leg to Australia for three months or more. We will need to depart Australia by the first of October to have a decent trip to the Solomons.

We have people to contact in both the Solomons and New Guinea. They are friends and relatives of people we have met along the way.

We hate to see you sell that beautiful house that we enjoyed with you. It won't be the same place when we get back.

Thank you both for being friends of and helping Coral and family all of these years. We think of you often. Remember you are always welcome here.

Love, Buf & Jerry

*****

Jerry volunteered to collect goodies from the cruisers in Pago Pago, American Samoa, to send back to the Kanton locals on a Coast Guard ship that stopped there regularly. She collected toys for the kids, candy, T-shirts, paints, and fabric for the women, labeling a gift for each individual on Kanton. When she learned that the ship was not going there, she repackaged the items into two boxes and spent $90 to mail them.

April 16 is a holiday in American Samoa called Flag Day. It celebrates the day the country came under United States jurisdiction in 1900. Buford and Jerry went to the park to watch the dancing and singing, involving a representative from each village in costume. It was good, but "no better than Kanton, though."

Letter 15

Solomon Islands, South Pacific
November 1992

Well, I swore I would never write another of these dreaded form letters, but sloth has won out over good intentions. We've moved many miles since we left Kanton last April. There was a lot of very welcome mail waiting for us in Pago Pago, Samoa, and I meant to answer each and every one promptly—"mañana." By the way, we've found the South Pacific equivalent of that great Mexican catchall. Buf was having a repair made and asked for a pick-up time. It was "tomorrow or sometime." That about covers all contingencies.

We passed back through Fiji in May, replenished our stores, and ate a lot of good Chinese food. We had a slow passage with light winds. One night it was completely calm, so we turned on the anchor lights and radar alarm and went to bed at midnight. We got up at dawn and had moved eight miles in the right direction. I'm trying to persuade the captain that this is the civilized way to sail, but no luck so far.

We arrived in Port Villa, Vanuatu, in June. Its pre-independence name was New Hebrides, and there was a lot of Allied activity here during WWII. We spent a month in Port Havannah, where the Allies formed large convoys and had airfields for the island assaults further north. It was a large bay with several small villages around it. We became acquainted with the locals and were kept well supplied with fruit and fresh veggies. Some of them we didn't recognize, but we try to keep an open mind. We haven't found an adequate substitute for fresh broccoli yet, but we're still looking. There were lots of Coca-Cola bottles circa 1942, as well as pieces of old airplanes, ships, and ammunition.

Port Villa is a nice town with a definite French accent. Lots of good food and wine, but pricey. It's a tourist mecca for Australia and New Zealand.

121

Buf and I even went to the charity horse races held during their twelfth-anniversary Independence Day celebration. A veddy British atmosphere at that event. Everyone was dressed to kill, except the yachties and the Ni-Vanuatu (the name the locals prefer). We were our usual scroungy selves. We bought a lunch from the Rotary Club that included a bottomless wine glass. That insured a good time. I must report that we lost money on the horses.

Cindy and Roger rejoined us on August 22 after a seven-month driving tour of Australia and a couple of months in the United States. We were glad to have our crew back on board.

Vanuatu is a strange country. A collection of numerous islands, big and small, but only two towns of any size—Port Villa on Efate and Lugganville on Espiritu Santo on the northern end of the group. The rest of the country is quite primitive, literally. There have been recorded incidents of cannibalism as recently as 1979, and most of the bush people live with none of the trappings of the twentieth century, except T-shirts and a few outboard motors. The same is true here in the Solomon Islands. It's truly mind-boggling. Trading is the accepted method for getting fruit, veggies, lobster, fish, and any handicrafts. Money is not valuable because they have no place to spend it. They love T-shirts (old and new), old clothes and linens, perfume (!), soap, thread and sewing supplies, fish hooks, batteries (very important for flashlights), and balloons and candy for the kids. They are family-oriented and treat their children very well. They are not quite aware of the relative value of these foreign contraptions. A young man with two lobsters came by and wanted a radio cassette player—when we declined, he shrugged and said, "Okay. How about a ballpoint pen?" We accommodated him in a hurry.

While on Espiritu Santo, a Ni-Vanuatan took us way into the bush to a "kustom village," a community that is living in the old tradition. We met a man named Jimmy Stevens, now in his seventies, who is a former revolutionary for Vanuatan Independence. He had spent some time in prison for his activities and had two sons killed in the fighting. Another son is now a high government official. Anyway, he worked with U.S. troops during WWII, and when we told him about ourselves, he broke into song. Try to picture us standing in a jungle clearing surrounded by naked women, men wearing only penis sheaths, dogs, pigs, chickens, and children of all ages, listening to "Deep in the Heart of Texas." Amazing. They still do all their hunting with bows and arrows and slingshots. Needless to say, they have large gardens and eat mostly fruit, vegetables, and rice.

And now for a change of pace, as they say. Buf and I left Cindy and Roger on board in a beautiful bay in Espiritu Santo in September and took a three-week vacation touring New Zealand by auto. It was magnificent. The South Island is covered with the snow-capped peaks and glaciers of the Southern Alps. And millions of sheep. We took a float-plane tour from an icy lake and flew over the tops of the peaks—barely. It was just us and the pilot, who delighted in scaring Buf to death when he found out he was an old colleague. We just wandered around and spent each night wherever we happened to stop, including a couple of guest houses on sheep stations. We call them ranches in Texas. Wine making is becoming a big industry there, and we did a lot of tasting. Spring was just arriving, and the flowers and fruit trees were blooming on the North Island. We hung around Auckland for a few days, buying the ever-needed boat parts. We found a Wendy's and a Kentucky Fried Chicken. It may sound prosaic to you guys, but we were thrilled.

We moved on north to the Solomons in October. We have a copy of Michener's Tales of the South Pacific *on board and are in the areas he describes in the book. It's a lot of fun to try to identify the places and peoples. The southernmost island is Vanikoro. We stayed a week and enjoyed it thoroughly. We had vague directions for finding a French frigate that ran on the reef here in 1788. The* Bousolle, *captained by LaPerouse. It is quite a famous wreck (at least in this part of the world) and has been salvaged twice, once in the '60s and again in 1990. Anyway, we snorkeled down the face of the reef and found the thing. We couldn't believe our luck. We zipped back to* Beachouse, *threw on the dive gear, and poked around for an hour or so. Not much left; a cannon and copper sheathing off the hull are the big things. Lots of pottery shards and small bits and pieces. It was enough to give us a thrill. Does that tell you something about our lifestyle?*

We are moving into the Solomons now and will mail this from Honiara, Guadalcanal. November 10 is the Marine Corps Birthday, and Roger, an ex, is pleased to be here. Lots of nostalgic activities going on for the 50th anniversary of the big battles.

Coral; Joe; Molly, age six; and Matt, age four, are flying in December 19 for a month's stay. We expect to be very busy for Christmas. Should be lots of fun and excitement. There are a dozen or so other boats wintering here, so we will have back-up, including one doctor. It's always a comfort in these remote spots to have a few friends close by.

Buf and I are well, still functioning totally, albeit a bit slower. I like to think it's the climate. Mad dogs and Englishmen and yachties. Please drop us a line and tell us everything. We really long for news from home. We listened to the election news with great interest. It seems strange to be so isolated from all the big happenings and to have to hear it on a shortwave radio that cuts out at the crucial moments. On the other hand, we don't have the minor hassles of city life. We have our own brand of problems, mostly mechanical. None of us will get out of the world alive.

Hope it's all going as smoothly as possible for you and your families. Remember, Coral is coming in December, so send us a note through her.

*****

Vanuatu

Buford and Jerry spotted whales for the second time during their circumnavigation while sailing to Port Vila, Vanuatu.

May 30, 1992. The big excitement was a gam of pilot whales, at least ten or more. They played with us for forty-five minutes. Just like dolphins, only bigger. They were sounding, and one turned a complete flip. It was great.

The nation of Vanuatu (the name means "Land Eternal") is comprised of eighty-three islands, sixty-eight of which are inhabited by 94 percent indigenous Melanesians. About 30,000 live in the capital, Port Vila, on Efate. Another 9,600 live in Luganville (or Santo Town) on Espiritu Santo, with the remainder living in rural areas. With over one hundred languages, Vanuatu is one of the most culturally diverse countries per capita in the world. Christianity has had a profound influence on Ni-Vanuatu society, with an estimated 90 percent of the population affiliated with a Christian denomination.

Buford and Jerry immersed themselves in the local environment during their five months in Vanuatu, a place not normally visited by yachts. Men, women, and especially children surrounded *Beachouse* in their canoes, bringing fruits, vegetables, fish, lobsters, prawns, beautiful rare shells, and coconuts to trade, mostly for T-shirts but also for old equipment like fish hooks, dive masks, fishing line, and hacksaw blades. In return, Jerry passed out lots of candy. The people were friendly, but many spoke only French.

Sailing from island to island, Buford and Jerry met the chiefs of each one, usually took a gift, and signed the chiefs' guest books for visiting yachts. One book revealed that only twelve to eighteen yachts had visited in five years. The chiefs, sometimes surprisingly well educated, usually visited *Beachouse* with their families and escorted Buford and Jerry to their villages, which were neat and clean though primitive.

Chief Johnson and kids, Lacona Bay, Santa Maria, Banks Islands, Vanuatu

One chief served Buford and Jerry Lap-Lap, Vanuatu's national dish—a doughy paste made from taro or yam mixed with coconut milk. It can be stuffed with meat such as wild boar, fish, or chicken, wrapped in leaves, and cooked over an open fire. Jerry made a pie from the local fruit they call "rose apple," which tasted more like a pear.

Making water music on Vanuatu

126

At Lakona Bay on the west coast of Gaua Island, Buford and Jerry experienced the world-famous Vanuatu custom of water music. Women create the amazing music by clapping under the ocean water; they perform it to welcome foreigners.

Though island exploring sounds fun and easy, Buford and Jerry spent time every day performing maintenance on the boat.

June 26, 1992. It's never ending. I get so discouraged, and I know he (Buf) does, too. The boat demands every minute of our time.

Jerry, determined to add to her artifacts collection, was always looking for a trade in these remote islands. In one handicraft shop, she kept eyeing a boar's tusk, which is worn as a necklace and had a price tag of $300. The lady in the store had seen Jerry's molas from the San Blas Islands, which cost $10 each. Soon two pieces of embroidery and the tusk had changed places on the counter. Each woman stood there smiling at the other, each believing she'd gotten the better end of the deal.

While in Espiritu Santo, Vanuatu, Jerry made a scuba dive on the SS *President Coolidge*, a massive 22,000-ton luxury liner converted into a troop transport for service in World War II. In October 1942, during her seventh military mission, the ship struck two U.S. mines and sank as she entered the harbor of Espiritu Santo. It took just one hour and twenty-five minutes for the *Coolidge* to settle onto the channel floor. It is the world's largest, most intact, and most accessible WWII wreck.

September 25, 1992. I was with one other diver and one dive master. The Coolidge *wreck was fantastic—really good. Lots of coral on it—plus guns, tanks, rifles, all kinds of stuff from WWII. Also saw two big lion fish, lots of reef fish, and clown fish while we were decompressing. We went to 110 ft. I also petted a rock cod. Incredible.*

On the first attempt to leave Port Olry, Vanuatu, a hose broke, spilling hydraulic fluid everywhere. After ordering a new one, Buford waited for the part to be mailed to this remote place. Six days later, the hose arrived, at a cost of $338. As they again tried to leave, the windlass pump blew up. Another part was ordered and installed. Ten days after the first attempt, *Beachouse* finally left Port Olry. Not only was maintenance frustrating, but it dictated changes in their schedule.

Jimmie Stevens, Vanuatu activist for independence, August 1992

"Kustom Village," living in traditional style, Santo, Vanuatu, August 1992

New Zealand

Buford and Jerry took a three-week "vacation" to New Zealand in September 1992, "traveling like real people." They flew from Espiritu Santo, Vanuatu, to Auckland, rented a car, and drove around the North and South Islands. It was one of their favorite places to visit, even though it meant being cold again!

Flight over the Southern Alps, South Island, New Zealand, 1992

Letter 16

Hi Guys,

I know you'll be surprised to get another letter so soon, but we had such a wonderful time reading the letters Coral brought that we decided to keep a little momentum going. We are still in the Solomons, but we'll be leaving the first of February, weather permitting as always. Rabaul, Papua New Guinea, is our next stop. We hear great things about the city and the sights around there, both above and below water. We are looking forward to playing tourist and buying some much-needed stores.

The Solomons have been interesting. Most of the islands we have seen are covered with very dense jungle right to the water. There are hardly any beaches but many beautiful and exotic birds and a few crocodiles. There are lots of reminders of WWII—the Big War—including a new memorial on Guadalcanal near Honiara, built for the 50th anniversary of the battles here. For those of us old enough to remember, the area abounds in buzz words that bring instant memory identification—Henderson Field, Tulaghi, the Slot, Iron Bottom Sound, Bloody Ridge, Red Beach. We will skip Bougainville because there is more fighting there now. A rebel group wants to secede from P.N.G. and rejoin the Solomons. They have a great name—the Bougainville Revolutionary Army. We saw one tough-looking young man with BRA tattooed on his forehead. It gave BC quite a start. Anyway, if you don't remember all these places and names, watch a few old war movies on late-night TV and catch up.

There is WWII junk everywhere—ranging from tanks and airplanes and vehicles of all kinds, to helmets, mess kits, bullets, and the ubiquitous Coca-Cola bottles. We anchored deep in a remote bay on New Georgia, and a local took us to an old Japanese airfield deep in the bush. Fascinating junk there. We have been surprised at the number of Japanese tourists here for the 50th anniversary. Kinda like Napoleon revisiting Waterloo. The big hotel in Honiara is owned by a Japanese company and flies a Japanese flag with the Solomon Island flag on the lawn. The tough old ex-Marines who were here for the official ceremonies in August made it clear that if it wasn't taken down voluntarily, it would be removed by force. It was lowered forthwith.

Cindy and Roger have been in Honiara for a couple of months, house-sitting for an English official who went home for the holidays. They are rejoining us for the trip to Rabaul. It will be good to have our crew on board again.

Coral, Joe, Molly, and Matt joined us on December 19 and were here for three weeks. They stayed a couple of days in Honiara with Cindy and Roger, coming and going. We picked them up at Seghe, New Georgia. They flew into an airfield that was built in 1942 by the SeeBees in ten days—their record. BC was impressed at how well it has endured. It's still in great shape.

The weather did not cooperate, and we had lots of rain and the threat of a cyclone. BC and I loved every minute of their visit anyway, and we trust they did, too. The kids are amazing—at six and four they are real water babies and can swim and snorkel and dive to the bottom in two or three feet of water just like the pros. We managed to have the traditional Christmas dinner, even if our twelve-pound turkey cost $55. We stayed in Marovo Lagoon while they were here. It's a large area with lots of islands inside a huge lagoon at the south end of New Georgia. The locals were mostly Seventh-day Adventists with a Methodist outpost at the village of Seghe. The SDA missionaries have encouraged them to preserve their crafts and culture. Consequently, they do a lot of carving and weaving. Some of it is inlaid with shell and is quite beautiful. They are happy to take trade goods as well as money, and we have amassed more wooden bowls, masks, carved fish, and baskets than we'll ever find a place for. We got several pieces from a guy named John Wayne! His grandfather was a converted headhunter who invited the SDA in for his people in the 1920s. He was looking for a religion that would ban liquor and betel nut. SDA fit the bill. We Methodists lost out on the betel nut criterion. Betel nut chewing is a really nasty, disfiguring habit. They must be peeled and then mixed with lime, which they make by burning coral. Consequently, it rots and discolors the teeth and turns the mouth bright red. UGH! The men carry a woven *bag around their neck for their paraphernalia. What they ought to carry is a spittoon. The markets here have large areas devoted to selling the nuts. Such strange habits we human beings can devise!*

We moved on to Rendova Island after Coral and Joe left. Rendova Harbor is where Kennedy's PT109 was stationed. We visited the tiny museum—nothing much on display except a picture of J.F.K. The islands inside the reef were lovely, and the water was spectacular. At last, we found a few sandy beaches. The locals showed us a TBF (BC informed me it was a Navy torpedo bomber) in forty feet of clear water. It was completely visible from the surface and was totally intact except for a bent prop.

The diving has improved as we've moved north. We are now in Gizo, and the water is quite clear. We made a couple of dives on a beautiful wall off Kennedy Island. It used to be Pudding Island until J.F.K. was shipwrecked there. Gizo itself is not a viable metropolis. One of the boats we are traveling with does occasional chartering. They got a package of info about a couple arriving this week, and it included food likes and dislikes. French and Thai cuisines were mentioned. When they went to the few small stores in this miserable little town, they couldn't even find flour. Then their fridge system blew up. Should be an interesting week for them. Luckily, we have enough storage capacity to carry most things we need and lots of things we think we might want "tomorrow or sometime." We may be deep in water, but we eat well. By the way: we are just about to get our fill of lobster. It is forbidden fare for the SDAer's, so it has not been fished out. We can buy it, trade for it, or shoot it ourselves. I never thought I'd get sick of it.

Most of the yachts have headed to Australia, New Zealand, or north to Micronesia, Japan, and around the north Pacific to Canada and down to California. Only a few of us nuts are going all the way around. There are two boats leaving for Rabaul at the same time we are. One has two doctors aboard (husband and wife). Then there's us—one mechanical genius and one cook and laundress. The trip is only four hundred miles and will take three days or so. We'll be there about six weeks.

I'm thinking of forming a pyramid club for movie cassettes and old movies copied from the TV. Everybody sends us one, but I haven't worked out what you'll get in return. We are in a part of the world that uses a whole different TV system, and nothing works on our equipment.

This must be an exciting time of change at home now, with a new Democratic administration. It's hard for us to keep up with the changes, although Coral brought us a stack of Newsweek *magazines, and we did a lot of catching up. Not all of it was good news. Rabaul may be big enough to have a newspaper, or at least a source for newspapers from the United States or Australia.*

One of BC's favorite clichés while we are sitting in the cockpit having our happy hour: "Of all the places in the world, this is a funny place to be." And some of the places we wind up are really strange. We are now anchored in an isolated harbor, all alone except for one inhabitant on shore—a shy young man named William who brings us pineapples and green beans. We give him canned tuna, onions, and Cokes. We are surrounded by dense jungle and watch the cockatoos and parrots fly by—we also hear them; they do a lot of squawking. The water is a trifle green inside, but just outside on the reef, it is beautifully clear and teeming with life. Across the straits, we see Kolombangara Island. It's a tall volcanic cone covered with brilliant green foliage. I sound like an overwrought travel agent, but I do want to convey to you that it's certainly different from Dallas and Mission, Texas. Not necessarily better, just different.

We think of home often and hope you and your family are going strong. We send our love and regards.

*****

Seghe Airport, New Georgia, Solomon Islands

Letter 17

Dear SSCA Members,

We are currently in Gizo, preparing to leave for Rabaul, P.N.G., as soon as weather permits. We spent the last cyclone season in Kanton, in the Phoenix Islands of Kiribati. We were there for four months with Dave and Linda on the Rebecca, *another SSCA Commodore boat. We've spent this cyclone season in the Solomons. We've had no significant problems in either year. Just want you to know that there is an alternative to the long, hard sail to New Zealand or Australia. We went to New Zealand by air for a month last year and plan to do the same this year to Australia. To quote: nothing goes to weather like a 747.*

The Lucas guide for the Solomons is helpful but certainly not infallible or complete. There is no substitution for local knowledge and just poking around the backwaters. There are many lovely anchorages in these islands that aren't mentioned in his book. He recommends giving Rendova a miss, and we found it to be a beautiful, safe place to anchor. It would not be good in a west wind, but otherwise it has clear water, a white sand bottom, and lots of small islands with beaches. Beaches are rare in the Solomons, our only complaint. We personally have had no problems with mosquitoes, but we have used screens and lots of repellent and have stayed on board after 5 PM.

Neither Honaira nor Gizo has a lot to offer for stocking the larder or boat parts. We are hoping Rabaul will be better. We will send an update if we find any significant changes since the report from Viki last April. We have been advised by both the Solomon Island government and the Papua

Coral Beach

New Guinea Consulate in Honaira to keep at least fifty miles off the coast of Bougainville. The problems there seem to be heating up.

We wish fair winds to all,
Commodores Jerry and Buford Beach

*****

The Solomon Islands

The Solomon Islands, a nation of nearly one thousand islands just south of Papua New Guinea, are the most westerly islands in the South Pacific. The official language is English, but Solomon Pidgin English, a shortened, childish form of English, is spoken most often. A typical Solomon Islander is of average height, black-skinned, with frizzy black hair. Even though the islanders were fierce warriors in their time, Buford and Jerry found them to be friendly, polite, and honest. They are totally immersed in Seventh-day Adventist beliefs, so they spend Saturdays quietly, with no visitations.

A Sunday afternoon visit to watch *Cinderella* and taste Jerry's chocolate cake

There are hundreds of small villages throughout the country. The villagers live in thatched houses with grass mats on dirt floors; many are without walls, which helps the houses stay cool and renders them less costly to build. Only one or two buildings, such as a church or school, are made of European materials.

The Solomon Islands are famous for their high-quality wood carvings; the carving center is Marovo Lagoon in the New Georgia Island group. Unlike in other Pacific countries, only hardwood, well seasoned and almost indestructible, is used for the Solomon Island carvings. The best carvings are made of local ebony from the core of the Riche Tree, which is super-hard and jet-black in color. Delicate inlay work is done using the Nautilus shell, the thinnest of all shells, which requires less sanding and shaping.

Beachouse and other cruisers had the advantage of being able to sail to Marovo Lagoon. Jerry threw her version of a Tupperware party, where carvers displayed their wares in the hopes that cruisers would buy them.

Marovo Lagoon carver on *Beachouse*, December 1992

The most well-known group of carvers was led by a man named John Wayne, one of many islanders named after the American movie heroes of World War II. He was a polite man who spoke English well. His group, located in Telina Village, had elevated carving to an artistic form of expression rather than producing general carvings of sharks, dolphins, and so forth. Jerry and Buford commissioned him to custom-carve pieces for display in *Beachouse's* saloon. One of the most prized carvings is called *The Spirit of the Solomons*; it portrays an obelisk with images of all the sea creatures that are indigenous to the islands.

Yachtsmen traveling around the world usually sail through the Solomons southeast to northwest when southeast trade winds blow. The northwest monsoon winds blow through the islands from January to April. Cruising guides tell yachtsmen to forget about sailing through the Solomons northwest during this period.

Beachouse, not following this advice, got stuck in Gizo in February 1993, and she was forced to wait several weeks through the rain and northwesterly winds. Buford and Jerry attempted several times to leave for Papua New Guinea, only to turn back. When they finally left, they endured six miserable days of sailing.

February 20, 1993. Today was a miserable day. We had to motor sail all day into rough seas and a very hard beat. It was miserable, and we wound up only making fifty miles toward the destination, Breton Bay on the south end of New Ireland, P.N.G. Everyone was in a foul mood. It was too rough to cook.

February 21, 1993. Another day of disasters. We've had more things go wrong on this one trip than ever before. The engines are both sick—the starboard the sickest—but the port one completely. Now we can only motor at a reduced speed.

One day they made fifteen miles in eight and a half hours. Another day they progressed two miles in three and a half hours—backward—and sixteen miles to the good in sixteen hours. When they finally arrived at Breton Harbor, P.N.G., all on board—Buford, Jerry, daughter Cindy, and Cindy's husband, Roger—were exhausted.

Letter 18

Madang, Papua New Guinea
May 9, 1993

Dear Coral, Joe, Molly, & Matt,

It's 5:00 AM here, so this letter may not be legible or comprehensible. The Riva's daughter and son-in-law are headed back to the U.S.A. today—I didn't know their flight was at 6 AM—and I wanted to send this letter along for the mail.

We are in Madang now. We got here last Thursday—three days ago. We had a really fast trip from Garove Island, north of Rabaul. We spent three days there. It was very pretty, and the diving is first-class; we were going to stay longer, but, for the first time, we weren't comfortable with the local people. They were pushy and persistent, but, worst of all, we could not stop them from coming up on the boat. They would board and walk right into the cockpit. It was disconcerting.

Right now we are really disgusted. We hauled out in Rabaul, painted the bottom, and had some mechanical repairs done on the props and drives. They were leaking oil. The repairs by the locals were a failure, and they are leaking worse than ever—so we have to haul out again here. Not only is it expensive, but I just hate it—so does Buf, of course—and he has to do all the work. Oh well; such is the life of the carefree sailor. We ordered new parts from the U.S.A. this time. Waiting for arrival.

The Savant *is still in Rabaul. Kim is doing some work there. He is having trouble getting his insurance to cover him in Indonesia. We don't have that problem, of course. Ho, ho! The* Riva *is here, and the* Wind Dancer, *another doctor—so we have three doctors alongside right now—and Ellen, the wife of the* Wind Dancer, *is an audiologist. She can test our hearing—but can't do anything about it. The* Wind Dancer *is going to New Zealand in a few weeks. He plans to work there for a year.*

We are staying in a bay next to a Jais Aben Resort. It is quite nice. The grounds are lovely, and the manager and his wife are young Australians who are quite helpful. The fax machine is great—but expensive! $7.50 per minute, so our letters have to be short. It costs nothing to get a fax, though.

We will be leaving here around June 15, so you can send mail to us: c/o Jais Aben Resort, P.O. Box 105, Madang, P.N.G. Phone calls prices are also much higher than U.S. rates, so I might call collect someday. The Riva calls, hangs up, and has his stateside party call right back. That seems to work. Anyway—we'll be here a few days—or weeks. We hope to get up into the Highlands for a few days to see the country.

Madang is a nice town but not as pretty as Rabaul—or as big. There is a grocery here that stocks American goods, and I found Springfield shortening—it's not Crisco, but it's close—and other assorted goodies. We find it incredible that Old El Paso Mexican foods are available everywhere we go, from salsa, bean dip, and taco shells to everything in between. Amazing. While we were in the grocery, a guy came up, asked us where we were from, and introduced himself. He's from Oklahoma and is a Bible translator. He and his family have been here for sixteen years. They were very friendly, and we went to their house for awhile. They seemed glad to meet people from the United States. Not many tourists here—and most of them are from Australia and New Zealand.

In downtown Madang, the fruit bats (flying foxes) are all over town, hanging upside down and making a terrible racket all day long. They must be insomniacs. The trees look like they are full of large black fruits—except they squeal and move around. At dusk, they all fly out to feed. They come right over our anchorage. We are about three miles out of town by dinghy, but ten or so miles by road because of the bays and inlets everywhere. We rode in and out by van the other day. The local transportation is by bus. Quite an experience. The locals at first were very shy but opened up after awhile and were full of advice and questions. It's about a thirty-minute ride. The market here is fair—lots of coconuts, bananas, and root vegetables but not much else. Have to open up the old cans.

The Riva and the Wind Dancer are divers, and we're hoping to get some dives in while we are waiting to haul. The resort here is a diving resort, so they know all the spots, and, hopefully, we can make a deal to get a good rate for us.

141

We've had a couple of the locals from the village nearby come to the boat. They seem very nice. We had met one young man in town. He works at the museum here. It has a good collection of artifacts and is in a beautiful, contemporary version of a local house. He's quite articulate and knows a lot about the local customs. There is a craft shop in town with very interesting carvings and stuff. It's not particularly pretty but really interesting stuff. It all looks very authentic. Most of it is from the Highlands and the Sepik river region.

This letter seems a bit disjointed, but it's awfully early. We have nine hours difference from your time—and one day, of course. Hard to figure out—at least for me. I think tomorrow (today here) is Mother's Day. Hope Molly and Matt have planned a big day for you.

Hope you are all well. We're fine—and will be better when the boat is back in shape. Please take care and let us hear from you. We must get this over to the Riva *quick.*

Love,
Mom and Dad

*****

Rabaul, Papua New Guinea

Beachouse spent almost four months (from late February to mid-June) of 1993 in Papua New Guinea, the first half in Rabaul. At the time, Rabaul was the provincial capital of the East New Britain Province and a big commercial and travel destination for the South Pacific.

This all changed one year later when it was devastated by the falling ash from a volcanic eruption. Rabaul is built on the edge of a large volcano and is constantly threatened by volcanic activity. After the tragedy, the capital was moved to the nearby town of Kokopo, and Rabaul never regained its prominence.

The harbor and volcanoes of Rabaul, Papua New Guinea, March 1993

Buford and Jerry took a full-day excursion around the island with local guides.

March 16, 1993. We went on a long tour today with a guide named

Henry and a driver, Edward, and helper, Ellis. They were Seventh-day Adventists, so no betel nut—but we did listen to religious tapes all day, In the Garden, Old Rugged Cross, and so forth. This is a beautiful island. We circumvented the whole Gozelli Peninsula. It took from 8:30 to 4:30. We were pooped. We saw hot bubbly springs, many guns and gun emplacements, and a couple of lookout points that gave us a great view. It was easy to see that this was once a huge volcanic crater. Also went to a very extensive war museum in Kokopo—the next town.

During World War II, Rabaul was the base for Japanese activity in the South Pacific and the sight of the well-known Battle of Rabaul in January 1942. Military debris is scattered all over the island.

Japanese landing barges, used during WWII to drop supplies, are still housed in tunnels and caves in the hills surrounding Rabaul.

Buford and Jerry had a frustrating time in Rabaul—and not just because it was monsoon season and rained almost every day. Engines had to be repaired, old sails mended, new sails ordered, outboard motor fixed, television repaired, awnings mended—you get the picture.

March 20, 1993. We're ready for the monsoon season to be over! I'm sure getting antsy to go swimming, diving, sailing—or something.

March 27, 1993. We decided to hell with it all this AM, picked up anchor, and motored to the Duke of York Islands.

The Duke of York Islands

After days of nothing going right, depression set in—and finally they'd had enough. In part to celebrate Jerry's sixty-second birthday, *Beachouse* went to Kakabon Island, one of the thirteen islands that make up the Duke of York Islands found in St. George's Channel between New Britain and New Ireland group of P.N.G. islands.

March 28, 1993. The water is clear, and the scenery is lovely. Lots of canoes came by. Many people in the village nearby. It's great to be out of the harbor to a beautiful sunset and a nice calm anchorage.

Buford and Jerry mixed right in with the Kakabon locals, which was typical of their experiences everywhere. Henry Lardi, a local electrician, stopped by, and Jerry typed a job application for him. When an oar from *Beachouse* went missing, Ellison, a local man, came by to report that it had been found and taken to the village's community house. When Buford and Jerry arrived in the village, they met two school masters, Isaac and Henry, and one member of the town council, July, who had their oar. Later that day, July stopped at the boat. Jerry gave him magazines for the school and a cake for his family.

The Kakabon locals lived on one island and crossed a shallow reef on foot to work in the gardens of a smaller neighboring island; *Beachouse* was anchored in between. Lots of canoes filled with friendly villagers rowed by daily; at times, close to one hundred canoes surrounded them. Jerry handed out "lollies" to the children until she ran out. She and Buford even resorted to staying inside the boat on some afternoons to avoid all the canoes! When Buford took garbage ashore to burn, he was surrounded by children who worked in the gardens. One day Buford took the kids back to their village in two trips of his dinghy. They were thrilled!

The water in the lagoon was clear and blue, satisfying Jerry's need for swimming, snorkeling, and diving. At cocktail hour, they could see the volcanoes of Rabaul against the sunset.

While moving to a nearby anchorage, Buford had a real scare.

April 2, 1993. We decided to move to the north side and left around 8 AM. Went out the narrow pass to the west. It was about ten miles to the place we picked on the chart. The coral was shallow, but we worked our way in—didn't like it and started out. We ran up on a reef and touched the main hull. We were able to back off without hitting the props, but it scared us both. I was on the bow, and the water looked six inches deep. I couldn't believe we got off. A miracle.

Back in Rabaul, *Beachouse* was hauled out in the Tobai Shipyard. It took a crew of six men two hours to lift her out of the water—easily and efficiently. For ten days it was a beehive of activity—workers fixed propellers, repaired and painted the fiberglass bottom, installed new parts and fiberglassed over them, tore them out again, replaced the parts, re-fiberglassed, and so forth.

One morning, Jerry spent two and a half hours at a "sing sing," a colorful local ritual where the people paint themselves and dress up with feathers, pearls, and animal skins to represent birds, trees, or mountain spirits.

Letter 19

Madang, Papua New Guinea
May 27, 1993

Dear Cindy and Roger,

We are sitting up on the rail in Madang. We had less than a foot of clearance on each side when we pulled out. They had to move some rocks and cut down some bushes. BC had to wield a machete over the side to cut away the branches. You can imagine the shape I was in. A basket case. There is something to be said for morning drinking. We've been up for two days and expect to get back in the water tomorrow morning. An Aussie machinist has been helping Buf put the drives back together with the new parts, and they both feel good about the repairs. It's been two years since we had the first problems—I'm sure you remember waking up in Bora Bora with your feet in water. We're more than ready to have everything back to normal— whatever that is.

The Savant is still in Rabaul, having its own travails. Kim and Deb got a bunch of bad diesel, and it ruined every seal in their engine as well as their injectors and injector pump. We talk to Kim almost every day, and he was bordering on hysteria. They have sent a bunch of pieces to N.Z. for overhaul and are waiting for them to return. We had to send the Trimble GPS back—it packed in on the way from Rabaul. Doesn't this all sound like fun? And people wonder what we do all day long.

We have made some really good dives here in the big Madang Lagoon. The water is quite clear most of the time, and the coral is alive and beautiful. The locals keep trying to steer us to old wrecks. BC tells them we won't look at junk on land, so why should he put all that crap on and go underwater to see it? We really enjoyed our trip to the Highlands. We only spent three days in Mt. Hagen, but we were on the go all the time. There was no one else at the lodge, so we had private tours. We drove way out

147

one day and came to a town where they were holding an election. All the outlying villages had come in to vote. At least half of the men had put on their local costumes and body paints. It was great. We took a lot of pictures. They didn't seem to mind—in fact, some of them posed and asked to have their photo taken. The highland valleys reminded us a great deal of the high valleys in the Andes. It is very fertile and covered with small farms, gardens, and huge coffee and tea plantations. The market was fabulous. I bought fresh strawberries and broccoli. That alone was worth the plane fare. The flight was fantastic. We left the coast and in forty minutes had passed over a range of 14,000-feet mountains and had landed in the valley at six thousand feet. It was great to be cool, but you know Buf—he kept complaining he was cold all the time. We still haven't met any hostile people here. We told you about the island where we had them all over the boat without permission. That's the only bad experience we've had. Our visa is good until June 15; then we will check out and start for Indonesia. We expect to take a month and spend most of it in the Hermits. We got a good chart from the U.N. Fisheries guy here. By the way, he doesn't know Paul but is familiar with this book.

We had a long talk with Kurt on the Hayes *the other night. He was anchored in a bay on Kyushu, the south island of Japan. The* Fait Accomplie *was on one side of him and the* Kavenga *on the other. They are all well and moving slowly. He said they have been treated royally and have been written up in the local newspaper. The* Kavenga *had its two folding bicycles taken from the deck, and a local bike shop supplied them with new ones. Maybe* Beachouse *should pile a bunch of old equipment on deck and see if we can get lucky. The* JD *had just moved on to Hiroshima. Otherwise we have lost touch with most of last year's crowd. Hope we can stay in touch with the* Rebecca*—they are special friends.*

We are still totally out of touch here. Is Clinton doing any good at all? It certainly was embarrassing to confess being from Texas while the Waco thing was going on. Of course, the only news that filters down to us is always bad. Let us know when the interest rate gets back to 10 percent. After all these haul outs, that's the kind of news we need. Everyone asks us where we are hauling next month. Comedians everywhere.

We have a package out at Jais Aben from Coral. It arrived the day we came into town. I can hardly wait to open it. A new bathing suit better be one of the items, or I'll be swimming in my clothes like the rest of the locals.

She has mentioned coming to Biak, which is our first stop in Indonesia, but I know nothing for sure yet.

We trust you are all well and having a good time there. As I said, your name is on our Indonesia CAIT (Clearance Approval for Indonesian Territory), so you can come on back anytime. The Riva is still in the States but will be back around July 1. Their P.N.G. visa is good until August, but their Indonesia permit starts July 20. They expect to be right behind us into Biak. The Savant is planning to meet us in the Hermits. They are taking the island route over and skipping Madang. Seems a shame to come all this way and miss the mainland of P.N.G. completely. We at least can say we got into the Highlands for a few minutes.

If you haven't already sent the mail on to Madang, better save it and see if Coral is coming. Otherwise, I don't know where the next drop will be. Anything important you can fax us about. Please, no bad news. Tell us the farm sold for half a million. That's the kind of news we want to hear. We miss you and would love to see you soon. Happy hour is a little boring without you—however, we persevere. Got lots of scotch left. We may have to switch soon. Let us hear how things are going with you all. Give Glen and Charlene our love and thanks. Also, Ron and the other Charlene when you see them.

BC is under the boat hollering for tools, so I must stop and get on with reality. Again, we love you much. Keep us in your thoughts.

*****

Madang, Papua New Guinea

Beachouse hauled out a second time in Madang, Papua New Guinea, resulting in more problems.

May 5, 1993. We got back in the water this AM. It was a really rough ride. I heard a loud crack about halfway down. And sure enough, later in the day, water began to seep into the root cellar. I was sick—BC, too. I am really discouraged. We can't seem to get it all together. The leak took the heart out of us.

May 30, 1993. It was a subdued day. The leak has us down. We can live with it—but it won't be fun.

A tight fit—haul out in Madang, Papua New Guinea, May 1993

Buford and Jerry attended a local party in Madang with fifty or sixty people called a "Mao Moo," named after the mumu, a pit dug into the ground to cook chicken, fish, pork, and tons of local vegetables. They also attended a custom dance troop led by Simon, a local school teacher they had befriended. They thoroughly enjoyed the "comedy with dancing," even though it was totally in the pidgin language.

Custom dance troop at Madang Museum with lead dancer Simon, the local school teacher, June 1993

Tok Pisin, a creole pidgin, is one of Papua New Guinea's three official languages and the most widely spoken. English is the language of the government and the educational system, and Hiri Motu is spoken in the southern region of Papua. Next to Vanuatu, P.N.G. has a greater density of languages than any other nation on earth, with an average of only seven thousand speakers per language.

During their trip to Mt. Hagen in the Highlands, a region formed by a spine of mountains that runs the length of New Guinea, Jerry made two prized purchases. She bought a necklace made from a kina shell, which was traditionally used as currency until 1933. The Kina (named after the shell) was introduced as the currency in 1975, replacing the Australian dollar. She also purchased a Bird of Paradise plume, often used in local dress and rituals, which has been prized as far back as five thousand years. They became extremely important in early eighteenth-century European millineries.

Buford and Jerry celebrated their forty-forth wedding anniversary in Madang, P.N.G.

May 14, 1993. We had an ordinary lunch and an ordinary day for our anniversary. BC brought some bananas as my gift.

At the end of their stay in Madang, Jerry and Buford met an Australian couple, Allen and Phillipa, and their twelve-year-old daughter, Heidi, on the S/V *Sumurun*, which had just arrived. Of course, they were immediately invited to *Beachouse* for happy hour, where they discovered that both boats would be going on to Biak, Indonesia.

Several days later, the *Sumurun* was robbed in Sek Harbor, about five miles up the coast.

June 10, 1993. They were tied up to the dock at Madang Resort Hotel and boarded by two men. Allen was tied to the mast for three hours. Phillipa and Heidi were below. Phillipa's clothes were cut off by a bush knife, and the robbers held guns and knives on them while they searched the boat. The robbers took money (not much), cameras, a stereo, and rum. They didn't take the VHF and HF, but they pulled the microphones out so they couldn't call for help. They next day Allen found out they were escaped murderers from a prison. They took a gun from the Sumurun *and shot a policeman with it. Very scary!*

Allen, Phillipa, and Heidi were all fine. The Beaches were thankful it had not been them.

Letter 20

Dear Dave and Linda,

We got a package of mail from Cindy the other day, and your letter and the picture were in it. It was great to hear from you. We can hardly believe it's been so long. This year has really passed fast. We love to talk to you on the radio. Now, for our "broke boat" saga. The lower drives never fully recovered from the work we had to do on them in Fiji after they were damaged by the wrong paint. Anyway, they both suddenly began to leak oil around the shaft seals. We hauled in Rabaul and had a local engineering company do a repair job. It turned out he did a number on us instead of a job. Anyway, when we left Rabaul for Madang, the seals let go, and we were pouring oil instead of leaking. Another haul out in Madang was a necessity. You know how much fun it is to be on the hard. Well, one a month is really the pits. Hard on the psyche as well as the pocketbook. We went up on a rail that was adequate but narrow, less than a foot clearance on each side. They had to move a few rocks, and Buf stood on deck and used his machete on the bushes as we went up. Buf had ordered new parts from the States, and the work was done by an expat. He did a good job, and that problem is all cleared up—however, the workmen were unfamiliar with yachts in general and fiberglass in particular. They put a small crack in the hull, and I now have a very small but extremely annoying seep of water in the root cellar. About a half cup a day. Needless to say, Buf was not interested in going back up to have it repaired. We have every hope that the miracle goup you sent will do the job. I forgot to mention that we had the bottom painted in Rabaul, so that is over for another year or so. So much for the gay, carefree life of a sailor. This crap is never mentioned in Cruising World. *Linda, I think we should collaborate on a book telling it like it is. We might not make any money, but we would be able to find a place to berth in any marina.*

153

Enough of the rotten stuff; on to the fun part. We have had a great time here in P.N.G., with the aforementioned obvious exceptions. The people have been super, and the weather has been great. Hot, but no unpleasant surprises. It's been very tame compared to your tales of Tonga. Sounds like a whole season of Dallas. *Glad you and Dave escaped unscathed. We were proud of you, Linda, and the way you handled the* Rebecca *in the storm. I only hope I can do half as well if the need ever arises. Things are pretty quiet around here. We are anchored off Jais Aben Resort and Christensen Research Center. The people who run both places are very nice to us, let us use their facilities, and generally give us the run of the place. It is a ways from town but only a ten-minute dinghy ride, and I go to the grocery and market with the girls from shore. We've done quite a few dives here. This is a diving resort, and they are very generous with their information and an occasional freebie. It's a very pleasant place to hang out for a while, but I think we'll be ready to move on when our visa is up on the fifteenth.*

We went to the Highlands for a few days before we hauled here. It was very beautiful and reminded us a lot of the valleys in the Andes. It was great to be cool for a change. The country wasn't as spectacular as you will see in South Island but quite a change for us. The people there look like the pictures you see of P.N.G.ers. We had a stroke of luck. We went into the country with a guide for a day tour, and it was Election Day in the town where we visited. All the people from the outlying villages had come in to vote, and a good portion of the people had donned their cultural garb and body paint. They were a wonderful sight to see. We were the only white people in sight, but when Buf asked if he could take pictures, they vied with each other to get in the photos. We ran out of film but got some great shots.

We will leave for the Hermits when we check out and spend a few weeks in the wilderness. Then on to Biak. We finally have all our paperwork done for Indonesia. Quite an ordeal. A Commodore boat named the Riva *is going with us, as well as the* Savant, *carrying a young couple from California. A boat from N.Z. came in today named the* Sumurfun *and is heading in the same direction. So we may have a small armada. We are a little apprehensive since this will be the first time we will be dealing with a general populace that speaks very little, if any, English. We've been reading all the old SSCA bulletins and look forward to a good cruise. Sounds like we'll be doing a lot of motoring, but fuel is supposed to be cheap. So are we, after all these haul outs.*

We also got a letter from the Inshallah *in our mail packet. Sounds like they may be getting serious at last. I hope we don't get so out of phase with the rest of you people that we never cross your paths again. I can't stand to think of it—so I won't. By the way, aren't you impressed with the fact that I am finally coming to grips with this damned computer? Cindy and Roger finally shamed me into it. They are fine, by the way, and still in Texas, trying to figure out what to do next. We told them to come on back, but I think they want to go to work, if only they could find a job that appealed to them. God knows what that will be. Something international is what they are hoping for. Coral and her two, Molly and Matt, are going to meet us in Biak for a couple of weeks before school starts. Molly will be in first grade this year. We can't get far enough away to hide from our kids, but aren't we lucky that they want to come and see us?*

Enough rambling on. I'm enclosing U.S. cash in this letter. If it doesn't arrive, let us know—and no cheating. You're on the honor system. Ho ho. Just because we don't write and forget to come up on the radio doesn't mean we don't love you both and miss you like crazy. Please tell Stan, Nancy, and all the rest of the group there hello for us. Give them our best regards.

We'll be listening up on Monday mornings.

Love and Kisses,

*****

Election Day in Mt. Hagen, P.N.G., May 1993

155

Letter 21

Beachouse—60' Horstman Trimaran
Ambon, Indonesia
August 20, 1993

Dear SSCA,

We left Texas in 1985, and, after six years in the Caribbean and two years making our passage from Panama via the well-known routes, we decided to sail around the north side of Papua New Guinea to use the road less traveled. The trip from Gizo, Solomon Islands, to Rabaul, P.N.G. parallels Bougainville, and we were warned to stay well off-shore because of the political problems there. We stopped at Mono Island well off the west coast of Bougainville in a lovely and well-protected cove. We were met by Roy, an SSCA associate, who led us all the way into the anchorage. He was a mine of information and proud of his membership in our organization. At the south end of New Ireland in P.N.G., we anchored in English Cove. It's an isolated area with no land access except foot trails. The bottom was covered in coral, but we held well in an unusual west wind that turned us stern to the shore. The locals were very friendly and generous, as they have limited contact with the outside world. We picked the wrong day to head up St. George's Channel, and it lived up to its bad reputation. We had fifty-five miles of strong currents and high winds on the nose. While tacking numerous times, we lost four miles in a one-hour period. We made for the west side of the channel and motored very close to shore. That worked better than anything else.

Rabaul is a very nice place. We took the normal precautions and had no trouble of any kind, and we heard of none from any of the ten or so yachts that passed through in the month we were there. The Yacht Club is almost inactive for cruising boats. Lunch and happy hour for the local expats are about its only functions. Lunch is much better at the New Guinea Club—a *great bargain and very pleasant. There is a laundry and good provisioning at Anderson's Supermarket. Lots of American products, including the junk food we all crave on watch. Fuel is available at the Shell Dock for US$1.30. We hauled Beachouse at the Toboi Shipyard and had a good experience. All the haul out facilities in P.N.G. are owned by shipping companies and are relatively inexpensive. John Seeto is the manager and has been there for twenty-five years. He was most helpful and was very careful. We got good international bottom paint from Taubman's Paint Co.*

We had a good sail around the northern coast of P.N.G. to Madang, with a two-day stop at Garove Island. We were not comfortable with the locals, who insisted on climbing aboard uninvited. We found Madang smaller and less cosmopolitan than Rabaul. We anchored about five miles from town by the Jais Aben Dive Resort. It is a lovely place, and Tim and Susan, managers of the resort, were very accommodating. We were treated just like their guests—except we were nonpaying. We used their phone and fax and caught rides into town with their transport. It seems a safe spot. The Riva, another SSCA boat, was left there for six weeks while the crew flew home, and we left Beachouse for a trip into the Highlands. There is lots of good diving within a dinghy ride. There is a small haul out facility at Lee shipping and a Shell dock for fuel in Madang.

We got our CAIT for Indonesia through agent Kartasa Jaya in Jakarta and sailed for Biak, a large island north of Irian Jaya, with a stop at the Hermit Islands of P.N.G. They have been covered before in the bulletins, but we would like to add an update. Chief Joseph and the whole population of 103 people are still as friendly and helpful as reported. Their yacht log dates back to 1983 and reflects very few cruisers annually. We found only one anchorage where we felt completely safe in all weather. It was in good white sand off a lovely beach and five miles or so from the village. We had lots of friendly visitors by canoe in the three weeks we were there. We bought lobsters for two dollars each and were presented with a haunch of venison from the deer left by the early German settlers. A delightful place.

We arrived in Biak, Indonesia, to find an open harbor with a submerged barrier reef that doesn't stop the seas at high tide. Very rolly. The bottom is a uniform fifty feet, with spotty sand and lots of hard pan. The most disconcerting problem is the lack of any landing place for a dinghy. There is no beach, only iron shore, and the tides of five feet or more can leave you two hundred yards up on the rocks. There are no piers except the main dock, which is very high and very busy with large ships. It was a challenge every time we went to town. The restaurants are inexpensive but mediocre. Provisioning is not good—buy in P.N.G. Fuel is unavailable directly from the oil companies. It must be purchased through an agent, and the fuel dock cannot be used. We bought five drums; it was delivered by canoe and took all day to load. We had guests arrive via a Garuda International Airways direct flight from Los Angeles. It runs four times a week and is relatively inexpensive.

We visited the group of islands twenty miles to the east of Biak. They are lovely sandy atolls, and the fishing, swimming, and shelling are good.

Our five-day passage around the Bird's Head of Irian Jaya to Ambon was erratic. The wind was highly changeable both in direction and velocity. We motored 75 percent of the 640 miles. Currents varied from all directions and reached a maximum of two to three knots. We were never in really bad conditions but never comfortable, either. We were glad to see Ambon. The annual Darwin to Ambon race had arrived one week earlier, and there were still a few boats in the harbor. We found Ambon to be a fascinating place, our first truly Asian city. Most things seem to be available with the exception of fuel, which involves the same problems as Biak. We have now checked in at two Indonesian cities and have had no hassles and no bribes or charges. Hope our luck holds.

We are following the crowd to Bali, Singapore, and Phuket, but we enjoyed our detour from the "Yellow Brick Road." We send best wishes and greetings to our many SSCA friends.

Fair Winds.

*****

The Hermit Islands

When *Beachouse* anchored in the Hermit Islands, Chief Joseph, representing 109 locals, boarded the vessel to welcome Buford and Jerry and introduce them to the islands. The Hermit Group, comprised of four islands, is part of the thirteen islands that make up the chain of Western Islands of the Bismarck Archipelago in the western Pacific Ocean, twenty-five miles north of Papua New Guinea. The group is a circular reef with three small peaked islands that stand in the center of a big circular lagoon. In the late nineteenth century, it was settled by a German trading company.

When Jerry and Buford explored the islands on foot, they discovered the foundation of an old German manor, as well as deer tracks of deer that had descended from those brought by the Germans. Buford received venison in exchange for helping repair the town radio. Jerry cooked it as a pot roast and found it tender and quite good—better than she expected. The villagers fed them local fare, including a four-year-old crocodile hatched from an egg.

On a gorgeous day with a light breeze, Buford and Jerry decided to go to Bird Island, about four miles away.

June 25, 1993. It is covered with birds and nests of boobies, frigates, and a local small black seabird with a white head. Thousands of birds.

Bird Island, Hermits, P.N.G., 1993

Jerry spent much of her time in the Hermits in pain, recovering from a pulled muscle in the right side of her chest. After taking medication, she began to feel better but still had no appetite. She pulled the muscle again while getting a stool from the back of a closet. Then she laid around and moaned.

Health care can be spotty at best for a cruiser. Most yachts carried medicines on board for all nonurgent care. If you were lucky, you'd meet a fellow cruiser who was a doctor or nurse who could give you advice. Otherwise, cruisers tended their own nicks, bumps, and infections.

Biak

Once in Biak, Indonesia, Jerry exchanged US$1,900. She was showered with four million Indonesian Rupiah.

July 9, 1993. Always wanted to be a millionaire!

Biak is the largest of the Biak Islands, also known as the Schouten Islands, after Dutch explorer Willem Schouten; it's to the northwest of New Guinea but part of an Indonesian province. The largest population is located in Biak City on the south coast. The rest of the island is thinly populated with small villages.

Beachouse was again constantly swarmed by canoes.

July 10, 1993. Hopefully, we will cease to be a novelty soon.

Coral, Molly, and Matt flew to Biak in July 1993 to join *Beachouse* for a month. During their visit, whenever Jerry took Matt and Molly ashore, locals surrounded them; they'd never seen white-faced children. In the local market, which was dirty but offered lots of vegetables, women wanted to touch the children and pinch their cheeks. Soon, Matt dreaded leaving the boat.

While they were anchored off the deserted islands of Nusi and Konori, they spent their days shelling on beaches inches deep in shells. Back on the boat, Coral and the kids cleaned and tried to identify the shells from collectors' books. Matt was more interested in fishing with Grandpa.

Living on the Indian Ocean

July 1993–September 1994

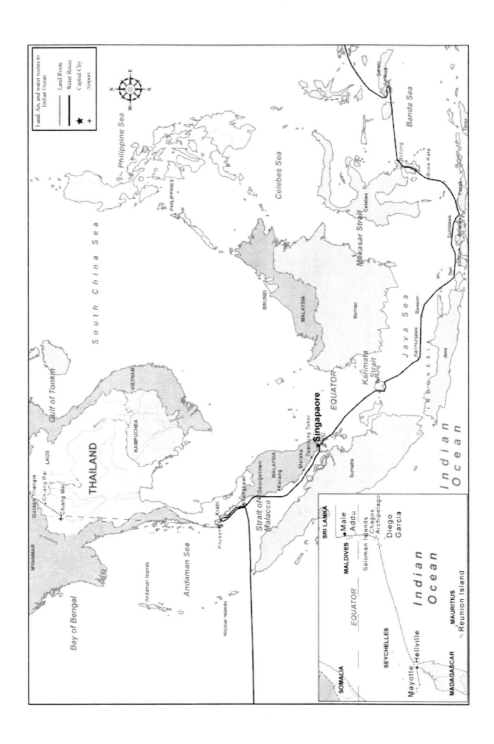

Letter 22

Dear Ones,

We are sailing up the Andaman Sea, fewer than fifty miles from Phuket, Thailand, the Mecca for boats in Southeast Asia at this time of year. Yachts funnel in here and then disperse after the holidays for the Red Sea and the Mediterranean, South Africa and Cape Horn, or just hang out in this part of the world for one more year. It is gorgeous cruising ground, plus the inland travel is cheap and diverse. We have sailed five thousand miles in the past year, so we are now officially half-assed circumnavigators on the downhill run home.

We were in Papua New Guinea from March through June. We cruised the north side and had a wonderful time. There were very few yachts there, and most of us were moving at the same pace and going to the same places. We enjoyed Rabaul and the diving there and then moved on north and west to Madang. We did a Highlands mini-vacation and saw the primitive interior of New Guinea that is pictured in National Geographic. *It's rapidly becoming totally Westernized, but we were fortunate to be there on Election Day, when the rural clans come to the small communities in full regalia. It was a spectacular sight to see them covered with paint, shells, feathers, and little else. We thought they might object to strangers taking pictures, but they crowded into the photos. We had a local driver whose uncle was one of the candidates. BC and I were the only white faces in a crowd of hundreds. We had heard bad stories about P.N.G., but we stayed away from the large commercial centers and were treated with kindness and concern. We hauled* Beachouse *on a small rail in Madang for a bottom paint job. There was only one foot of clearance on each side as we went up, and BC was on the*

*bow hacking brush with a machete—shades of the African Queen! Jerry
was cowering in the cockpit close to incoherence.*

*We stayed a month in the Hermits, a small island group off the north
side of P.N.G. It was an interesting time. A German settlement was
established there before WWI, and they had stocked the four main islands
with deer and pigs. The Germans are long gone, but the deer are thriving.
There are only 109 locals, and they kept us supplied with lobsters, fish,
and a couple of venison haunches. It was surprisingly good and certainly a
change of pace gastronomically.*

*We rounded the "chicken head" on Irian Jaya (get out your atlas and
look it up) and sailed to Ambon in eastern Indonesia. Being woefully
ignorant of the geography of this part of the world, we were astounded
to learn that Indonesia is the fourth most populous country in the world.
It's sure spread out. We spent three months sailing through, and we were
moving fast. We met the rest of the sailing community here, all headed
for Phuket (see paragraph 1). Even boats we had known from the Virgin
Islands and Venezuela.*

*We saw komodo dragons in the wild while anchored near the beaches
of the only islands they inhabit, along with many monkeys and deer. Bali
was one of our disappointments. Although the island itself is gorgeous, the
tourist carnival atmosphere is disconcerting. At one point, BC was beating
his way through a crowd of persistent sidewalk salesmen by flailing his hat
willy-nilly. The anchorage by the main city was a disaster. We were only
there for four nights, but we were hit twice by local boats, and a third
picked up our anchor and set us adrift. We began to feel like a ping-pong
ball, so BC gave up and we left without doing half the tourist things. We
did see some beautiful Balinese dancing and had a day ride through the
countryside. The Indonesian people are very friendly—almost too much so.
It's the first place we were unable to discourage people from marching onto
the boat without invitation. We found it unnerving to look up from chores
and find a couple of smiling locals standing in the cockpit looking us over.
We were never caught au natural but had a couple of close calls.*

*We island-hopped to Singapore, taking our time and making lots
of stops. Singapore was a revelation. Modern, clean, and full of all the
familiar products of home. We pigged out on ice cream, pizza, hamburgers,
fried chicken (KFC must have thousands of outlets in Southeast Asia), and
first-run movies. We stayed almost a month and spent untold amounts of*

money on boat parts and provisions. Also, we both had complete physicals, dentistry, and new glasses. We were pronounced perfectly healthy—then given the added zinger "for your age." Don't you just hate that phrase? Arriving and leaving Singapore is like rush-hour traffic on the freeway. It's the world's second busiest port, and I was a total wreck. BC found it exhilarating. Being under sail, we had right-of-way, but try telling that to a supertanker bearing down on your bow. We didn't try to press the nautical niceties and made a lot of unorthodox maneuvers to avoid ramming or being rammed.

We moved up the west coast of Malaysia through the Malacca Straits. It is a very shallow body of water, and I never got used to sailing at full speed with thirty feet of water under the boat. That's anchoring depth, for God's sake. We day sailed the whole six hundred miles between Singapore and Phuket, stopping at several interesting cities. The city of Malacca was founded by the Portuguese in the late 1600s. Many old buildings are still intact, serving as museums. Also, there are lots of beautiful Buddhist and Hindu temples and mosques, both new and old. It was a lovely layover, and we stayed five days. Georgetown on Penang Island was another city with preserved British colonial buildings plus Chinese and Muslim antiquities. One temple had a sleeping Buddha over one hundred feet long, covered with gold leaf—gorgeous. We spent several nights just pulling over to the side of the Strait and dropping the hook in about twelve feet of water. It was a gooey mud bottom everywhere, and the holding was great. The major problem was getting the damned stuff off the anchor and chain every morning. We ran an obstacle course every day through the fishing boats and their nets. It was incredible. At times there would be hundreds of them in sight, ranging from one-man canoes to pretty good-sized commercial boats. It got pretty exciting every once in a while. BC skillfully worked us through without picking up a net. We weren't so lucky back in Indonesia. One night we hit a bamboo fishing platform that had broken free and was floating in the shipping lane. I got to put on my scuba gear and cut the net off the propeller at 4:00 AM while BC kept the boat steady. It was not my idea of a night dive.

We are leaving all those travails behind and heading into Phuket, the fabled playground of the rich and idle. The beaches are supposed to be white sand, the water clear, and the coral growth fantastic. Since we have heard this story before, I am reserving judgment until we have seen it all for ourselves.

A phonetical sidelight. In Thailand, the Ph *in* Phuket *is pronounced with a soft* P, *as in* Poughkeepsie, *thank God. The English alternative would be disastrous. Our next stop is Phi Phi Island, and that's bad enough. Speaking of urine: I spilled some hydrochloric acid down one leg but washed it off quickly so it didn't burn. However, it left long yellow streaks all the way from mid-thigh to my foot. People kept eyeing it surreptitiously, and BC threatened me with adult diapers. It gradually wore away, but it was a major embarrassment for a few weeks.*

Now for the family report: Coral; Joe; Molly, seven; and Matt, five, are joining us for Christmas. We always enjoy their visits, and this should be a great place for the kids. Cindy and Roger are working for an oil company in Europe. They spend half their time in Amsterdam and half in Moscow. They don't know how long it will last, but it's a wonderful way for them to see the world. We still don't have a definite itinerary or timetable for working our way back home, but sooner or later we'll show up again. Until then, we hope you are well and happy and that your family and loved ones are thriving. Please keep in touch.

We miss you all and send love and kisses.

*****

Indonesia

In the fall of 1993, *Beachouse*, with six other boats, cruised from one Indonesian island to another, all the way to Singapore. Starting at Ambon in August, they sailed eight days on the Butung Straits to Taka Bone Rate Islands, twenty-one coral islands that form an incomplete ring surrounding a large lagoon.

August 23, 1993. The anchoring here is weird. You go right up to a coral wall (!), drop the anchor in thirty feet, and back off. We are hanging in 125 feet!

Bone Rate has a long history as a boat-building port. Jerry and Buford attended the launching of a newly completed boat for Frenchman Phillipe and Isabel, his wife.

Phillipe and Isabel's boat launching, Bone Rate, 1993

August 25, 1993. First, we had a meal at the house where they are living. We sat on the floor with a crowd and had goat, chicken, fish, and rice. They fed a large crowd of men. Then we all trooped to the beach. The launching was very crude. It was done by sheer manpower. Must have been more than a hundred men pulling on ropes and pushing to keep it upright. Just dragged it over the ground on wooden planks to the water. The tide was down, so they just laid it on its side. It was kind of a party. There must be fifty or more boats under construction.

Beachouse anchored for a week in Ginko Harbor on Rinca Island, where Buford and Jerry ate saddle oysters for the first time. The oysters do not attach themselves to hard surfaces but live in the mud of tidal pools, growing up to seven inches in diameter. They are valued for their translucent shells.

On Komodo Island, Jerry attended a feeding of komodo dragons, the world's largest living lizard—they devoured a whole goat in a hurry. A type of monitor lizard, the komodo dragon inhabits only this island and some of the smaller surrounding islands. Jerry and one couple were the only people over thirty years old, with the rest being "scroungy backpackers."

Next was Senggigi Beach on Lombok Island, the poor man's Bali, with several four-star hotels.

September 14, 1993. There must have been three hundred boats out fishing just off the coast. Beautiful sight with their bright sails—but very daunting—we have to pass through that line to leave.

September 15, 1993. Lots of very new, very pretty government buildings. The towns are reasonably clean. Lots of carts drawn by tiny horses. Very picturesque. Went to the King's Water Palace—a pavilion and garden complex—and a couple of temples. Also, went to watch native weavers and the big market. Made another palace built in 1744 and had lunch in the Highlands. A beautiful countryside.

Wild "top-knot" monkeys by the side of the road, Lombok

In Bali, a place Buford hated except for its spectacular sunsets, a chartered catamaran came into the harbor at full speed at 10:30 PM. Having trouble anchoring, it hit *Beachouse*, bending the bow roller. The next morning, the captain, who had not been on board at the time of the accident, claimed he would bring the boat's owner by the next day.

September 20, 1993. The guys from the catamaran that hit us came over with sledge hammers to try to bend our bow roller back. BC ran them off—so much for compensation.

After Bali, *Beachouse* stopped at Bawean Island, with a population of around sixty-five thousand. They received a radio call from a fellow cruising boat, the *Stylapora*, which had lost her propeller. Jerry and Buford towed them into the anchorage. Don Chilcrest and Robyn Boase of the *Stylapora* chronicled the incident, "A Tale of Two Props," in their book, *Here Be Dragons*.

September 25, 1993. It was only three or four miles, but BC and I did a professional job of picking them up. I was proud.

The sail from Bawean to Karimunjawa, an archipelago cluster of twenty-seven islands in the Java Sea, was treacherous. Karimunjawa, located on the busy trade route beginning at the sea ports along Java's northern coast and running through the Malacca Straits, is the home of many underwater shipwrecks.

September 27, 1993. Lots and lots of fishing boats in the night. I find it very scary. In the daytime, some of them head straight for us to take a look. Very disconcerting. The island is very lovely with water that is many, many shades of blue.

The next stop up the shipping lane for *Beachouse* and her traveling armada was Mendenau Island off of Belitung.

October 1, 1993. It's a lovely small spot between coral ledges, right under a huge lighthouse. Good white sand bottom.

The next day, the crowd jumped into Buford's dinghy for a snorkel in a small bay islet and then motored to shore for a tour of the lighthouse, built by the Dutch in 1883. After a beach stroll, Jerry invited all to *Beachouse* for a chili supper.

The last stop before Singapore was Batam Island on the Batam Strait. It was a quiet stretch of water except for a military boat that circled *Beachouse*; its crew waved and laughed, enticing Jerry to put out all her flags. At Batumpal Dock on the north side of the island, Jerry went from store to store trying to buy provisions, but the language barrier made for fiascos.

Singapore

Around noon on October 8, 1993, after a scary ride across the shipping straits, *Beachouse* anchored in a Singapore marina. Buford and Jerry were enjoying their one-half circumnavigation champagne lunch when Phillipe, of the boat launched in Bone Rate, paddled up. His boat was also in the marina. They scurried over to see it and had tea and cake. Jerry described it as "very rudimentary—like camping out."

Buford and Jerry were in awe of Singapore, though they found it extremely frustrating to get things done in such a vast foreign city. It took one and a half hours on land to get from the marina to the immigration office in the World Trade Center.

October 11, 1993. Getting all our business done here will be a big battle because of the size of the city. It is gorgeous and clean—but huge!

October 12, 1993. Singapore is a city composed of large apartment high-rise buildings with shopping areas nearby. Each is a separate village with its own name. The bus and rail system is great.

They were excited to find all kinds of American goods and meats. Between having health checkups; finding boat parts; getting electronics and engines repaired; copying nautical charts of Malaysia, Malacca Straits, and Thailand; and socializing with the other twenty boats in the marina, Buford and Jerry were "on the dead run" the whole time.

Strait of Malacca

Leaving Singapore, *Beachouse* entered the Strait of Malacca, a five-hundred-mile stretch of water between the Malaysian Peninsula on the east and the Indonesian island of Sumatra on the west. The strait connects the Pacific Ocean and the Indian Ocean, making it one of the most important and busiest shipping lanes in the world. It is an important trade route among China, India, and the Middle East.

The Strait of Malacca's geography has made it prone to the threat of piracy. It's narrow, contains thousands of islets, and is an outlet for many rivers—it's an ideal place for pirates to hide and evade capture. However, pirates usually ignore small personal yachts such as *Beachouse*, which carry little money, in favor of large tankers, which have large amounts of money in safes.

Beachouse first anchored overnight in Palau Pesang and Tanjung Tohor and then passed the Water Islands en route to Malacca (also known as Melaka). There, Buford and Jerry checked in with Malaysian Immigration and Customs. They were pleasantly surprised by the number of tourists in Malacca and the beautifully restored sixteenth-century churches and forts. They took a river ride through the city and toured a replica of the Sultan's Palace and botanical gardens.

River ride through the city of Malacca, Malaysia, 1993

Progressing through the Malacca Strait, *Beachouse* anchored one night at Port Langat and then spent all day trying to maneuver around the river complex outside Port Kelang.

November 9, 1993. It is a vast, swampy delta with lots of banks and shallow water. It's very well marked, but there are also lots of fish nets and boats.

After spending a night in Burong, they passed some lovely islands, the Sembilans, which were too steep for anchoring; then they sailed on to the resort at Palau Pangkor. Buford and Jerry hired a taxi, costing US$12, for a ride around the island.

November 10, 1993. It's a pretty place but will soon be full of tourists. There are new hotels going up all over—and the airport was opened last August.

True to this prediction, today Pangkor is known for its fine beaches and mixture of accommodations, from low-budget to five-star. It is extremely popular with travelers from Europe.

The City of Georgetown, the capital of Penang named after King George III of Great Britain, was a big surprise.

November 13, 1993. It is very large and modern, but they have preserved a lot of the old Victorian buildings.

Penang, formerly known as the Prince of Wales Island, is Malaysia's most populated island; a large bridge connects it to the mainland.

November 13, 1993. It is supposed to be one hundred feet tall, but it sure looked close as we approached. We passed under with no problems.

Buford and Jerry visited a large Buddhist temple surrounded by ten thousand Buddha statues.

November 15, 1993. Beautiful, but they have almost ruined it with crappy little stands lining the steep steps leading up to it.

Buford with ten thousand Buddhas, Penang Island, Malaysia

Completing their harrowing journey in the Malacca Strait, *Beachouse* finally arrived in Kuah Harbor on the island of Langkawi.

November 17, 1993. It is a gorgeous place, with rock formations that are fantastic. Lots of rocky islets coming right out of the water. Still no clear water, but better.

The town was small but had markets for provisioning fruits, vegetables, drinks, booze, and fuel. In the harbor was a Swedish boat that had visited Kanton. Buford and Jerry invited them for happy hour—they watched Buford's film of the Kanton singing and dancing and laughed about their experiences with the native people.

On Wednesday, November 24, 1993, *Beachouse* declared it Thanksgiving on Langkawi and invited fellow cruisers for a turkey dinner with all the trimmings. The next day, *Beachouse* left for the Butong Islands and finally found clear water. Buford and Jerry immediately jumped in for a swim and snorkel. Jerry had returned to heaven.

November 25, 1993. Lots of reef fish and live coral. Great to be in the water again!

Thailand

Beachouse spent a wonderful two and a half months in Thailand, beginning in December 1993. The first stop was the island of Ko Phi Phi in the Andaman Sea, where they were surrounded by fourteen cruise boats plus a mass of bare boat charterers that came in to anchor at dusk.

Here they got their first introduction to the longtail boat native to Southeast Asia. It is a simple craft that uses a common automotive engine mounted on an inboard pole that can rotate 180 degrees for steering. The propeller is mounted directly on the long driveshaft, the "tail," which keeps the engine relatively dry. Locals use these brightly decorated canoes as transportation, while visitors use them as taxis.

Longtails on Phi Phi Island, Thailand, 1993

Twenty-five miles north of Phi Phi, *Beachouse* anchored at Ao Chalong. Traditionally the first port of call for visiting yachts, Ao Chalong is a year-round anchorage at the southern end of Phuket. It was only ten kilometers to Phuket Town by taxi, or tuk-tuk. There, Buford checked in with Immigration and Customs, and Jerry went to the market.

They'd arrived just before the annual Phuket King's Cup Regatta, Asia's biggest and most popular regatta, which attracts boats and crews from all over the world. The prestigious event, which starts on Phi Phi Island, was established in 1987 to celebrate the sixtieth birthday of King Bhumibhol. Buford had no interest in watching the race, so afterward they rode a tuk-tuk to the bay, which was full of the anchored racers. There was a wide range of boats in all shapes and sizes.

A fellow lady cruiser "boat sat" *Beachouse* while Buford and Jerry flew north to Chiang Mai, Thailand's second-largest city. Surrounded by green hills and lazy rivers, it is full of friendly people and a staggering number of temples. It is also the center of Thailand's arts and crafts scene, making its night bazaar a shopper's heaven.

Buford and Jerry treated themselves to a four-star hotel.

December 12, 1993. I couldn't believe it—next door to a new mall with a KFC and a Pizza Hut!

Just outside the city, they visited an elephant work camp. Tourists can ride the elephants, which are trained to move large timbers in the jungles.

December 13, 1993. We arrived just behind two buses of Germans, so we got a teenaged, undersized, undertrained elephant. It was not a lot of fun, but it was interesting. He kept pushing at the elephant in front.

Elephant riding in the jungle outside Chiang Mai, Thailand

They flew further north to Chiang Rai, a slow-moving, medium-sized city near the Burma and Laos borders. After visiting ruins, including a twelfth-century temple, they took a brightly colored longtail to the "Golden Triangle," where Laos, Burma, and Thailand meet on the Mekong River.

December 14, 1993. We never thought we'd see Laos and Burma, the once opium capital of the fabled area—makes a great story. The river was dark red with mud but was a smooth ride.

Buford approaching a twelfth-century temple, Chiang Rai, Thailand

Coral; Joe; Molly, eight; and Matt, six, arrived just before Christmas 1993, staying for two weeks. *Beachouse* cruised under a full moon all through the Phi Phi Islands, the Krabi and Koh Dam group of islands, the Koh Rang group, and the Phang Nga Bay area, including James Bond Island (Koh Phing Kan). The James Bond film *The Man with the*

Golden Gun was filmed on the island, making it famous; hundreds of tourists visit daily, most of them arriving by longtail boat.

From November to April every year, the weather in the Phuket area is consistently sunny and dry, with calm seas and winds that are ideal for sailing. The cruising area, sometimes called the Caribbean of the Orient, is one of the most spectacular in the world, with gigantic limestone sculptures set in shallow, milky green water. Inside some of the islands are hongs, or rooms, the result of collapsing cave systems. They are accessible only by dinghy.

December 27, 1993. We went around the island to the hong (cave) on the north side. Entered through a narrow slot into a big lagoon with sheer sides—absolutely beautiful.

Hongs in the Andaman Sea

After cruising the islands of Thailand in the Andaman Sea, *Beachouse* anchored on Patong Beach, one of the world's most famous beaches, for New Year's Eve. The harbor was full of boats, and the cruisers held a "dinghy raft-up," where some twenty dinghies were tied together off the beach for a party. They could hear the constant popping of red firecrackers being thrown all over the city. The next morning, the streets were inches deep with the remains.

At midnight, all were asleep on *Beachouse* when noise erupted.

Coral poked her head outside a porthole and spotted a gigantic display of fireworks, covering 180 degrees around the huge bay. She woke everyone up to witness the show, the likes of which they'd never seen before. It seemed to go on forever—perhaps because they were half asleep!

Once the family left, Buford and Jerry spent several weeks provisioning, fixing problems, and waiting for more visitors—Gene and Grace Smith from Galveston. They, too, were treated to the beautiful cruising area of the Andaman Sea and then a return south to Langkawi, Malaysia, arriving in time for the Chinese New Year. While cruising, they came upon the wooden boat from Bone Rate again, with the French couple, Phillipe and Isabel, on board.

After the Smiths left, Buford and Jerry spent several frustrating days filling the freezer and refrigerator with vegetables and fruits, performing general maintenance, and fueling up in preparation for a long twelve-day sail to the Maldives.

They left Langkawi, Malaysia, on February 20, 1994, and were glad to be out of the harbor and on the go. The trip was slow going, as the winds came from the west, which was highly unusual; but they were under a full moon and witnessed gorgeous nights. Few ships were in sight, which meant that they were out of the shipping lanes at last.

February 25, 1994. Yesterday's log is a combination of two days. You can tell how boring it is. The days all run together. I like it this way. I love boring when we are under sail.

Letter 23

Chagos Archipelago
April 20, 1994

Dear Coral, Joe, Molly, and Matt,

We are anchored off Boddam Island in the Salomon Atoll of Chagos Archipelago. Maybe you can find it in an atlas. We have been in the lagoon here for two and a half weeks. It is quite beautiful, and the water and reefs are great. We left Male and made day trips through the Maldives to Addu, on the last island south. It took us six days, and we stopped at some lovely spots. We didn't bother to put the dinghy in the water, so we did our snorkeling from the boat. The islands are mostly uninhabited, so we saw very few people. The weather was good, so we had an easy trip. We started with the Savant, *but they dawdled longer while we pushed on to Addu. It was a very neat and picturesque little town. Not much in the way of provisions, but the people were very friendly and spoke lots of English. They were all Muslims and had beautiful schools. There was a string of five to six islands connected by causeways. It had been a British military outpost at one time, so it had an airport and a pretty good dock. We filled up with diesel there. We were there six days and enjoyed it all. We hired a taxi for a couple of half days and saw the whole thing. Not much to see except sand and palm trees. They are low-lying islands—like Galveston.*

The water was clear but deep, so we anchored close in by the reefs—great for swimming. We left April 1 and took three nights to make it here. We had very little wind at first, and it was very slow—then the wind quit completely, and we had to motor the last full day. At that, we were really lucky. The weather changed just after we got here, and the Savant *and others who were behind us had storms and rain and a really bad trip*

183

down. Our calm trip was unusual for an equator crossing. It's ordinarily pretty unsettled.

When we got here, we had an engine problem just three miles out. It was totally calm and flat, so BC put the dinghy in the water and towed us in—another lucky break that it was calm enough. Anyway, we (rather, he) got the problem all sorted out, and we joined the other boats in the anchorage. There were five others here then—but they keep arriving. There are now twenty-two, of which about ten are French. They are in another anchorage across the lagoon. We call the center the English Channel. We have six Americans, four Brits and Aussies, one Chinese, and one German here. Two of the Brits are from South Africa, and we have gotten some good info from them and hope to get more. There are six of us going around Good Hope this season. It's nice to have company. We will head for Madagascar sometime in the last of May or early June, depending on the weather.

There are four boats that have been here since last November. Their supplies are really running low. We had twenty-four people over for a party last Saturday night. They were thrilled to see ice. Our fresh stuff is slowly disappearing, too. We have cabbage and carrots, tomatoes (getting soft), limes and oranges, a few apples, and lots of cans! We have eaten much fish. We fill scuba tanks for a couple of boats, and they bring us fish. The long-time boats here have built a nine-hole golf course. They cleaned out some jungle, put in holes (tin cans), and have it all marked with painted coconuts. It's a riot. BC and Kim shot a round yesterday. They said it's like playing in a sand trap.

This island used to have a village and copra plantation, but when the Brits made a military base in Diego Garcia—the island sixty miles south—they moved the people off. The base at Diego Garcia is now leased by the American military. It was used as a NASA tracking station, and there are still around three thousand Brits and American men there. The atoll where we are (Salomon) is a marine park, uninhabited except for the yachties. The Brits come on a chartered American cargo ship every month or so to check us out. There is a US$55 fee to anchor. When they come, they throw a big BBQ and feast on shore. They also bring mail and will mail this to you—we hope. We are looking forward to the get-together. Should be fun and interesting.

We don't know what to tell you about visiting this year. We have to move with the wind and weather from now on. It's almost impossible to plan ahead very far. There is no communication from here—except this mail. We will try to contact you as soon as we can. Hope all is well there. Please send a copy of the letter on to Cindy by fax. We don't have their address. We love you all. Give the kids and Joe a big hug and kiss.

Your wandering parents—
Mom and Dad

*****

The Maldives

The check-in process in Male, the capital of the Maldives, was a major hassle. After arriving at 8:00 AM, Buford called the Coast Guard and waited until 1:30 PM to get their security clearance; then he waited all day for Customs to come to the boat. When Customs wouldn't answer the phone, a frustrated Buford went to town, but he was run off and told to stay on board. He and Jerry went to bed at 9:00 PM. Customs finally arrived at 10:30 PM, and they were cleared for entry.

The Republic of Maldives is an island nation consisting of 1,190 small coral islands that are grouped into twenty-six atolls, encompassing eighty island resorts and two hundred inhabited islands. It is the smallest Asian country by population and the smallest predominantly Muslim nation in the world. English is widely spoken for commerce and for instruction in the government schools.

Buford and Jerry arrived on Friday, which is the Muslim Sunday, and Ramadan, when there is a ban on eating and drinking from sunrise to sunset. When they went to shore, they bribed the hotels to let them eat. They changed U.S. dollars for rufiyaa, the local currency, and wrote the government asking for permission to sail the Maldives island chain. They anchored at the Bandos Island Resort in incredibly clear water; the bottom was visible at sixty-five feet. They treated themselves to a $33 hamburger at the resort (including ice cream!) to offset their frustration over attempting to get parts to fix engine problems.

Jerry visited the fresh-market ship.
March 15, 1994. It has huge cool rooms and freezers. It supplies all the outlying resorts and gets fresh stock flown in twice a week.

Soon after receiving their permit to tour the southern islands, Buford and Jerry took *Beachouse* on a six-day sail; they dodged reefs through many of the Maldives atolls until they reached the southernmost Addu

Atoll. They found it much prettier than Male, and very clean. They had no trouble with Customs.

Post office in Addu, Maldives, 1994

When Buford woke Jerry up the next day, on her sixty-third birthday, he presented her with her usual morning glass of juice and a birthday gift—a mother elephant carved from sandalwood, with a baby elephant inside. They hired a taxi and toured the island, finding it one of the prettier places they had visited; the people were friendly. The driver stopped by a private home, where they met the driver's brother and nineteen-year-old sister, Minha, who had finished school and was going to teach English. The only downside they found to Addu was that there was no telephone or fax.

Chagos Archipelago

Buford and Jerry fell in love with the Chagos Archipelago, a group of seven atolls comprising more than sixty individual tropical islands roughly in the center of the Indian Ocean. It is a British Indian Ocean Territory (BIOT), so British Troops often arrive from a large cargo ship to check boats in; they usually provide a barbeque lunch to the cruising boats that are anchored there. The Salomon Islands, one of the atolls, is located in the northeastern part of the archipelago, with Ile Boddam the largest island surrounding the lagoon. These islands are among the favored anchoring spots for cruisers sailing through Chagos on their passage across the Indian Ocean.

Lagoon and pass in Chagos Atoll, Salomon Islands

Buford and Jerry spent seven and a half weeks on Boddam Island, doing the usual maintenance chores but mostly socializing with the numerous cruisers who were constantly coming and going. The socializing excluded the French boats, which stayed across the lagoon, separate from the other cruisers. Cruisers referred to their part of the lagoon as the "French side." Weekly Friday beach barbeques, meal sharing, book trading, game playing, reef diving, island exploring, and fishing kept them busy. One cruiser had tapes of football games, including Dallas Cowboys games, Super Bowls, and college Orange Bowl games, which provided afternoon entertainment.

The cruisers created a golf course on shore and organized a tournament called the "Great Boddam Open." Buford made a hole in one, which was commemorated with a flag marking the spot. Jerry awarded prizes—one large chocolate bar to the adult winner and a lunch box for the juvenile winner. *Beachouse* hosted a large turkey dinner; a Mexican feast of fajitas, tacos, rice, and margaritas; and numerous happy hours, with one of these soirees celebrating their forty-fifth wedding anniversary.

Buford and the guys golfing, Chagos Atoll, 1994

After several weeks of socializing in an extremely close-knit setting, friction began to develop.

May 20, 1994. There seem to be a lot of funny tensions and back biting going on all of a sudden. Everyone was congenial at the Friday BBQ, what with all the intrigue. BC and I call it "Peyton Lagoon." So we have decided we are ready to leave soon.

They began preparing for their trip to Madagascar. When Buford entered the route into their global positioning system, they discovered the journey was 1,476 miles. Luckily for them, Neil Ericsson and Scarlett Duffy on the *Lebenho* decided to make the journey with them.

Letter 24

Dear Coral, Joe, Molly, and Matt,

We made it here from Chagos in ten days. The first eight days were great, but the last two were really bad. The worst seas and winds we have seen. We had water all inside the boat, as waves were breaking into the cockpit. Quite a ride—but no real damage. We were glad to get here. We heard from Tony in Kenya that you talked to him. I'll bet that was a surprise at 6:00 AM! The phone system here is not viable. We have tried and will try again—but we won't plan on it. We are trying to get money on Visa, and they can't reach their capital city on the phone to get authorization.

It is quite primitive—more so than Biak, even. However, the buildings are old French colonial, and it is very picturesque and surprisingly clean. The people are black but with fine features, and most are a handsome lot. Things are cheap here—at least the local items. Imports are expensive, naturally. The market is good, with lots of veggies and fruits. They have lots of cattle—zebus—with a hump like a Brahma and long horns. The meat is quite good—at least the tenderloin is tender and tasty.

The Savant left us at Chagos and is headed back to Thailand for another year. They have a job there doing God knows what. We are traveling with the Lebenho and will be with them until at least South Africa. They are going to the Caribbean, too. We hope to do a little inland traveling but haven't found a place to leave the boat. One of the yachts had its outboard stolen last night.

We will be leaving the town in a few days and visiting other islands and bays. Call Tony if you need us.

We love you,
Mom and Dad

*****

Letter 25

Dear Coral, Joe, Molly, and Matt,

Sorry the phone call was so short. We have gotten here with very few backup dollars and are trying to keep a reserve for any emergency. We cannot get cash on credit cards and no collect phone calls. Soooo! The local communications office is in a guy's private house, and he has the setup to make calls and send faxes. If you get another quick call, we may ask you to call right back—to a phone booth. One of our friends is trying that today. Now, how is everybody? Molly, do you like the second grade? And is Matt doing well in kindergarten? Such a big boy to ride the bus all alone! We assume Big George is doing well. And you, too, of course. We are envious of your trip to Europe. Hopefully we will get the chance to go before Cindy leaves for somewhere else.

Unbelievable that there is no international calling from Nosy Be in Madagascar. A friend asked about it, and they said the line was "broken" but might be fixed in September. What can you expect in a country that has no running water in the hospital! It was very primitive. Since the French left in the early '70s, it has been sliding backward at an ever-increasing rate. The fresh food was a real bargain, with local fruits and vegetables selling for pennies. Quite a contrast to Mayotte. Here we saw tomatoes for sale at US$5 per pound. Other veggies are on the same scale. French bread is a big bargain. We got lobsters in Madagascar for old T-shirts and bottles. They even covet empty tin cans. We took a long trek into the hills in Madagascar with a guide. Most interesting. Saw lots of lemurs, held and petted a boa constrictor, and saw a vine that has the biggest beans in the world. We got one to show you when you come to see us. A bean, not a snake!

We had an easy thirty-two-hour trip to Mayotte. Mostly motoring. This is a big lagoon, with a coral reef around two large islands and a bunch of small ones. We have only been here a couple of days, but we hope to get out and about soon and do some snorkeling and sightseeing. The French Foreign Legion is much in evidence. Also, the French Navy in their cute uniforms with the red pompoms on their berets. We are at a big disadvantage with the language—or, rather, without the language. English is not spoken much at all. We did meet an Englishman in the Legion. Shades of the old desert movies. Our second day here, we met an Indian officer from an oil tanker, and he invited us out to see his ship and have lunch. Most interesting. It was a new one, so it was all computerized, and Buf considered the engine room a marvel.

We expect to be in South Africa in early October and will be hauling out for extensive work. Repainting the whole boat, plus the normal mechanical repairs and redos. We have heard nothing but good things about the country since the elections. Think about coming to Durban for Christmas. The Yacht Club is right across the street from downtown, and the beach is next door. Also, at least three game parks within a day's travel. Supposed to be cheap against the U.S. dollar.

We love you all and hope to see you soon.

*****

Madagascar

Beachouse's first landing in Madagascar, the fourth-largest island in the world, was Nosy Hara (nosy means island in the Malagasy language).

June 3, 1994. A beautiful, unique-looking, rocky place. Really spectacular.

Beachouse sailed on to Hellville (today known as Andoany), the capital of the island Nosy Be (means "big island"), Madagascar's largest and busiest tourist resort. Located just off the northwest coast of Madagascar at the start of the Mozambique Channel, Nosy Be is easily accessible. It has a jagged coastline containing numerous bays, gorgeous coves, and deserted beaches, and it is surrounded by many small islands, including Nosy Komba, Nosy Mitsio, Nosy Sakatia, and Nosy Tanikely.

Zebu pulling a cart in Hellville, Nosy Be, Madagascar

Once again, *Beachouse* received many visitors in canoes, including kids who wanted to trade T-shirts, candy, plastic and glass containers, and anything else for lobsters. Buford and Jerry introduced themselves to the Hellville port captain and proceeded to argue loudly over extra port fees. Several days later, a Port Office representative visited the boat, requesting a great many more dollars for a cruising permit, which Buford unsuccessfully tried to negotiate his way out of paying.

June 17, 1994. Well, the place lived up to its name today!

Ten days later, the port captain insisted they owed still more dollars for cruising fees, making them pay more than any of the other cruisers. I guess it doesn't pay to get in shouting matches!

They exchanged US$350 for 1,282,000 Malagasy francs. Millionaires again! They found eating out extremely cheap and often bought lobsters for seventy-five cents apiece. Today, that US$350 would exchange for only 587,650 Malagasy Ariary, which replaced the franc as the official currency in January 2005.

Beachouse was lucky enough to be in Hellville for Independence Day festivities. The Republic of Madagascar, after its time as a French colony, was proclaimed an autonomous state within the French community in 1958 and claimed full independence on June 26, 1960. Jerry claimed that things had gone downhill since then, referring to its crumbling infrastructure and primitive state—they considered it the saddest place they'd visited.

While anchored off the mainland in the town of D'Ankify, Buford and Jerry made land excursions.

June 21, 1994. We saw two large plantations, one about six thousand acres with diversified crops of cocoa, coffee, pepper, raffia, and vanilla owned by a French corporation and all exported. They even mine quartz. The other place grew some plant we couldn't understand the name of, used as a base for perfume, also exported. It was made in a beautiful old rendering plant with all copper vessels.

A Burial at Sea

They encountered three disasters during their stay in Madagascar: the outboard motor quit, one battery bank quit, and they discovered a tear in the sail. Buford spent several days working on the batteries, changing them slowly, trying to find the bad one. It took all day for a slow charge.

July 1, 1994. BC had a flash and remembered putting a strange bottle of water in the batteries. It turned out to be ospho—that's what's wrong—a real disaster.

Buford took a quick dinghy ride to the nearest hotel and a taxi to town to buy battery acid and distilled water. Back on the boat, he spent the afternoon working with one of the batteries to see if he could salvage it.

July 1, 1994. A really disgusting situation and a very expensive mistake. We won't know for several days if it will work. It is very time-consuming, and we must run the "Blue Monster" (generator) for hours trying to charge it up. Just trying to cope with this.

After several days of work, they declared the batteries dead and gave them a burial at sea.

The tear in the sail was at the top of the mast where the foil had come apart. *Beachouse* settled into a quiet anchorage behind Manoko Island for the repairs. Buford traversed the mast three times to screw the foil back together. Jerry's sewing machine would not handle the heavy fabric, so she sewed some by hand, with Buford drilling holes for the hand stitching. They borrowed a heavier machine for the rest—a very time-consuming task.

Buford and Jerry held a Fourth of July celebration on *Beachouse* for fellow cruisers, providing the American fare of hamburgers and hot dogs cooked on the grill, potato salad, and beans. The crowd sat on deck, anticipating the launch of six bottle rockets, but they fizzled—which was funnier than if they'd actually worked. The annual showing of the movie *1776* was the evening's finale.

Nosy Komba

Buford and Jerry spent eighteen days anchored with other cruisers On the island of Nosy Komba, home to a colony of black lemurs. Madagascar's separation from other continents has resulted in a unique mix of plants and animals, many found nowhere else in the world. The lemur is its most famous endemic animal species. Since Buford and Jerry were there at the height of the tourist season, boats came in and out on day trips from Nosy Be to see these animals.

Mother lemur with baby, Nosy Komba, Madagascar

One of the boats that was anchored with *Beachouse* was a big power charter boat called the *L'Estranger*, owned and captained by Harry and Robyn Teste. The Testes asked if they could send some of their belongings with *Beachouse* to South Africa, which turned out to be much more than the Beaches expected. Buford asked the Testes if they would like to ride along, since a hired crew was handling their next charter. After thinking it over, they accepted the invitation, agreeing to meet *Beachouse* in Mayotte for the journey to South Africa.

August 3, 1994. We have mixed emotions. It will be great to have them, especially since Harry has made the trip many times and is very knowledgeable—but it's always a drag to have someone else along.

Since leaving Chagos together, *Beachouse* was still traveling with Neil and Scarlett on the *Lebenho*. The day before leaving Madagascar, a young local man who spoke only French came by the boat. Jerry sent him on to Scarlett, who spoke French and had practiced emergency medicine.

August 18, 1994. He whipped out his penis and asked for medicine. He has the clap. How hysterical!

Mayotte

After two and a half months in Madagascar, *Beachouse* sailed under a full moon to Mayotte, a territory of France, located at the northern end of the Mozambique Channel. It consists of a main island, Grande-Terre (or Mahoré); a smaller island, Petite-Terre (or Pamanzi), located about a mile to the east; and several islets around them. The two islands are connected by a causeway, and ferries run every hour. Geographically, it is part of the Comoro Islands but has been politically separate since the 1970s.

Beachouse anchored in the harbor of Dzaoudzi on the small island. For shopping and supplies they rode the ferry, took a taxi, or borrowed a car to cross the bridge to Mamoudzou, the largest city and the capital of Mayotte. Jerry described a typical taxi trip, which took an hour and cost US$3.

August 31, 1994. A pleasant ride through several villages, all poor-looking and unattractive because of the red clay, with no vegetation around the huts. We caught a truck back, and it was an experience. We had a drunk on board who got thrown off, a young kid who discovered his wallet was stolen, and two guys who spoke English and who were very curious about our lifestyle.

Buford spent most of his time on Mayotte fixing problems, and Jerry did household chores while they waited for Harry and Robyn Teste to arrive.

September 17, 1994. Things keep breaking faster than BC can put them back together.

He fixed the plumbing, repaired a hatch, and then found a leak in an exhaust hose that was allowing saltwater to dribble in. He took it all apart and discovered that a bronze metal elbow had corroded. He had to make a trip to town to get it repaired. He fixed both hot water heaters, overhauled the water-maker pump, and discovered that the refrigerator was not cooling properly.

Meanwhile, Jerry did all the laundry in freshwater from a waterfall; keeping the clothes away from the coarse black sand surrounding the area was a challenge. She washed out the root cellar, cleaned all the bed linens, and made a new computerized inventory list.

Finally, after ten days of this, Buford and Jerry decided to relax and try some diving. It took twenty to thirty minutes to get to the reef by dinghy, but Jerry wrote that it was well worth the trip—it was the best dive they'd had in a while, with lots of reef fish and coral. They wore their dive skins, but the water was still cold. The next day they arose early, ready for another dive. On the dinghy ride out, however, the police stopped them and informed them that they couldn't take the small boat out to the reef. Disgusted, they turned around.

Once Harry and Robyn arrived in Mayotte, the four borrowed a car and spent eight hours driving around the big island. There were no good beaches, just one mediocre sand hill with a hotel. Lovely, abundant baobab trees, sometimes called upside down trees, were the best thing about the island; their branches look like underground root systems. Their swollen tree trunks store water so the trees can endure the harsh drought conditions.

Baobab trees in Mayotte

A Hard Sail

After five weeks in Mayotte, during which they spent their last franc and organized watches for four people, the Beaches left on September 26, 1994, eagerly anticipating Durban, South Africa. They were glad to have Harry and Robyn on board, though they promptly got sick. Robyn couldn't take her turn on watch, so they devised a new system for three, where each person had two shifts every third day.

The weather turned bad, with high winds that caused water to constantly get in the boat.

October 4, 1994. The weather fax shows no relationship to the wind. The boat is a wreck, and I am, too.

Jerry had to change Harry's bed mattress and sheets for dry ones and keep towels on the floor to absorb water. One day *Beachouse* went backward at two knots per hour. That night, they lost fifty-five miles; they had to make it up as well as try to keep to their original mileage schedule. Jerry pulled out their cold weather gear—it was quite chilly now, especially at night.

October 6, 1994. BC looks tired, but so are we all.

On the twelfth day at sea, as they were approaching the entrance to the bay leading to Durban, they spotted several whales, some jumping out of the water. They sailed on to the international dock at the Point Yacht Club.

October 7, 1994. What a joke. It has room for three small boats and us.

Buford, Jerry, Harry, and Robyn had champagne to celebrate their arrival in Durban after such a hard sail. Buford and Jerry were looking forward to settling in for a few months while the boat was being refurbished, visiting with some of the cruisers they'd met from South Africa, and visiting wild game parks. They could not know that a devastating disaster awaited them.

Living in Royal South Africa

October 1994–December 1995

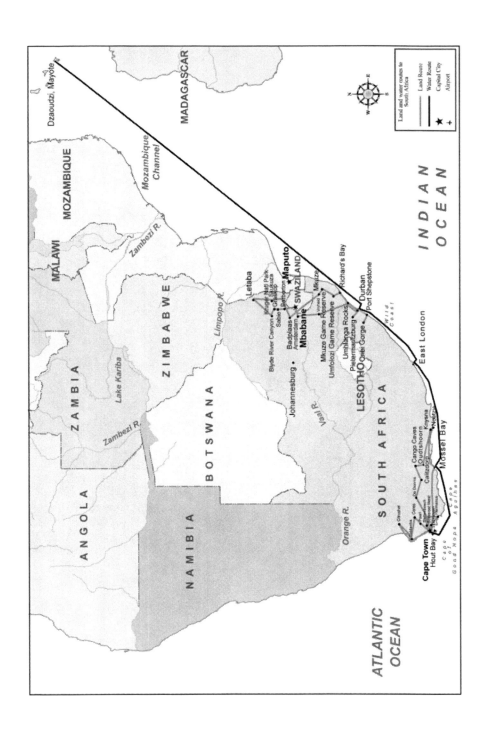

Durban

Beachouse docked in October 1994 at the Point Yacht Club in downtown Durban, within walking distance of the old city center. Tall buildings towered on two sides of them, with large, ship-filled piers around the other two sides. The weather was miserable—windy, cold, and rainy—but it didn't deter them from getting settled in. They set up a bank account and rented a late-model Mercedes from Rent-A-Wreck.

October 21, 1994. Buford was a menace on the road. The car steers hard, and he can't remember to stay left.

They applied for a television license, which was required for purchasing a set. Jerry bought a small black-and-white television in order to watch local programming—and then promptly declared it all very bad! She could walk to the public library and drive to the American Consulate, where she read old *Time* magazines to catch up on current events.

Then they discovered movie theaters. They could actually see first-run movies instead of their taped movies, of which they knew the dialogue by heart. It was a good way to spend time while waiting to hear from the boatyard when they could haul out of the water. All of their cruising friends were docked at Richard's Bay, a short drive up the coast.

Buford and Jerry desperately needed shoes; they hadn't worn real ones in years. Jerry's habit of going barefoot had caused her feet to spread to a size eleven. She couldn't find any women's shoes in South Africa to fit her, and the men's shoes were too wide. It was a good excuse for Jerry to go barefoot forever!

When it was time to lower the mast in preparation for the haul out, Buford and Jerry moved *Beachouse* across the bay to dock at a small out-of-the-way marina. The large crane arrived and took just over an hour to get the mast off the deck, with many sightseers watching. Finally, on

November 2, the crane operator and "strapping man" (the straps used to lift the boat off the ground were supplied by a third party) met at the boatyard at 3:00 PM to raise and stabilize the boat.

November 2, 1994. The wind was really strong up the channel. The strapping guy made a botch of it and took over an hour—then didn't get it right. BC had to stay on the crane. The boat was swinging wildly in the air. I couldn't watch. They couldn't get it on the stands, so they had to set it on the ground. The rudder is right on the ground and so is the center hull. We were complete wrecks.

The painters began working on the boat anyway. Several days later, they were able to raise the boat eight inches off the ground, but they were still unable to lift the boat.

November 16, 1994. They are just tearing the boat up. What a fiasco. They have changed their minds over and over on the method.

Finally, the boat was placed on racks Buford had made; it was still only one foot off the ground, but it was braced. Everyone was relieved and much happier.

On Safari

Two days later, Coral; Molly, eight; and Matt, six, arrived for a two-week visit. It was a nice respite from the stressful environment for Buford and Jerry. They rented a condominium in Umhlanga Rocks, a resort town on the Indian Ocean north of Durban. From there the itinerary took them north to Mkuze Game Reserve; to Badplass, a mineral spa and resort; and through the Drakensberg Mountains to the internationally renowned Krueger National Park. In Krueger they visited the Berg-en-dal, Skukuza, Satara, Letaba, and Sabie camps and then drove through Blyde River Canyon and MacMac Falls.

On safari in Krueger National Park, South Africa, 1995

In each camp, the routine was to leave the cabin around 6:30 AM to drive the roads for several hours looking for wild animals. Once it cooled off again, around 5:30 PM, another drive was in order. Sometimes they took a guided "night drive" in a large Jeep, huddled under blankets (it was cold!), to search for nocturnal animals. By the end of the trip, they'd seen all of the "Big Five"—cape buffalo, elephant, leopard, lion, and rhinoceros—along with cheetahs, kudos, springbok, nyalas, elands, dik-diks, waterbucks, impalas, zebras, spotted hyenas, vervet monkeys, hippopotamus, crocodiles, warthogs, giraffes, baboons, wildebeests, ostriches, a giant ground hornbill, and, Buford's favorite, a secretary bird.

Cape buffalo seen while driving through game parks in South Africa.

Buford drove the family through the countryside to the Swaziland border, past the patrol, and on to Mbabane, the capital city. You could immediately see a difference in the quality of the roads and infrastructure of this poorer country. Because of the conditions, they decided not to spend the night; instead, they headed back into South Africa. Jerry took the wheel and drove on the back roads, which turned into dirt roads, for hours to get to the Hluhluwe and Umfolozi Game Reserves. The crude, bumpy ride provided a close-up view of the South African people in their beehive-shaped mud huts called rondevals. The Beach clan had the only white faces in these remote areas, but they never felt uncomfortable.

Mud huts called rondevals in the South African countryside

The last stop was Shakaland, a resort built on the set of the movie *Shaka Zulu* that provided an educational experience focusing on the Zulu nation, people, and customs. The rooms were separate beehive huts, and in the late afternoon a program began with a presentation on Zulu customs. After dinner, the men performed a tribal dance, featuring the characteristic high kick followed by in-unison stamping that literally shook the ground. After breakfast the following morning, grandson Matthew participated in a spear-throwing contest; then the group returned to the Umhlanga Rocks condominium.

Once the family left, Buford and Jerry lived on the boat for the completion of the haul out, but there were constant frustrations. The varnishing was done poorly, so Jerry took charge of redoing most of it. Daily rain and southwesterly winds in the afternoons deterred progress and helped Buford develop a throat infection. When the port propeller was removed, Buford found it to be a mess and had to order a new one.

December 6, 1994. We are getting deeper and deeper in this mess. Hope I can cope with it.

After another several weeks of taking the same safari trip—this time with Cindy and Roger—the inside and outside painting of the boat began in January 1995, requiring that the boat be emptied. By the end of January, the painting was finished, everything was put away, and the boat had an overall cleaning. Several days before the boat was scheduled to be put back into the water, Buford tried to start the engines—to no avail. He worked on them for several days, becoming more and more disheartened and exhausted. Finally, he called in a mechanic. It took the mechanic two days to get both engines operational, with Buford watching over his shoulder like a hawk.

Buford and Jerry were on board all day on Sunday, February 5, doing last-minute preparations for the scheduled water reentry the following day. They kept busy enough to stay calm. Even the weather was cooperating perfectly, with only a light breeze in the afternoon. They had their usual evening cocktails and were even able to sleep a little that night.

Letter 26

Durban, Royal South Africa
March 9, 1995

Beachouse 60' Trimaran 5' Draft

As some of the members may have already heard, we have run into a problem in Durban, R.S.A. On February 6, after a three-month haul out and overhaul, we were dropped while being lifted back into the water. The crane was owned by Portnet, the Port of Durban, but the strapping was done by an independent contractor. One of his straps broke, and we fell about fifteen feet. The aft cabin of the center hull took the blow. The rudder and steering mechanisms were driven up through the aft bunk and left a good-sized hole in the sole. Also, a couple of holes on each side of the deck as it came down onto the stands below. The boat is currently being repaired and hopefully will be back in the water in time to get around the Cape before winter. Buf was on board and unhurt. The damage was not covered by insurance, so we are bearing the costs.

Everyone in the Durban yachting community has been supportive and helpful. Our renovation was done at Marina Yacht Lift, and we were most satisfied with the original work. However, we didn't plan on doing it twice.

Anyway, we would like to tell all our friends that we are alive and well, and Beachouse *is on the road to recovery. Hope to see the Caribbean later (much later) this year.*

Fair winds to all, and we hope to rejoin you on the high seas soon.

Jerry and Buford Beach
Commodores

*****

Total Disaster

Damage after the boat drop in Durban, February 1995

February 6, 1995. Total disaster! They dropped the boat while they were lifting it up. There was a two-and-a-half-hour delay in the proceedings. The crane was being repaired and didn't arrive until 10:00 AM. I left to drive around, doing a couple of small errands. When I got back at noon, the crane was gone, and the boat was still here—dropped on the stern. The rudder is up through our bed, and the aft lower hull is demolished—plus all the work we had done on the bottom. The stands have come up through the deck, and we have two big holes—one on each side. BC wasn't hurt, but there were four guys on board, and all were injured some. One has a bad ankle, one has cracked ribs, and two guys have slight problems. What a disaster. BC and I are in shock. We couldn't believe it. I don't know what we'll do now. Repair it—as soon as we can get it lifted.

The next day, temporary lights were rigged on the powerless boat. Still not able to comprehend the whole problem, Buford and Jerry spent the day trying to come to grips with the situation. Jerry found the original blueprints for the rudder, and Buford began devising a new plan for jacking up the boat again, another big deal. That night, they tried to sleep on the slanted floor of the boat.

Jerry worried about Buford.

February 8, 1995. This will be a lot of work, and I worry for him. He stays on the boat all day. No energy to do much or go anywhere.

The Durban Daily News printed a story with two large pictures of *Beachouse*, one labeled "before" and the second, with Jerry looking over the damage, labeled "after." The large boldface title read, "Crash goes a yacht—and their dream. Sailing couple watch in horror as hoisted catamaran smashes into ground." That says it all.

Knowing there was little she could contribute, Jerry decided to get out of the way by flying to Texas for five weeks and then going on to Amsterdam to visit Cindy and Roger for another two weeks. When she returned, she was happy to be back with Buford, but nothing had changed.

April 3, 1995. Same old grind—just like I hadn't been gone. I am trying to stay calm about the work. So is BC.

Letter 27

Durban, R.S.A.
April 6, 1995

Dear Carol and Shel,

A voice from the past—or, should I say, a letter from the past. I apologize for not keeping up with our correspondence, but this gay, mad existence we live is very time-consuming. I guess you have heard about our disaster. In case you missed it, we were reentering the water after an extensive haul out and were dropped. The back sling broke, and we fell fifteen or so feet. BC was on board but braced in a helm seat and was unhurt. We had been out for three months getting a complete facelift—all new paint outside, new varnish inside, the mast down and completely serviced (new roller furling system), plus all the regular stuff. It was not a happy day. We planned to dazzle you with our beauty when we got back this year. So much for vanity. Instead, we may have to borrow a few bucks. We have no insurance, you know, and the strapping company had disclaimed any responsibility before they undertook the job. BC had accepted that condition on a "gentleman's agreement." I suppose we could get involved in a long, time-consuming, expensive, and stressful lawsuit, but at this time in our lives, it isn't worth the hassle. Just less to leave the adorable children. They are all great, by the way, and I will get to them later.

This personal Armageddon took place on February 6, and we have been busily rebuilding ever since. The damage was confined to the rear of the main hull. We fell onto the rudder and pushed it up through our bed, pretty much destroying the area aft of the cockpit. Fortunately, the engine mounts held, and the engine room was undamaged. You've heard of having a sore ass? Beachouse had it to the extreme. After two months of work, we are slowly coming back together. The work ethic here is a little lax, and they seem to have an inordinate number of holidays. Buford has to oversee the work personally and is afraid to take his eyes off the guys for more than a few minutes at a time. But enough complaining and bitching for the moment, although I do reserve the right to return to this mood. By the way, I am not trying to minimize your engine problems and hope your problems are solved by now. Isn't yachting fun? I'll be glad when things are back to normal; we are sitting around on the back of the Rainbow *in the Caribbean, listening to the* Katufa *and the* Watermelon *trading lies.*

Now on to more pleasant stuff. I took this opportunity to take a six-week vacation. I left BC here working, which is what he gets for talking me into this entire scenario, anyway. I spent five weeks in Texas with Coral, Joe, and the kids and visited friends. I covered the state and had a great time. It's amazing how all those guys have aged while we still look the same. Cindy and Roger are now working in Perm Russia, eight hundred miles northeast of Moscow. They have a beautiful little seventeenth-century house rented in The Hague, Netherlands, that their company provides them for R and R. I stopped off and spent two weeks there doing Holland and Belgium. The flowers were just beginning to bloom, and it must be gorgeous by now. However, I had to come back to the "dirt pit," as we fondly refer to the yard.

In defense of South Africa, I must tell you that we have traveled the parks and a lot of the other scenic places, and it is truly a lovely country. Both girls and their families have visited, Coral over Thanksgiving and Cindy over Christmas. So we did Krueger Park twice. Loved it both times and have seen all the animals in the wild, including leopard and cheetah. That is very lucky. They can be hard to spot. Prices here are very reasonable, so traveling is a pleasure instead of a pain. Nothing like the old days in Venezuela, but we'll never find that again, I'm sure.

Most of the cruisers have moved on. We'll wind up being Tail-End Charlie. The majority of the boats we were traveling with went up through the Red Sea. We do have a very special single-hander coming your way. He is a delightful young Chinese from Hong Kong. He has traveled with us off and on for two years. The boat is named the Cadenza, *and his name is Terence. He is on the fast track, moving through the southern Caribbean, and should be there in June sometime. Keep a lookout—you'll enjoy his company.*

Speaking of people, the whole South African community has rallied to our side, and we have gotten a lot of sympathy and also lots of help and advice. They are trying to cope with this "new South Africa," and most of them are doing quite well. Every once in a while we will hear a few remarks that cause us to doubt our hearing, but most of the thinking populace realizes that the old system was not defensible in this new world of mass worldwide media.

I have not been good about keeping up with the old crowd. As you can attest, I hate to write letters. Anyway, if you see some of the gang, let them know we are okay and coping. In this day of the aforementioned mass media, rumors to the contrary might be circulating. We will be here for a couple more months, but sending the mail to Borger will be safer. Then we can have it forwarded to any current address.

We send our love and hope your engine problems are solved.

Pray for us.

*****

Letter 28

Dear Carol and Shel,

Well, I thought I'd send a broke boat report. We are sorry to hear about all your engine problems, but the old saying that misery loves company is certainly true. I would really hate it if everybody else I know was having a wonderful, carefree life. Think of your travails as therapeutic for Buf and me. The major repairs to the structural damage are finally finished. After four months. The cosmetic work is now underway. The holes in the deck are fixed. They look good, and after a few drinks and snacks are ground into them, we won't be able to tell the difference. They will start rebuilding the furniture in our aft cabin this week. No work today. They have more holidays in this country than they do in Venezuela. Today is Youth Day. Put the little bastards to work is my solution to all their traumas. They don't know what problems are. Buf has a project going most of the time. I'm the one at loose ends. I need you to go shopping with me. The Indian market is huge and lots of fun—but not with you-know-who. He's always looking at his watch and sighing.

The yard workers are a funny lot. Our chief carpenter is an Indian named David who is quite competent—but meticulous and very slow. Buf says the rest of the guys just walked in from the jungle. They are shy with us but talk in loud Zulu to one another all day long. They have terrific smiles and really appreciate any little thing we do for them. We have been here so long that the area covered by our hulls has become the dressing room, lunch bar, pissoir, and general meeting hall. We have told Dave, the English yard owner, that when we leave he will have to build a shed here for the guys. Dave is a wonderful host and shows us every kindness. His girlfriend (lady, live-in, significant other, or whatever the current vernacular is. I can't keep up)—anyway, her name is Kate, and she is the local rep for epoxies and Airex that we have been using. Last Sunday she took me to a small airfield about sixty miles out in the country. I went for an ultra-lite flight and also a glider ride. Buf and Dave were too chicken—they stayed behind and watched rugby. I had never been up in either contraption, so I had a marvelous time. The glider was particularly fun. We were over a beautiful area of rolling hills, farms, and lakes. The pilot asked if I wanted a plain ride or acrobatics. You know me—I bade him to do his worst—and we did a series of loops and chandelles that was scary but exhilarating. Kate had a tamer ride with her guy. We both had a great day and met some interesting people. Kate has a glider license, so she was acquainted with a number of them. Anyway, it was a break from the dirt pit, as we fondly refer to the yard.

Buf is enjoying the World Cup rugby. All the games are televised, so we are weekend couch potatoes. I don't know what we'll do when the games are over; weekends are boring. The yard is locked up at night, and there is a guard dog. His name is Starboard, and he rolls over and lolls his tongue if he is spoken to or petted. He's a sweetie pie, but we don't feel he has the killer instinct in case of a break-in. We like to be on board most nights. We've about covered the local and nearby tourist traps. We don't know how much longer we will be in the yard, much less how long it will take to get the rig up and all the onboard systems back in working order. Everything has been shut down for seven to eight months, so we are bound to have glitches. The big fly in the ointment is a place to settle down and do the work. The Yacht Club here won't let us come to their piers. They are floating docks, and they say we are too big. Almost all the many, many boats in Durban are small day sailors. Not many alternatives for us, and they are all unattractive.

The South African winter is setting in, and, unaccustomed as we are to anything below seventy-five degrees Fahrenheit, we are freezing at night. Normally, the days are warm and beautiful, but the nights are chilly; today is rainy and cloudy, so it's colder than kraut. (I wonder where that saying comes from. I've heard it all my life, but it actually makes no sense at all.) Anyway, you know how cheap we are. We have few clothes that are warm enough but hate to go buy stuff we will need only for a very short time. Layering has become a big thing, and our nightdress is a sight to behold. We are slowly getting accustomed to the idea that we will be in R.S.A. until next fall and will probably sail to the Virgins, bypassing the *southern Caribbean until next season. Cindy and Roger are leaving Russia in September and may join us for the Atlantic crossing. They are eager to do it if the timing works out. They have been in Russia for two years, working. He is heading a partnership of U.S. and Russian oil companies, trying to get production going. Cindy is his assistant. They hate it there. Between the weather and the confrontational style of doing business, they have become most disenchanted and are looking forward to R and R. They admit that it has been a once-in-a-lifetime opportunity to see that part of the world. However, they now say—been there, done that.*

We are looking forward with trepidation to making the rough sail around the Cape and settling in Cape Town for a month or so. God knows when it will happen, and this is definitely the wrong time of the year. Oh well; yachties are known for going against the flow. Everyone we have spoken to here raves about Cape Town. Hope we aren't disappointed. The scenery may not live up to expectations, but the wines will probably make up for any other shortcomings.

I hope you notice that I have made a supreme effort to keep the whining tone out of this letter. At least Buf and I are together and healthy. I might add that I am referring to physical well being. Our mental attitudes vary wildly from day to day. Depends on the weather, if the guys are working, whether the costs threaten to pauper us, and other various and assorted outside influences. As I am beginning to detect a distinct whine in the tone of this letter, I will close with much love and many kisses. Let's stay in touch. Keep using the Borger address. Glen is very good about forwarding our mail.

Keep the faith.

*****

Life in the Boatyard

Life in the boatyard became very routine and reminded Buford and Jerry of a time eleven years earlier when they built the boat on Bolivar Peninsula. Buford supervised the workers, a full-time job, taking its toll on a seventy-two-year-old. He cut an artery in his hand while installing a bilge pump, which required several stitches. Jerry began to notice Buford's diminishing enthusiasm for maintaining the boat.

April 16, 1995. This predicament we're in has taken a lot of the fun out of it for BC. I think he's getting about ready to sell Beachouse *and relax.*

May 1, 1995. We are really getting low and depressed. It's hard to stay enthused.

May 11, 1995. It's very boring in the yard. I'm tired of sitting and sitting. Haven't seen anyone we know for weeks.

During the week, Buford and Jerry were usually the only ones in the yard. They continued their evening routine of having happy hour and watching TV or one of their taped movies. Weekends were quiet; only the local boat owners were in the yard working on their boats. Every Sunday morning, as a treat, Buford bought a newspaper and ice for the day. They usually spent the afternoon shopping or at a movie theater—except during rugby season.

Buford became addicted to watching South African rugby on television every weekend, and he eventually came to regard American professional football as a "sissy sport." He watched the 1995 Rugby World Cup Tournament for weeks, which South Africa hosted and won at their first attempt, in overtime. There was pandemonium throughout the country; even Buford and Jerry joined in the excitement.

Most Saturdays, Buford and Jerry took sightseeing drives to get away from the city and boatyard. They rode through spectacular scenery to the Drakensberg Mountains, the highest in South Africa, and saw centuries-old cave paintings by bushmen. They visited Pietermaritzburg, the capital and second-largest city of the KwaZulu-Natal province, best known for its Victorian city buildings that are 100 to 150 years old. They drove one and a half hours south of Durban to Port Shepstone, situated on the mouth of the Mzimkulu River, the largest river on the south coast of the KwaZulu-Natal province. There they took a round-trip tour bus to the Oribi Gorge, followed by a narrow gauze train through the canyon. The tour treated them to a braai lunch—barbeque in the Afrikaans language—a social custom in South Africa.

The boat reconstruction was finally finished in mid-July 1995. Having everyone off the boat was a great relief. Jerry began to varnish and paint the inside. Buford began devising a scheme for preventing damage to the boat during the lift back into the water.

On July 27, 1995, more than six months after the boat had been dropped, the big reentry day arrived. Jerry followed her usual routine of leaving the boatyard during the process and returned to find *Beachouse* at the dock.

July 27, 1995. It was great to see it in the water. BC said the lift out took a long time because they were so slow and careful.

Buford was not allowed to stay on board this time. The cradles he had made for lifting the wires on the wings were a life saver. They rinsed off the boat and, having been strongly warned about theft, put away everything on deck. They opened champagne to celebrate, happy to be back in the water at last.

Beachouse returns to the water after fifteen months in Durban, South Africa.

Back in the Water

The next day, Buford bought ten gift certificates to a nice restaurant for the crane workers, who seemed thrilled. With the boat in the water and the structural repairs and painting completed both inside and outside, Buford began to supervise the various mechanical specialists who would help return the boat to top working order. They put the mast back into place and installed a new hot water heater. However, the roller furling wasn't working, the refrigeration had problems, and a crack was discovered in the windlass for the anchor. When these problems were corrected, a leak in each ama was discovered.

August 10, 1995. We are really discouraged. There is no end in sight to our problems. We don't feel like we're making much progress.

After a month of frustration, Buford and Jerry took a week off for another safari trip to the Hluhluwe and Umfolozi game parks. When they returned, they learned a "big blow" had come through while they were gone.

September 1, 1995. The boat is absolutely filthy with black dirt. It has never looked so bad. We were very depressed.

Delays upon delays, short work hours, unmet schedules, and slow workers kept Buford and Jerry frustrated. Jerry attempted to provide some kind of organization, but it was impossible.

September 4, 1995. This country is beyond belief with its lack of efficiency.

Finally, in mid-September, they began stocking the boat for sailing. Jerry was excited to find Pringles potato chips at one store. They had just arrived and were expensive, but she bought some anyway as a treat.

After being in the water for eight weeks, *Beachouse* was finally ready to leave Durban on September 20, 1995. Now she had to wait on the weather—for the winds to be light and moderate from the southeast.

Buford and Jerry, anxious to be on their way, became bored just sitting around. Ten days later, all systems were go. Buford checked out with Immigration, Customs, and the harbor captain. After one year, *Beachouse* was finally leaving Durban for the famous Wild Coast and treacherous Cape of Good Hope, recognized for hundreds of years as the graveyard of ships.

The Wild Coast

On the morning of October 1, 1995, Buford and Jerry threw the lines off the boat. Just as they began to leave the dock, however, the engine overheated—it was a broken fan belt. A friend drove Buford all around town to find a replacement—not an easy assignment since it was a Sunday morning.

Beachouse set off again, passing whales outside the Durban harbor just as she had when she'd arrived one year before. But the day soon got worse, and the following day was not much better.

October 1, 1995. The radar didn't work, the fridge quit, and the starting cord on the Blue Monster quit. It turned cloudy and drizzly, with wind on the nose. We ran over a fishing net at sunset, and I went down in the dark to cut it loose but couldn't get it because of the sloppy sea. What a day!

October 2, 1995. Our saga continues. The starboard engine overheated again—so we are running on one propeller. When the sea calmed, I went below and cut the line off the propeller, losing two knives in the process. It is worrisome because of the problems.

They decided to make an unscheduled stop at East London, a pretty seaside tourist town known for its beaches and surfing competitions. Buford immediately dove into the engine room. When Buford was certain he'd fixed the belt, *Beachouse* set out again. Two miles out of the harbor, however, the engine reheated, prompting them to turn around and retie at the dock.

The arrival of *Beachouse* in the small coastal community of East London created great excitement. Just as Buford and Jerry were leaving for lunch, a carload of well-dressed men drove up and insisted on taking them to lunch at the Tug and Ferry, a local pub on the dock. The group leader invited them to the Yacht Club the next night for dinner.

Docked in front of the pub, *Beachouse* had visitors and sightseers every day. One morning it took two hours to get rid of a group of fifty drill team members and sponsors. Locals at the pub and Yacht Club kept stopping to visit and inviting Buford and Jerry to various social outings.

October 7, 1995. This is a very friendly place, almost too friendly. People really are curious about the boat.

Two weeks after *Beachouse* arrived in East London, the weather finally looked favorable for another attempt around the Cape. The night before their departure, Buford and Jerry said good-bye to their friends at the pub. The owner placed a plaque bearing their name on the wall, which surprised and touched them.

The following morning, when they sat down for their last breakfast at the pub, they found themselves on the front page of East London's daily newspaper, *The Daily Dispatch*. They were the subjects of a story entitled "Retired U.S. Couple Enjoy Luxury at Sea," which included three large color photographs. The only direct quote in the article was from Jerry: "We have liked the lifestyle very much and have met wonderful people all around the world. Our philosophy is you have to get off and go inland to meet the people." Amen.

Beachouse left around 10:30 AM on Saturday, October 15, 1995. The weather forecast for Sunday morning predicted light easterly winds, increasing to twenty knots later in the day.

October 15, 1995. We turned the corner, and the current had us really flying. The wind kept building all day and really got strong. We were miserable, and it got worse. The wind finally got to forty-five knots in the middle of the night. We got one big wave over the side and a huge one completely over the stern and the top of our cabin. What a mess. Everything is wet, and we were really miserable.

The next day, they arrived at the ship dock in Mossel Bay. *Beachouse* fought off a big surge motion with terribly loud noises that made life uncomfortable. Jerry spent the day wiping up the water in the boat. Buford toiled on the little problems—the refrigerator was not working, the engine reheated again, and the cooling water tank was empty.

Mossel Bay was a great place to spend two weeks waiting for the southeasterly winds they'd need for the 244-mile sail around the Cape of Good Hope to Cape Town. They visited an extensive museum complex that included a full-sized replica of the Portuguese explorer Bartholomew Diaz's ship. In 1488, he discovered the Cape of Good Hope, which he originally named the "Cape of Storms." The discovery proved that Africa had a southern tip, which made it possible to sail from Europe to India.

The day of their departure finally arrived.

October 27, 1995. I didn't sleep well at all. We are so uptight about getting around the corner. There is a good chance of southeast winds tomorrow—but maybe a little strong. I guess we'll go even though it's stronger than we want. I'm a nervous wreck!

At last it was time for *Beachouse* to undertake the journey past the southern tip of Africa and the menacing Cape of Good Hope.

Letter 29

Cape Town, R.S.A.
December 1995

Here we are still in darkest Africa, which is apropos, as it has been the darkest year of our cruising adventure. I'm behind in my correspondence because my arm is in a sling. At least it's a change, as it has been our ass in a sling all year. We have Beachouse *all repaired after our disastrous drop in Durban last February and in good sailing condition. We are at the dock at the Royal Cape Yacht Club in Cape Town. The club itself is a very classy facility, but we have been delegated to the far reaches of the perimeter and are right next to a pile of barricades that are used in case of an oil spill in the harbor. We have to go outside the fence and walk down the street to get to the clubhouse. It is not a true walk-on dock. The scenery makes up for the other shortcomings. Table Mountain is off our portside and is a magnificent sight. Better than the pictures. The city is as lovely as advertised, and the region all around is quite spectacular. The tourism industry here has been overwhelmed by the visitors, mostly from Europe. It is the beginning of summer here, and the weather is slowly turning warm. I had always visualized Africa as hot, but this place is cold!*

Our voyage around the Cape of Storms from Durban to Cape Town turned out to be just that. It was the pits. Weather forecasting in this country must be done by a witch doctor rolling bones. We took over a month, but every time we stuck our necks out of a harbor, the wind gods were laying for us. Forty K's became normal, and we got into a real whizzer approaching Cape Town. We diverted into Hout Bay, thirty miles south, with the help of the NSRI (National Sea Rescue Institute) in sixty to seventy K's. The NSRI guys said they saw gusts to eighty-five K's. I don't know if it's true—but suffice it to say, it was more wind than we wanted. They sent two boats and led us into the dock. Hout Bay is a small harbor without many navigational lights, and, of course, this all took place in the dead of night. These men are volunteers, can you imagine? They do this for fun.

For the first time since we started this caper over ten years ago, we had an injury on board. I fell on deck as we were tying to the dock and dislocated my right shoulder. It's been in a sling for a month but is coming off soon. Beachouse was undamaged, except a couple of cleats ripped off. The real damage was to our egos. The commander of the operation has since become a good friend. He and his wife have taken us to dinner and on trips to the wineries and have given us freely of their time and advice. Very nice people and a lot of fun. We have been treated with kindness and consideration everywhere we have been in this country and find the people to be more like home than anyplace we have been since we left the Caribbean.

We stopped at East London for two weeks and were docked at the tourist waterfront development. We had shops and two pubs within a few steps. Freedom from cooking, a lot of sightseers, an abundance of free drinks, invitations to private homes and all the Yacht Club functions. It was great. We even made the front page of the local newspaper. Next stop was Mossel Bay, just short of Cape Agulhas, the southernmost point of the continent. We spent another two weeks or so waiting for a good weather forecast (ha!). Ate lots of seafood and watched the seals.

We had to motor on to Cape Town two days after our dramatic entrance into Hout Bay and expect to be here for Christmas and New Year's. The Cape to Rio Yachting Race leaves for Brazil on January 6, and we plan on crashing as many of the festivities as we can. Then we'll take off for Trinidad and the Caribbean, officially finishing our circumnavigation.

Cindy and Roger have joined us for the long Atlantic crossing. Having two extra hands on board will make for an easy passage, and we'll have time to play a lot of bridge. They have been here for a few weeks now and did some inland traveling while waiting for us to arrive in Cape Town. We have rented a car and driven the "Garden Route" on the southern point of the continent. The juxtaposition of sea, flowers, and mountains makes for spectacular scenery. There are many sights to see, and we stayed in small accommodations that had a lot of atmosphere. Visited a huge ostrich race. My bird lost—surprise. I have been fighting a faulty camera ever since we got to the African continent, and it has finally won. I was too cheap to buy a new one, and I have paid a price of more than money. I don't have a decent picture of anything that we have seen in the year we have been here.

Incredible! When we show you pictures of our African adventures, please don't remind me that I have had to copy pictures from our kids and friends. It really hacks me off. Especially since we saw so many animals really close. It has been a real experience. There is a small beach not far away that has a colony of jackass penguins that are totally oblivious to humans. It is possible to walk within two or three feet of them and watch and take pictures to your heart's content. The sound they make is just like a donkey. Also, colonies of seals are common. Even here in the inner harbor, there is the occasional seal wandering by. We had one by the boat yesterday morning. Californians may not be impressed, but we South Texans are thrilled.

We are planning a trip north of Cape Town soon, toward the desert regions. And we are busily making short wine route trips into the vineyards that are nearby. There are hundreds of them, most with free wine-tasting facilities and inexpensive good wines. We usually buy a few bottles at each place so we won't feel guilty for depleting their bar.

There are few American boats here. Most everybody we know took the Red Sea route. We plan to stop by St. Helena, a possible stop at Ascension, hopefully Fernando de Noronha off the coast of Brazil, French Guyana with Devil's Island, and on to Trinidad.

Meantime, we all hope you have a Merry Christmas and a marvelous New Year. Maybe we'll see you in 1996. At least we are going to be getting closer. We send our love and affection. Coral, Joe, and kids won't be coming this Christmas, but we expect a long visit from them next summer.

Love,
Jerry and Buford

Addition to friends Gene and Grace Smith:

Hello there, it's the real me! I find it too easy to send the form to keep from having to repeat myself. Now to get down and dirty!

We really are enjoying Cape Town. We finally got around to riding the cable car yesterday—us and two cruise ships. It was a long wait but worth it. The Victoria and Albert Waterfront is a fantastic area. We are working our way through the restaurants. We even tried Carlos Cantina. Any resemblance to Mexican food was an accident. Truly bad. You'd think we had more sense. Muy loco! We have found jalapeños, taco shells, and nacho chips—at a very dear price. But what the hell—sometimes you've just got to have a fix. We also tried Morton's, named for Jelly Roll and touted as genuine Cajun. They got the names of the dishes right, but the food was unrecognizable to any in New Orleans. The wineries are great. We are trying to work our way through the best ones—but it's a hard job. There are hundreds. Some of the wine is not too grand, but most of it is really good. I'm not much of a judge—if it doesn't take the enamel off my teeth, I'm satisfied.

We have a little black-and-white TV to watch the news. I'm not sure why we thought that was important. The news is all bad and leaves us depressed. The local programming is pathetic, and the imported U.S. programming is worse. Can you believe they are showing The Jerry Lewis Show *from twenty years ago? I hated the sombich then, and he hasn't improved.*

The political situation here is interesting to an outsider. I'm glad we don't have to cope with it. Except for the Zulus, who hate everybody not in their tribe, and the far-right Afrikaners, who just hate everybody, everyone seems genuinely contented at the least with President Mandela. He doesn't have a clear-cut successor, and God knows what will happen when he goes. We have been surprised at the tribal animosity still alive among the blacks. I don't know why that should come as a shock. Look at Bosnia. We met a South African cruiser three years ago in Vanuatu who went to work for the United Nations in Bosnia. We heard from him a few weeks ago, and he will be here for Christmas. We hope to get the real scoop from someone who has been there for two years. Enough digressions—back to South Africa. The major problem looks to be many-sided. There are millions of black people whose expectations have been raised to impossible levels and a minority of whites who are frightened and would like to leave the country. The tax base is very small considering the vast numbers of country people to be educated and brought the barest amenities, such as power, water, and schools. The tribal system didn't include a work ethic for men. They hunted, and the women did the rest. Even if there were employment for all, it will take a generation or so to bring everyone into the modern world. Enough political crap. The locals probably wouldn't agree, anyway.

We had a nice Thanksgiving here, turkey and all, but it would have been great to have been with the kids and you back in Galveston. We'll miss them at Christmas but expect a long visit this coming year. We are enjoying

Cindy and Roger, who have a lot of stories to tell about Russia. Keep in touch, and we hope to see you soon.

Love,
Buford and Jerry

*****

Rescued

Jerry's journal account of their rescue at Hout Bay included:

October 29 and 30, 1995. We passed Agulhas Point early this morning. The farthest point south on the trip. The wind began to build all day and the seas, too. It wasn't too bad until we rounded Cape Point at dusk, but then it really began to rage. The seas were horrendous, and the wind was terrific. When we called Cape Town, they advised us to come in at Hout Bay and called NSRI. Both our engines overheated, and we were powerless. The rescue boat came about 10:00 PM and then another from Cape Town. It took them two to three hours to maneuver us into the dock. There must have been ten to twenty guys. It was a terrible experience. Like a stupid fool, I fell and dislocated my shoulder. They took me to the hospital, and I had it resocketed and spent the night. We spent the afternoon kinda in a daze.

The National Sea Rescue Institute (NSRI), founded in 1967, is a volunteer rescue service charged with saving lives on South African waters. Today the NSRI has seventy-two rescue craft located at twenty-nine coastal and three inland rescue stations, with over 840 volunteers on call twenty-four hours a day, seven days a week. Their rescue of *Beachouse* was chronicled in the October 30, 1995, edition of the *Cape Argus Southern Edition* newspaper.

NSRI rescue yacht caught in fierce gale

HURRICANE-force winds had Sea Rescue boats battling to save a stricken American trimaran and its two elderly crew—one of whom was injured—near Hout Bay.

The 60-foot trimaran, Beachouse, *from Texas, crewed by Buford Beach, 71, and his wife Jerry, 64, ran into trouble about 10 km from Slangkop Lighthouse near Hout Bay yesterday.*

> *The couple left Mossel Bay at 2:00 PM on Saturday but sailed into the south-easter which began to build to gale-force by noon yesterday.*
>
> *When the vessel was halfway to False Bay, both engines overheated and they "couldn't cope," said Mrs. Beach, who fell to the deck and dislocated her right arm.*
>
> *The 70-knot wind (about 133km/h) made the rescue extremely difficult, said the Hout Bay NSRI, who had to call in their colleagues at Table Bay NSRI's Station 3 to assist them.*
>
> *Hout Bay NSRI coxswain Bruce Bodmer said that while trying to connect a tow to the stricken catamaran, the NSRI vessel began to drift.*
>
> *Table Bay's Rescue 8 vessel came in and also managed to connect a tow and helped bring the catamaran in at 1:00 AM today, but not before the bollard, to which the tow line was attached, snapped on the Hout Bay NSRI vessel.*
>
> *"This was probably one of the most difficult rescues we have ever done.*
>
> *It's a miracle we were able to bring the boat in—the wind was absolutely frightening," he said.*
>
> *Mr. Bodmer said that while they were trying to connect the tow, the catamaran "kept bearing down on us."*
>
> *"I'm just so glad to be in—I can't thank the NSRI enough," said Mrs. Beach, who was taken to Constantiaberg Hospital.*

Jerry was not embarrassed by the article, even though it mentioned her injury, referred to the boat as a catamaran, and included a photo of her being lifted off the boat on a stretcher. But she was humiliated that the article referred to her and Buford as "elderly."

Still in semishock, they awoke the following morning to a beautiful, calm, and sunny day. Since the weather was perfect, Buford decided to finish the trip to Cape Town. He left for the dock to organize the trip and returned to *Beachouse* with two girls in tow to help make the sail: one a member of the NSRI team and the second an experienced sailor.

It was a pleasant motor all the way; they watched dolphins, seals, and a few penguins.

With her arm in a sling, Jerry was having difficulty performing her usual boat chores and writing in her journal, and she couldn't drive, so she walked to town while Buford dealt with mechanical issues.

November 2, 1995. It was quite a distance and not through a great part of town. I stopped at the port customs building to ask directions. The guy asked if I was carrying a gun! Anyway, I made it to town and to the bank. The post office was next door so I picked up phone books. Always handy.

Buford hired a worker from the marina to clean the boat. He spent several weeks thoroughly cleaning both the inside and outside. Once Cindy and Roger arrived, Buford and Roger took on the time-consuming job of replacing all the boat's cleats.

Exploring Cape Town

The foursome made side trips to wineries south, east, and north of Cape Town, traveling through beautiful scenery. Upon returning from one outing, they were told that a body had been pulled from the water next to their boat. It was a boat owner who fell off his boat and drowned. Buford immediately hung his man-overboard pole on deck, which he'd been lax about doing.

They took a trip to the nature reserve on Cape Point where the two giant water masses of the Atlantic and Indian Oceans meet. Most people think that the Cape of Good Hope is the meeting point, but, geographically, Cape Point is the junction where the cold waters of the west coast meet the warm waters of the east coast. Both are promontories off of towering cliffs above the sea.

Boat reflections at the Royal Cape Yacht Club, Cape Town, South Africa

November 24, 1995. It's a strange countryside there. Looks like a desert with small, scrubby foliage and plants. The mountains are rocky, with very little top soil. Cindy and Roger walked up, while BC and I took the bus. It was a lovely view of the meeting of the two oceans. Sure looked benign, not like when we came around!

By mid-December, after a month in Cape Town, all were getting bored and tired of the endlessly strong winds.

December 9, 1995. This morning, the wind is still blowing gale force. It will make you nuts. At 6:00 PM, the wind is still howling. I didn't sleep until 3:00 AM. The noise is horrific. A sail got loose on a boat across from us. Really loud!

Stocking Up

It was time to start stocking up and preparing for their departure. First, they inventoried their food and discovered that not much was left except canned vegetables. Cindy and Jerry spent four hours buying all the necessary food, except for fresh produce. Both the manager and the butcher of the grocery store were very helpful, especially considering that the store was packed with Christmas shoppers. The manager agreed to vacuum-pack and freeze the meat, bread, and flour and deliver it all to the boat in two days. On the delivery day, Cindy and Jerry waited and waited for them to arrive.

December 22, 1995. They finally arrived at 11:00 AM. It took a lot of trips to get the stores on board. Six or so guys on the dock helped. They had already had a lot of beer, evidently. They were funny. One dropped a bag of cookies overboard.

Buford closed their bank account, bought Trinidad and Brazilian flags, and picked up their Brazilian visas. The day before departure, he turned in the car, while Jerry and Cindy bought the fresh fruits and vegetables. That evening, Buford and Jerry went to the Yacht Club to spend their last South African rand and have their last drinks at the bar.

Beachouse finally left Cape Town on December 30, 1995, passing a parade of seals and whales. It was a happy ending to their unexpected fourteen months in South Africa and a great beginning for the last ocean crossing of their circumnavigation.

Returning to the Caribbean

January 1996–November 1996

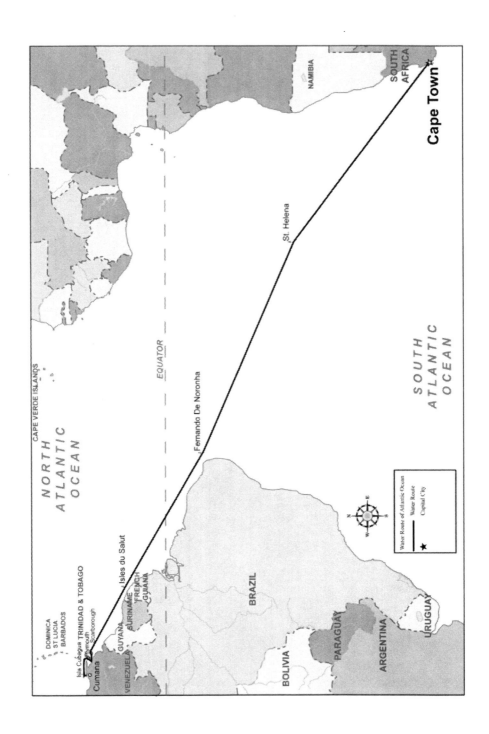

240

Letter 30

Trinidad, West Indies
April 1996

Another dreaded form letter from the Hellship Beachouse*!!*

Back in the sunny Caribbean at last. It was a swell six years, and we had a great time, but it's nice to feel at home again. There has been a big change in the scene here in Trinidad. We had not been here before, because it was off the beaten track when we left—now it is covered up in boats. There must be at least four hundred boats on the hard and one hundred or more in the anchorages. We were going to haul, but the travel lift in operation will only take thirty-one feet and six inches in width. We are thirty-three feet. Story of my life. There is a larger lift going into operation this summer, and we have made a reservation for September.

Our passage from Cape Town was slow but fun. Daughter Cindy with husband Roger were on board, so the watches were easy, and we had no weather until the coast of Brazil. We were fifteen days to St. Helena, where we had a problem with our auto pilot. We had the great good fortune to be anchored next to an Australian wizard named Allan on the S/V Savanika, *who got us back in business while regaling us with hilarious stories. His "down under" accent made Crocodile Dundee sound like he attended Oxford. St. Helena itself was a delight. From the ocean it looked like a large and forbidding rock, but the interior revealed a lush, beautiful island. They grow lots of fresh veggies, even broccoli and lettuce. We took a tour with Colin, who owns a 1929 Chevy pickup that he has outfitted for tourists. There were six of us, but the three guys were as interested in the truck as they were in the scenery. Napoleon's house was a surprise. Quite lovely. It is still owned and maintained by the French government as a museum. It is impossible to land a dinghy, so there is a ferry service on standby. It's a small motor launch that takes you to a cement landing that has a scaffold across the top with four large ropes dangling. The exercise is to grab a line and swing onto the dock without falling in or breaking something. Depending on the swell and weather, it could be routine, thrilling, or terrifying. We hit all three conditions during the two weeks we were there.*

Another sixteen days and we anchored in Fernando de Noronha. It is just off the coast of Brazil, near Natal and Fortaleza. We stayed six days, just long enough to tour the island, do a little snorkeling, and replenish veggies. It is a resort of choice for the Brazilians, so there were a lot of tourists. Also, with our usual impeccable timing, a cruise ship showed up and unloaded the customary lily-whites. Lots and lots of dolphins. Cindy and I were fortunate and swam with a group for fifteen minutes or so. They would come tantalizingly close, but we were never quite able to touch one. Another eleven days and we anchored at the Iles du Salut off the coast of French Guiana.

Devil's Island, the infamous prison, is one of the three small islands. There is nothing much left of the penal colony, but there is a hotel for the ubiquitous tourists. We stayed only three days, as we had the bit in our teeth and were headed for the barn. We took four days to Tobago, including our fastest day ever—213 miles in twenty-four hours. It was a little rough, but the current really whizzed us along.

We stayed in Tobago for a month. Cindy and Roger headed for the States shortly after we arrived. Back to the real world. Coral, Joe, and the grandchildren replaced them in a few days. They stayed eighteen days, and we had a great time. The water and anchorages in Tobago are good—not true Caribbean quality—but a lot better than anything we have seen in a long time. The two kids—Molly, nine, and Matt, seven—are totally at home in the water, and we swam and snorkeled endlessly.

Coral brought our mail, and we caught up on a lot of your travels and activities. We have no plans beyond hanging around in the lower part of the Caribbean this summer, out of the hurricane area, while waiting for our haul out. No use trying to make plans too far ahead—something always comes up, and flexibility is the key. Some people might call it lack of purpose—we prefer to think of it as preparedness for any eventuality. Meanwhile, keep in touch, if you can, and stay loose. Hope to see you soon, somewhere, sometime.

Addition to Gene and Grace Smith, May 1996:

Hi guys—this is the real us—the end of the dreaded form letter. We wanted to bring you up to date and let you know we got back safe and sound. We presume Coral has filled you in on most of the news. She said you had been in the hospital, Gene. Hope all is well and you are back on the road, selling superfluous hardware to the unwary public.

As for us, Buf has been engaged in an epic battle with one of the Perkins engines. He and half of the mechanics on the island have finally gotten it beaten into submission, and we will soon be on our way to somewhere. We've been in Trinidad for four weeks and haven't been to town but once. There is a small shopping center a few miles from here with a good supermarket, so that has been the focus of our explorations so far. Buf has seen the engine room, mostly. We exchange books and movies and have our sundowners, so it's easy to take it all in stride. We went to a pan (steel band) concert last week. It was put on for the yachties. Especially those like us who missed Carnival. It was fun. We are headed for Venezuela in the next few days—then on to Bonaire. Coral and the kids are coming again to let us play Grandma and Grandpa—probably mid-July to mid-August. We will meet them there. We are playing it by ear until then.

Please pass our best on to Trip, Pam, and Michael. We will probably be back in Texas sometime in the next year. At least we're a lot closer than we've been in a long time. Let us know what's happening.

Sent with love and affection,

*****

Letter 31

Trinidad, West Indies
April 1996

Dear SSCA Friends,

We are back in the Caribbean after five years and six months making our circumnavigation. It was a mixture of great fun, great stress, and great people. We wouldn't have missed it for anything, but it's wonderful to be "home."

Thought we'd send a few notes about South Africa and the Atlantic islands for those who choose "the road less traveled."

Our trip from Durban to Cape Town was the pits. The wind gods were really on our case. Our first port of call was East London. It is a very safe harbor in the mouth of a river. The Landing is the dock for visiting yachts and is just steps from two pubs, shops, and restaurants. We were a novelty, as few foreign boats stop here, most going on to Port Elizabeth. We stayed two weeks and made many friends at the Yacht Club.

We left for Cape Town but were blown into Mossel Bay by fifty-knot winds. It is a fishing harbor surrounded by a breakwater and has a lot of surge. The Yacht Club is a half mile down the beach and has three moorings. They were just completing a walk-on pier system inside the harbor for yachts. The town is very picturesque, and we stayed another two weeks.

On the 245-mile trip left to Cape Town, the wind built to sixty to seventy knots, and we were diverted into Hout Bay by the Cape Town harbor radio and the NSRI, the volunteer rescue service. They were reporting gusts to eighty-five knots. All in the dead of night, of course. The weather forecast had been for thirty-five knots around the Cape of Good Hope. Weather forecasting is chancy at best in this part of the world, as the patterns are so volatile. Two days later, we motored the remaining thirty miles to Cape Town in dead calm. We were at the Royal Cape Town Yacht Club for two months. It's very nice, but they were much preoccupied with the upcoming Cape to Rio Race and not too social to visitors. We provisioned for the long crossing at Pick and Pay in Constantia. The management was extremely helpful. They arranged an exemption from the 14 percent Value Added Tax since we were leaving the country—and they delivered dockside. The quality of the provisions was excellent, the meat superb. We bought cases of wine while tasting our way through the vineyards.

We sailed on December 30 and made St. Helena in fifteen days. A long, slow, uneventful crossing. The anchorage is a bit rolly, and the ferry landing is dangerous. It is almost impossible to land a dinghy, and we saw very few boats even try. We add our praise to that of other yachties for Ann at Ann's Place. Her restaurant is a haven for passing crews, and we found many boats we knew in the log books she has kept for more than ten years. We made the obligatory tour with Colin in his 1929 Chevy truck. A nice two-week stop.

Another slow, seventeen-day sail got us to Fernando de Noronha, off the Brazilian coast. We had gotten a visa in Cape Town, so the check-in was very casual. No time limit and no fees. Patrick, owner of Atlantis Dive Center, changed dollars for us and was very helpful. There is bare-minimum provisioning—and very expensive. We could not make a phone call to the United States.

We anchored off the Iles du Salut eleven days after we left Fernando. We didn't go to the coast of French Guiana—just rested and enjoyed the three small islands, including famed Devil's Island. Phoning the United States was not possible here, either. We stayed only three days and zoomed up the coast of South America to Tobago. The current and favorable winds made for our fastest twenty-four hours ever—213 miles. After a visit from the family, we have moved on to Trinidad, where we are getting the usual repairs.

We were disappointed to find we cannot haul at Peake's Yard. We are one and a half feet too wide. There is a new yard being built across the bay. The name will be Crews Inn, and it is due to open in June. They have a two-hundred-ton travel lift being assembled that will haul boats and multihulls with beams up to thirty three feet seven inches.

We hope to meet up with lots of new and old cruising buddies now that we are back. We fly our Commodore flag, so come on by.

Jerry and Buford Beach
Commodores
S/V Beachouse

*****

245

Crossing the Atlantic Ocean

The stops *Beachouse* made in the Atlantic in January and February 1996 are well-known among ocean cruisers. St. Helena, one of world's most isolated islands, was for several centuries vitally important to ships sailing from Asia and South Africa to Europe. It is a British Overseas Territory that was used as a place for exile; Napoleon Bonaparte was the most famous figure to be exiled there. He was brought to the island in 1815 and remained there until his death in 1821. His tomb was moved to France in 1840.

Tour guide Colin and his 1929 Chevy truck, St. Helena

Fernando de Noronha, an archipelago known as the Rocas Atoll, is part of a range of submerged mountains. In 1988, most of it was declared a maritime national park. Because of its unique flora, fauna, and geology, UNESCO declared it a World Heritage Site in 2001.

Buford and Jerry found this Brazilian tourist resort to be expensive and rudimentary, with no working phones.

Finally, the Iles du Salut (Salvation Islands) are a small group of islands off the coast of French Guiana, with the most famous being Ile du Diable, better known as Devil's Island. The penitentiary that opened in 1852 became one of the most infamous prisons in history; it was featured in the novel *Papillon* by Henri Charrier. Today the islands are a popular tourist destination, as Buford and Jerry found when they set out for an island tour.

February 15, 1996. A cruise ship had come in, and the place was crawling with tourists. A terrible day for our island tour. We made the beaches on the windward side. They are quite spectacular, but all were covered with people. We were in a four-wheel drive and open. The roads are dirt, and we were covered with dust. Not a pleasant day.

Devil's Island, French Guiana

Sailing across the Atlantic Ocean was slow, with little wind. It tended to be boring, with no sightings of any kind—boat, ship, fish, or bird.

February 5, 1996. Finally saw something tonight! We had four birds spend the night on the davits. They came in at dusk and stayed until dawn.

They would go days without touching the sails. The weather was gorgeous, with a beautiful, cloudless blue sky, a calm blue sea, and a nearly full moon. As they approached the equator, the temperature became noticeably hotter; the water warmed to above eighty-two degrees.

In contrast, the last leg from the Isles du Salut to Tobago was bumpy. The seas were confused and rough, making for an uncomfortable ride. It was hard for Jerry to cook and hang on at the same time. The weather was overcast, with rains that progressed from light to heavy. With all the leaks, keeping the boat dry was a real chore.

Wearing Down

As *Beachouse* crossed the Atlantic Ocean, it was fraught with mechanical problems that Buford and Jerry consistently attributed to faulty workmanship performed in South Africa. As they made their way from Cape Town to St. Helena, they found a dagger board leaking in one ama, keeping the dressing-area floor wet. The engine was still heating up, and the electrical power was not working properly, resulting in a low power supply. The generator, which they affectionately called "the Blue Monster," wouldn't start, requiring them to motor all night and hand-steer.

January 2, 1996. After all we paid to fix the boat—we're worse off than before.

January 7, 1996. We are still having all kinds of problems. The trip from hell!

All of the problems were beginning to take a toll on Buford. The effects of the year of repairs in South Africa were becoming apparent. Before the boat drop, he had been a strong decision maker, eager to solve a problem by studying the situation, taking a few minutes to weigh the alternatives, and then making a decision. Now he was slow to respond and tentative in deriving a solution.

Boat maintenance was wearing him down. The autopilot was not functioning, so steering had to be done by hand. Buford wanted to continue hand steering for the rest of the Atlantic crossing, but the idea was quickly overruled by Jerry, Cindy, and Roger. Once in St. Helena, by sheer coincidence, they met a fellow cruiser who was an electrician; he worked on the autopilot for several days, taking it apart and putting it back together.

Looking down on Jamestown, St. Helena

Buford placed an advertisement on the St. Helena radio station for a generator and, to his surprise, found one. With a new generator and a newly repaired autopilot, they seemed to be in good shape for the crossing to Fernando de Noronha, Brazil. However, once they were under sail, they discovered a leak in the forward shower.

January 29, 1996. The haul out was a total disaster. We are still finding things that got messed up.

Then the Blue Monster died, and they resorted to the new generator, which also quit; they named it "Horrible Hannah Honda." The depth sounder stopped operating as they were approaching the anchorage. Finally, the outboard engine wouldn't start.

February 13, 1996. BC is really discouraged. Everything we had fixed in South Africa is falling apart.

As they traveled from Fernando de Noronha to the Isles du Salut, they found a leak in the office that was causing water seepage. Paint began peeling off all over the boat.

February 25, 1996. Another South Africa screw-up. Absolutely disgusting.

Trinidad and Tobago

Once in Tobago, the South African hoses blew up, putting the propane system on the blink. Until Buford could repair it, there were no hot meals on *Beachouse*, making meal times simple.

Coral; Joe; Molly, ten; and Matt, eight, visited in March 1996. One day they all crammed into a small station wagon for a personal guided tour. The coastal bays, particularly Englishman's Bay and Portavlier Bay, were breathtaking. Then they all took a guided trek through the lush and densely wooded rainforest, followed by a climb to rocky Argyle Falls. They also celebrated Jerry's sixty-fifth birthday with a fancy lunch at the Mt. Irvine Hotel.

After spending March in Tobago, *Beachouse* sailed the sixty-six nautical miles to Trinidad, anchoring at Chaguaramas Bay—a large bay near Port-of-Spain. Being in Trinidad was like returning to the cruising social scene of the northern Caribbean. Buford and Jerry knew many of the boats, so they caught up on happenings with friends during happy hours. They listened on the radio every morning to hear the "yachtie news" from around the Caribbean.

Buford immediately started making boat repairs. He formulated a plan to haul the boat out in Trinidad in September. In the meantime, they would remain in Trinidad for a month, sail to Venezuela, move on to Bonaire, and return to Trinidad for the haul out. Once *Beachouse* was refurbished, he would have the option of putting her up for sale.

Now that they had a plan, Buford and Jerry were anxious to move on.

April 24, 1996. This place could depress a hyena if the work is not going well. I hope to get into town someday.

They had been anchored in Trinidad for three weeks before they ventured into town. They found Port-of-Spain full of old buildings and discovered a movie theater. A double feature, including two movies, popcorn, and Cokes, cost $2.00. Also, Jerry was again able to buy, rent, or watch on local television as many movies as she wanted!

Circumnavigation Completed

After a month in Trinidad, *Beachouse* arrived at the marina in Cumana, Venezuela, on May 13, 1996, officially completing her circumnavigation. Buford wrote in his Navigator's Log Book:

We left Cumana August 16, 1990 to start our circumnavigation.

Returned to Cumana May 13, 1996.

Sailed 30,446 Nautical Miles, an average of 14.5 nm/day

5 years 9 months, 2,092 days

The next day, Buford and Jerry celebrated an accomplishment that was equal to the world journey they'd taken together—their forty-seventh wedding anniversary.

Another Haul Out

The manager of the Cumana marina, Henry, and his wife, Barbara, were still there after six years. Buford and Jerry had a great time gossiping with their old friends. The marina, however, was different. It wasn't full of cruisers ready to party as it was before.

May 13, 1996. Very few cruising boats here and no other Americans. Strange.

The Cumana boatyard also had the same managers, Mike and Mark, so Buford decided to change plans and haul out there. It made more sense; this way, they wouldn't have to return to Trinidad unless they wanted to.

May 26, 1996. I'm getting enthused. BC is still wary. But any haul out makes us nervous, especially after the drop.

They prepared for a three-week haul out. Jerry inventoried the tool room. Buford made two trips up the mast to fix the antennae so Jerry could watch television with perfect reception—except it was all in Spanish, and they couldn't understand a thing.

The weekend before the scheduled haul out, Buford and Jerry, nervous, paced around the boat, trying to be patient. Monday finally arrived.

June 3, 1996. We thought we would haul out today. Mike wasn't there all day—so nothing went on. We got very discouraged. I had forgotten how unreliable the guys can be.

June 4, 1996. The yard had screwed up and had to reweld a part, so it's tomorrow now. We may never get hauled.

June 5, 1996. We were assured we would haul today. I wandered around on my own until noon, came back to the yard, but no boat. Talked with Mike—still on for today! Electricity problems. BC was still waiting, and we are trying to stay calm! We had given up when Mike called at 4:00 PM and sent a crew down to help with the boat. It was 7:30 PM before the boat was out of the water.

The marina manager offered Buford and Jerry the use of an apartment in town while the boat was in the yard. To get to the apartment, they had to take a twenty-minute hike from the marina then climb up nine flights of stairs thanks to a faulty elevator. However, air conditioning and a long, hot shower made it worth all the trouble.

Buford and Jerry immediately set up a daily routine. Buford went to the yard every morning at 9:00 AM. Jerry walked to town later to meet him for lunch, stopping along the way to exchange movies at a video store. They spent the afternoons together, running errands in town or watching movies in the cool apartment.

Once *Beachouse* was out of the water, Buford was shocked to see a mass of barnacles on the bottom of the hulls. The bottom paint applied in South Africa was supposed to deter adherence. The estimated cost of the repairs was adjusted for the paint removal.

June 7, 1996. It looks like most of the paint will have to be scraped off. How depressing—the time and money both. What a waste. The barnacles on the bottom were incredible. We were really given a bad job by Rob.

June 10, 1996. I was sick. The rest of the day was wasted. I feel so disgusted—just wasting all this time. We need to be doing something— anything!

When the repairs were nearly completed, an official internal and external survey was conducted. Buford and Jerry moved back onto the boat, which returned to the water on July 2.

June 30, 1996. We got a clean bill of health on the boat—no major problems. Only small glitches.

July 2, 1996. A day of triumph and disaster. We got back into the water about 8:30 AM—no problems. The guys came aboard to do the deck—what a circus. The color is still wrong, and they can't get the nonskid right. They were here until 6:00 PM, and it's still not painted. BC tried to start the starboard engine, and it wouldn't turn over—another big problem. We may never get to Bonaire.

Jerry loaded the boat with provisions. Buford restrung the rigging line, and a mechanic finally fixed the engine on July 6. The next day, *Beachouse* left Venezuela for Bonaire, where she'd stay for four months.

Beloved Bonaire

When Buford and Jerry arrived in Bonaire, they finally returned to party central. Many friends they'd known in their early Caribbean travels were there, including Carol and Shel Nemeyer on the *Rainbow* and George and Laura DeSalvo on the *Oscarina*. The cruisers socialized with two happy hours and a ladies' lunch every week. Jerry held several parties on *Beachouse*, with forty to sixty people on board each time.

August 18, 1996. We had a dandy of a party! We had fifty to sixty on board. It was a lot of fun. Everybody brought food and drink. I can't begin to name them all. Carol and Shel co-hosted. Everyone seemed to have a good time.

Carol, who, before cruising, had been the head librarian at the Library of Congress in Washington, D.C., interviewed Buford and Jerry for an article about their circumnavigation. It would be printed in *Port Call*, a weekly Bonaire newspaper published by the DeSalvos. Here are some excerpts from the article, titled "Trimaran Around the World":

> *Two of the most gregarious cruisers in the Caribbean, Buf and Jerry welcome guests aboard their gracious vessel, where Jerry enjoys showing folks the "root cellar," a spacious below-deck area fitted with food lockers and freezer. When they stocked 64 watermelons in Venezuela I asked, "Why only 64?" Buf's response: "That's all they had in the Mercado."*
>
> *"We never gave anything to anybody. We always traded. That way we all maintain dignity. It's the right message for cruisers to give to the world.*
>
> *"We never gave away beer or booze on the islands. On some they make their own 'toddy' from coconut blooms. Terrible stuff, but we still didn't give them imported spirits, except once in Kanton on New Year's Eve. The chief got zonkered!"*

Were the long passages difficult? Were you ever in real trouble? *"No. No. It sounds more daunting than it is. We stand three hour watches all night, and even during the day one of us is always alert in the cockpit. We record our position once every hour so we always know where we are, should the electronics fail. We believe in safety and the log becomes a wonderful memory-prod."*

"We much preferred the remote areas to the 'civilized' ones. Sure, Singapore and other big cities were great to see, but what we'll remember forever are the secluded anchorages, the small islands with their local happiness and sadness, and, for us, the most arrestingly beautiful place of all, Fatu Hiva, an anchorage in the Marquesas. The Indian Ocean was the worst, with confused seas and volatile weather."

They agree that going around the world is not hard to do. "It's easy. You just take it a day at a time, but we have more respect for those who have circumnavigated now that we know the sheer amount of hard work involved."

They advise, "Don't sell the Caribbean short. Overall, it's just as pretty and friendly as anyplace else in the world."

Touring Washington-Slagbaai National Park, Bonaire, 1996

Buford and Jerry's scuba-diving buddies from Dallas, with whom they'd taken lessons twenty-two years earlier, were in Bonaire on a scuba trip—Jon Dee, Rolinda, Craig, and Cathy Lawrence; Dick and Judi Littleton; and Marlene Clarkson. Also, Coral; Molly, nine; and Matt, seven, visited for a month, from mid-July to mid-August.

With everyone visiting, Hurricane Caesar passed just south of Bonaire on July 25, 1996, causing winds of thirty-five knots and big swells in the marina. Coral and the kids spent the night at a hotel to avoid sea sickness.

July 25, 1996. Disaster again! We pounded the dock for hours. All the boats came into the marina—a few went behind Klein Bonaire. They had the best deal. A small boat from Curacao tied up next to us. The guy had no big fenders and no big lines. We had to help him all day. We had big fenders donated by several boats to keep us off the dock—but a cleat broke on the bow and turned our stern in, and we have a big ding on the rear of the ama. We were sick. Also bent the stantions.

More bad news followed. *Beachouse* needed a new windlass, to the tune of $3,000, in addition to the repairs from the hurricane. Jerry reverted to her "blue funk" mood. When Coral and the kids left, they had the damage from Hurricane Caesar repaired.

Taking a Big Step

The boat was in pretty good shape by early September—except for the windlass. Buford was now ready to take the next step and put *Beachouse* up for sale. Anticipating a one-year process at the minimum, he signed a contract on September 5, 1996, with InterYacht, Inc., a yacht broker based in Annapolis, Maryland.

September 5, 1996. The broker, Jill Griffin, is fairly optimistic and seems interested in trying to sell. We faxed her back a signed contract—a very big step. Can't decide if I'm glad or sorry.

Jerry typed up a description of the boat based on sales information for the *My Way*, their sister ship chartering in St. Thomas. It had been for sale for two years.

Repairs had to go on. The windlass finally arrived on September 24.

September 24, 1996. It is beautiful—quite different from the old one. Hope it will go in the old spot.

September 25, 1996. BC is still pondering his windlass work. The mechanical and hydraulic parts don't match up with the old ones.

Buford ordered a bigger hydraulic motor, which didn't arrive for two weeks.

October 6, 1996. Well—as usual—nothing is easy! The parts BC got for the windlass don't work. They will need lots of alteration and adaptation. BC was very discouraged.

Three days later, Buford flew to Curacao to have hydraulic parts made. He finally got the windlass functioning on October 9, over two months after he discovered he needed a new one. This could drive anyone crazy. No wonder he'd put *Beachouse* up for sale.

Booby Lagoon

By late October 1996, Buford and Jerry were bored and ready to leave Bonaire. However, the wind was "blowing like crazy." They finally left on November 9, to return to the Aves de Barlovento, one of their favorite places; they anchored in Booby Lagoon.

November 10, 1996. The place looks as great as ever. There are two boats here, and we counted twelve total that we can see. Lots more than before.

Buford and Jerry went snorkeling and scuba diving in the same reef as six years earlier. It was just as full of live coral and reef fish as they remembered. Buford speared a fish, which Jerry cooked for lunch.

November 14, 1996. Great to have fish again! A large barracuda bit BC's toe while he cleaned the fish.

They couldn't find a trace of the palm trees they'd planted in August 1990. And remember the fishermen who used to offer lobster? The lobster was now $5 per pound. Cheap Jerry declined.

After eight days in the Aves, Buford was getting antsy to sail. Light winds and flat seas were projected for several days, so he and Jerry took the opportunity to set sail on November 19, 1996, even though Jerry hated to leave.

A Caribbean Reunion

Beachouse arrived in Hurricane Hole, Otter Creek, St. John, in the United States Virgin Islands on November 23, 1996, after putting ninety hours of motoring on the engine—there had been no wind. Buford was glad to be anchored so he could turn off the engine and get some peace and quiet. Buford made his last entry into the Navigator's Log Book and tallied up the total mileage for *Beachouse*: 41,239 nautical miles.

The next day, Buford and Jerry learned that Terry and Laurie Tittle on the *Inshallah* were in the next bay. They'd sailed with the Tittles in Venezuela in 1989 and traveled together to Ecuador.

November 25, 1996. We launched the dinghy and were getting ready to go to the Inshallah *when Terry came around the corner in his dinghy. He did a double take. We were all really excited to see one another. We rode to town with him to pick up Laurie. She was astounded, too. We all talked a mile a minute.*

The Tittles were now living permanently on their boat in St. John, where Laurie worked at a local hospital. Jerry had Terry and Laurie to *Beachouse* for Thanksgiving dinner.

November 28, 1996. We yakked all day and ate and drank. Dinner was delicious. Turkey, dressing, strawberry salad, pumpkin pie, mashed potatoes, and carrots. Typical Thanksgiving. We talked about everything. They left at 7:00 PM—and the TV wouldn't work—oh my God!

Buford fiddled with the television early the next morning and got it going—again. After lunch, Jerry turned it on to see what was playing.

November 29, 1996. Surprise! It was the Texas vs. Texas A&M game. I got BC up from his nap. He was thrilled.

The next day, Buford saw the Florida vs. Florida State game. He was in heaven, watching live college football after so many years.

December 7, 1996. Texas and Nebraska played on the TV. Texas won. Two more college games followed. We watched until our eyeballs and the batteries both gave out.

Beachouse had a fire on board—a boat owner's worst nightmare.

December 2, 1996. Real excitement this morning. BC started the fridge, and after five minutes or so, the alarm went off. Opened the engine room hatch, and there was a fire! BC put it out with the fire extinguisher. A first for us! A relay switch to the hydraulic pump was the culprit. BC worked all day getting the damage contained. Some burned wires and the pump were about all the damage. Very scary.

Waiting for News

Cindy and Roger arrived for a visit in mid-December and stayed until just after New Year's Day. As soon as they left, life returned to a boring routine. Jerry tried to keep busy and prod Buford into action.

January 3, 1997. I piddled around most of the morning. BC changed a light switch—ten minutes of work.

January 4, 1997. We were on the boat all day doing small odd jobs. It drives me crazy to sit and do nothing, but BC seems to be content with it. It's hard to get him to do the boring stuff.

This went on day after day while they waited for news from the boat broker.

January 11, 1997. Today was a total nonday. I did the rest of the laundry. We didn't get any faxes or messages from anybody. Sure wish someone would come up with a proposition for the boat. I think BC is ready to give it away.

Selling the House

December 1996–March 1997

Letter 32

Yachthaven Marina, Charlotte Amalie
St. Thomas, U.S.V.I.
March 1997

This is a difficult letter to write. We have sold Beachouse *and will be living ashore for the first time in twelve years. We have very mixed emotions. Partly relieved of the burden of yacht ownership and maintenance and partly regret at leaving the life we have loved so much. If we include the dreaming, planning, building, and cruising,* Beachouse *has been the center of our lives for almost twenty years. Mostly we hate leaving the friends we have made all over the world, both in the cruising community and in the countries we have visited. We have saved a lot of addresses, so don't be surprised if you get a phone call from us as we "cruise" by on land or air. We still have itchy feet and don't plan to settle down. We don't have a home to return to, so we aren't obligated to any particular plan or place. We will go to Galveston, Texas, first and have a nice long visit with Coral, our daughter, and her family. The only thing we own in the States is a car. Cindy (the other kid) and her husband, Roger, have moved to London, and we bought their car unseen. Sure hope it isn't bright red. They will be there for several years, and, with any luck, they'll have a house large enough for in-law visits. It will make a great base for touring the British Isles and the continent. We still hope to cruise the Turkish coast—in someone else's boat— and maybe the Greek Isles, too. Buf's idea of heaven is sitting in the cockpit telling the captain which anchorage looks good for the night, what he wants for dinner, and "I'll have a beer now." Also, we deliberately skipped Australia on our way around, thinking we could always fly there. Still a possibility. None of this mentions the U.S.A. at all. Lots of places to drive there, visit friends, and see the parts of the country that we have only passed over by air. Anyway, we don't plan to plop in front of the TV and vegetate. Buf hasn't been in the States for* almost eight years, and he'll probably see quite a difference. The fearless captain is already dreading the freeways.

Separating the "good" T-shirts and shorts from the ones covered with varnish stains, rust marks, and ground-in dirt of mysterious origin has been a chore. It has forced us to make some final decisions. Buf pitched a three-piece blue pin-striped suit that has been with us since we sailed away, unworn, of course. But it was there in case we had been invited by the king of some far-away country to a royal reception. It never happened. The problem will be to find a wardrobe suitable to get us as far as the Goodwill at home. Shoes are a particularly absent item. I always hated to wear them as a kid growing up, as an adult, suburban wife, and mother, and as a yachtie I could indulge my idiosyncrasy. As a little gray-haired old lady, I'm not sure how it will go over.

The number and variety of "souvenirs" boggles the mind. We have some lovely sculptures, various wood objects, woven pieces of both fabric and straw, and some things of unknown origin and material that even we don't know where they came from or why they seemed important at the time. Heaven only knows where we'll put all this stuff. The biggest single category of item to ship home is books. They weigh a ton and are all indispensable, to me at least. Buf rolls his eyes and tightens his lips but doesn't complain. You'll notice shells have not been mentioned at all, another ton!

The new owners are a family from Oregon. They are novice sailors and will have a captain for a while. It seems like a bit of déjà vu. Buf and I were nonsailors when we started out from Texas, and we made it. I'm sure they will, too. Sometimes, approaching a project with no preconceived notions makes it easier to conquer. Assuming you don't kill yourself or sink the boat. But, hey, you got to take a few chances in life! Anyway, we wish them well and hope they enjoy the old girl as much as we have.

Please forgive the unforgivable form letter, but we wanted to get the news out and about as quickly as possible. Rumors are already flying around, and we want to set the record straight. The Borger address will still be in effect until we make other arrangements. God knows what they will be. We promise we will keep in touch. Until we meet again. We hold you in our thoughts and always in our hearts.

*****

Preparations

Beachouse sold quickly. At 8:00 AM on January 18, 1997, the boat broker called by radio to warn them that a prospective buyer would be coming to see the boat that afternoon. Buford and Jerry leapt into action, getting the boat as neat as it could be. Bud and Sharon Smith from Oregon, with their ten-year-old daughter, Tiffany, arrived at 4:00 PM. Buford and Jerry went into their charming mode, guiding them through every nook and cranny of *Beachouse*. Bud, at age forty-nine, was a lawyer, and Sharon, age forty, was a grammar school teacher.

Having seen the sister boat, the *My Way*, in Florida, the Smiths had ordered a catamaran built, but they backed out because of construction problems. They wanted a multihull boat, as they were planning to share it with a second family.

The Smiths stayed on *Beachouse* for three nights. Buford explained all the mechanics to Bud.

January 20, 1997. We went for a sail at 9:30 AM. The wind turned out to be twenty-five to thirty knots—more than we had bargained for. The trip was short. They are real novices.

January 21, 1997. BC and Bud had a long talk this AM. They definitely want the boat—but will make an offer through the brokers. His and ours. Also, he must arrange for the financing—and insurance.

Jerry realized they were serious buyers when Sharon started measuring for carpets and pictures.

Buford and Jerry continued to repair small parts on the boat, such as a bilge pump in a shower, the water transfer pump from the rain catch tank, and a broken spring in the stove, which required them to tear the stove apart.

January 26, 1997. The boat is in good shape except for BC working on the antennae and radio—too windy to go up the mast.

The next day they made a new discovery.

January 26, 1997. We rushed back home to check on a large oil leak we saw as we left this AM. *Sure enough—the new windlass case cracked. We went back in and ordered a new one to be sent ASAP. We are immobile now.*

Buford signed a preliminary agreement for Bud on January 28. Soon afterward, Buford received a fax from the owner of the *My Way.*

January 27, 1997. He is pissed at our selling price. It upset me—but BC laughed and laughed.

Back to work the next day, Buford changed out an alternator in the engine room and then rewired a malfunctioning part.

January 28, 1997. Bud called in the middle of the job, told BC not to work too hard, it won't be our boat much longer.

Both parties signed an earnest money contract, and earnest money changed hands on January 30. The boat survey performed in Venezuela was determined sufficient for the sale.

Jerry took the ferry to St. Thomas to pick up the part for the windlass. She was excited, nervous, and going without sleep—big surprise.

February 2, 1997. We are torn between euphoria and fear. Afraid to believe the boat is really sold and afraid something is going to break.

Terry Tittle on the *Inshallah* expressed an interest in taking some of Buford's nautical charts. He and Jerry culled through the massive pile, separating the keepers from the giveaways.

On February 6, with no signed contract or money, Buford took a leap of faith and moved *Beachouse* to Yacht Haven Marina, the premier facility for large yachts in the Caribbean, located next to the Charlotte Amalie Harbor in St. Thomas. Here the boat would exchange owners. *Beachouse* was about as trouble-free as they could get her.

Waiting for a new owner at Charlotte Amalie, St. Thomas, U.S.V.I., February 1997

Boat School

A week later, Buford and Jerry received a box from Bud.

February 13, 1997. It was a bunch of smoked salmon! We would a lot rather have had a contract!

When Buford called to thank him, he learned that Bud had already shipped a container of belongings to St. Thomas, which would arrive in five days.

February 16, 1997. Still doesn't quite seem real. Be glad when the process is over.

While they were in the Yacht Haven Marina, a Royal South African boat anchored next to *Beachouse*. One of the crew was Tjarda, the girl from the NSRI in Hout Bay, South Africa, who'd helped Buford and Jerry take the boat to Cape Town following their rescue. She enjoyed visiting *Beachouse*; she was unhappy with her current job and anxious to return home.

The Smiths and their entourage arrived in St. Thomas on February 19.

February 19, 1997. They all trooped over to see the boat in the late afternoon—Bud, wife Sharon, mother-in-law Carmen, and ten-year-old Tiffany. Plus the other family—Jeff, his wife, Jerry, thirteen-year-old Jeremy, and ten-year-old Jamie. All very nice and very excited. It's going to be a huge crowd on board. Plus they have guests coming—chaos!

Bud and Jeff arrived on the boat for five straight mornings to attend Buford's "boat school." Bud took notes as Buford explained all the mechanics in detail. Bud had hired a captain to assist him part-time until he and Jeff felt comfortable. Sharon and her mother Carmen continued measuring for curtains and pictures.

Jerry tried to stay relaxed, but having nothing to do made her frustrated and bored.

February 25, 1997. Another long, miserable day of waiting. We are all getting a little nervous. Nothing to do but sit and brood. We don't know what we'll do if this all falls through.

Though no sale had been finalized and Buford had received no money, Bud kept assuring Buford that the sale was going to be completed by February 28. Wanting to believe it, Buford and Jerry sorted and boxed belongings to ship to the United States. On February 27, Bud caught the 6:30 PM plane to Florida to finalize his financing.

February 27, 1997. He assured us he would do it tomorrow or die in the attempt. We went to bed still not sure.

Beachouse Sold

Unbelievably, Buford made repairs on his last day as a boat owner.

February 28, 1997. BC worked on our head all day. We couldn't believe the thing completely broke down on the last day. It took him from 8:30 AM to 6:30 PM to get it fixed. An hour for lunch.

Jerry's job was packing, while Sharon's job was running between the marina office and *Beachouse* with papers for Buford to sign. By 4:30 PM, the bill of sale was complete, and money was in Buford and Jerry's bank in the United States. Bud had missed his flight from Florida, so there was no big celebration; this relieved the exhausted Buford and Jerry. After enjoying a bottle of champagne, they went to bed at 9:00 PM.

Jerry didn't sleep at all. The boat kept moving around, and her nest was completely torn up. Buford had no problem. The next morning, they began packing, filling up a dozen boxes and four bags to carry on the plane. The amount of stuff they'd collected over twelve years from around the world was incredible. At the same time, Sharon and the Smith crowd began to move onto the boat.

March 1, 1997. We couldn't believe it. It was an absolute circus.

With Bud still in Florida, Buford and Jeff moved all twelve boxes to a hotel room—on the ground floor—by 3:00 PM. Jerry paid the marina bill and transferred the utilities to the Smiths.

From their hotel room, Buford and Jerry called Cindy in London. She was horrified to learn that her shell-inlaid paddle from the Solomon Islands had been left on board. Jerry quickly ran to the boat to retrieve it, but she had no idea how to get it to her in London. Buford began thinking of other items he'd forgotten.

March 1, 1997. Buford remembered he had left his shoes in their drawer in the steps. When we went to help Jeff start the engine for refrigeration, I was going to get them. They had already thrown them in the dumpster. We had to go diving and find them. Just as we went to bed, we remembered we left the briefcase with our passports—hope they haven't thrown it away! We were too tired and numbed to enjoy the finality of the day. It will hit us tomorrow.

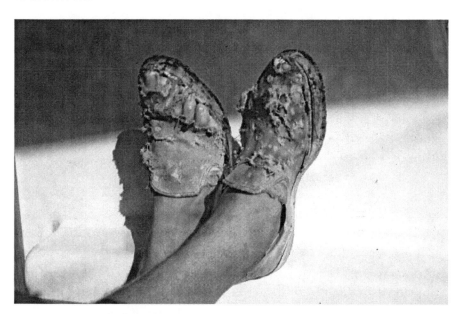

Buford's engine-room shoes—two pairs in twelve years

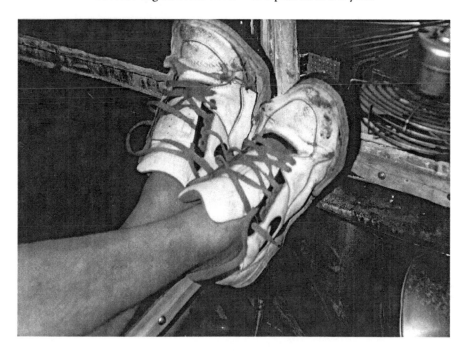

Off the Boat

Buford went to the boat first thing in the morning to retrieve the passports and help Bud maneuver to the dock for fuel. Jerry, too nervous to watch, arrived later. Buford had banged the rear of the boat as he got it out of the docking space. Oops.

They both left the boat depressed.

March 2, 1997. Our first day off the boat was a mixed bag. We didn't sleep well at all. They have piled crap everywhere, and their container isn't even here yet.

Buford and Jerry had to ship their twelve boxes of junk to Texas. After loading them into a taxi van in the rain, they stopped first at a company that wrapped the boxes in plastic then weighed and measured them. Their next stop was the shipping company, which would get the boxes to Texas by boat and van.

March 3, 1997. It was a pain to do it ourselves—but we saved over $1,000! Amazing.

The following day, Bud was still putting his belongings on the boat.

March 4, 1997. It's going to sink. I can't imagine how they are going to get all their junk on the boat. They brought three dinghies, plus we had one good and one lousy. Five dinghies, astounding! Not my problem.

The Last Happy Hour

Buford and Jerry spent a day on St. John visiting Terry and Laurie Tittle on the *Inshallah* for the last time. They drove to the Tittles' land in the mountains, where the Tittles planned to build a house someday.

March 5, 1997. It's hard to say good-bye—the day was a little strained.

Bud invited Buford and Jerry to happy hour on *Beachouse* for the last time.

March 6, 1997. The new carpet looks really good—but is very light. All my pictures are gone and new ones in. Bud's two sons were here, plus two friends—twelve on board. A madhouse. We probably won't see them again.

Before leaving for Texas, Buford and Jerry took the ferry to Road Town, Tortola, to visit their good friends Duncan and Annie Muirhead, the owners of the large trimarans the *Cuan Law*, docked in Tortola, and the *Lammer Law*, in the Galapagos. Buford and Jerry met the *Cuan Law* crew, and Buford couldn't resist poking around in the engine room.

Buford and Jerry's last day in the Virgin Islands was March 10, 1997. After having lunch with the Muirheads, they caught the 3:30 PM ferry back to Charlotte Amalie, St. Thomas, passing *Beachouse* on the way.

March 10, 1997. Kinda sad. We watched her motoring by—into the wind and pitching. Very sad and happy, too.

Epilogue

Letter 33

Galveston, Texas
April 9, 1997

GUYS!

This is just a short note to pass along our new mailing address in case any of you turkeys decide to write. I have included it below.

Our reintroduction into real life was traumatic. We flew into Houston, picked up our sight-unseen automobile, drove one mile down the freeway, and had a tire blow out in the middle of a heavy rainstorm. Welcome home! Buf was immediately convinced we had made a major error in judgment.

After creeping down the highway, being passed by everything except bicycles and pedestrians, we had a great family reunion in Galveston. The kids, Molly, age ten, and Matthew, age eight, are such fun, and we caught up on all the news with Coral and Joe.

We've spent the last month trying to get organized—talk about Mission Impossible. The shippers lost two of our boxes, and we are fighting with them—we're trying to get the address changed to all our business accounts, and we're shopping to upgrade our wardrobes to fit into polite society. BC has bought two pairs of new shoes but hasn't screwed up the courage to wear them yet. My shoe size has expanded, along with my girth, and I find it is almost off the charts. Suppose I could start a new craze? Barefoot grandmas in the park.

We have rented a storeroom for our "stuff." It will probably stay there and mold for years. We plan on living out of the car and Motel 6 for a while. Meantime, we are slowly adapting to life ashore. It's quite an adjustment. We still slip up. The other day I turned the sink faucet off so the "pump" wouldn't interfere with Buf's phone call. No longer a necessary procedure.

Sent with affection and the anticipation of your news,
Buford and Jerry Beach

*****

Letter 34

We are on South Padre Island, Texas, still homeless and with no worldly goods except the T-shirts and junk we brought off the boat. We have a townhouse in the works. It was supposed to be finished in December. With any luck, the pilings will finally be set on December 3. Meanwhile, we are hanging out in rented houses. The postcard shows the island, and "X" marks the spot where we will be. I hate to admit that we can remember when there was no bridge to the mainland and not a single structure. It is only seventy-five miles from our old hometown.

We drove eleven thousand miles this summer from June 1 to mid-September. The western states were gorgeous, and we visited eight national parks. We stopped at the Oregon, Washington, and California borders, as we hope to make that a separate trip someday. We found Idaho an unsung treasure. It is beautiful and unspoiled compared to some of the more well-known places. We were amazed at the foreign tourism. In some of the parks, they were 50 percent or more of the visitors. Must be great for the economy and brought home to us again how small the world is becoming. We kept on the move and never spent more than two nights in the same motel. We ate so much fast food, even our hair got greasy. BC certainly has honed his driving skills—but the traffic is still frightening. I'm afraid we are the proverbial little old gray-haired couple driving under the speed limit and getting the finger from the passing cars.

Life is so laid-back on S.P.I. that it can be almost comatose. Trying to fill up our days while waiting out the construction is a challenge. I'm taking an aerobics class, and BC walks the beach. I find some of my little old lady aerobic companions very intimidating. They bend and stretch into pretzels. I've never been able to touch my toes. I claim it's because my legs are so long.

BC has unkindly pointed out that my arms are long, too. However, it does give me a goal in life. Everyone needs a challenge.

We really miss the cruising life. Our advice: If you are on a boat, stay there. If you're not, buy one quick. We know that physically it was time to move back ashore, but that hasn't made it easier. We're close to water here, and that helps some. I find myself in the grocery store every day. When we were in Kanton in the South Pacific, we went four and a half months buying nothing. Incredible! Of course, it's nice to have lettuce and store-bought bread. I still find the range and variety of available products mind-boggling.

Buf has been in touch with the new owner of Beachouse and was relieved to hear she is performing well for the new family owners. They are still in the Caribbean but contemplating the Pacific. We still feel an attachment and a responsibility for Beachouse. We had some wonderful times on her.

One of the fun things about S.P.I. is the proximity to Mexico. We can go across for a margarita and fajita fix at the drop of a sombrero. The quality of the crap in the shops has been upgraded from the black velvet paintings of my youth, although it is still possible to acquire a portrait of Elvis. Actually, some of the clay pots, pewter objects, and wrought-iron pieces are quite attractive. We are going on a "Senior Special" bus to Tampico, Mexico, on December 8. We lived there as newlyweds in 1949 and are looking forward to seeing if we recognize anything or anybody. And please—no jokes about who is crying in the bathroom this time around.

We were fortunate enough to never have had an illness while we were cruising, and our luck is still holding—thank God. However, we have entered the medical system for tests and regular checkups. It is mind-boggling. We are lucky to have both Medicare and insurance, but the paperwork they generate is beyond belief. I get mail every day saying "This is Not a Bill." I guess I'll have to wait until I get a dunning letter from a credit agency before I'll be able to figure out which ones "Are a Bill."

Quick family report: daughter Cindy and husband Roger are now living in downtown London. We plan to visit next fall. Daughter Coral; husband Joe; Molly, eleven; and Matt, eight, are in Galveston, Texas, and we are happy to be able to visit regularly. The kids are a fun age. It is that nice time between babyhood and the terrible teens!

I promise this is the last address change you will get from us until we move into the home. We hope to be computerized soon and have an email address, but first we have to have a permanent telephone. Meantime, letters will have to do. I hate to write, but I love to receive, and we don't want to lose touch. If you ever get to South Texas, please come and stay with us. We are at the end of the line here, but we'll try to make it worth your trip.

We send love and kisses,

*****

Letter 35

South Padre Island, Texas
August 21, 1998

Hey guys, (Shel and Carol Nemeyer, S/V Rainbow*)*

I can't believe I just spent an hour writing you the most interesting, witty, and informative letter and then erased the sumbitch while trying to correct the damned errors. I should have printed it, misspellings and all. What a drag, but here goes again. It's hard to stay adorable for long periods of time.

First, I wanted to explain to you that the only time I am called Mary is when I am dealing with Medicare, Social Security, assorted bureaucrats, and insurance people. Even my mother never called me Mary. I always ask people if I seem like a Mary to them, and I have never received an affirmative answer. Should that tell me something?

Then, I want to ask if you can obtain a copy of the SSCA bulletin that had us as Commodores of the Month. Our one claim to fame got lost in the move from St. Thomas. I don't know what it is about seeing your name in print that turns you into mush. I wonder if Prez Clinton is feeling that way about now? And doesn't all that make you proud?

Also, I have to comment on the dinner with George and Laura (DeSalvo). Please give them our best wishes, but I couldn't help but wonder if a bird pooped in the hors d'oeuvres this time. One of my favorite memories. Remember that night in Charlotte's Armpit? There is a valuable lesson there. No matter how suave and sophisticated we think we are—Shit Happens.

We are headed for Europe on September 11. We will be headquartered there for about three months while doing the Eurorail on the continent. Then Buf lost his head and bought a round-the-world ticket, and we will come home via Singapore, Hong Kong, Australia, and New Zealand. We have talked to Linda and Dave (the Rebecca) and will be spending time with them. Also Terence (the Kadenza) in Hong Kong. We are all excited. We will be sending you postcards and hope you will keep in touch. Cindy's address is downstairs, and I will write it on the bottom of this letter.

Well, my dears, the other letter was longer and more clever, but the cocktail hour is calling and first things first. I hope to conquer this unholy beast when I get back home next year. Meantime, I hate technology, and Bill Gates should take a flying leap.

*****

Setting Up House Again

Buford and Jerry chose South Padre Island (S.P.I.), where they still owned land, to establish their new home. The island, at the southern tip of Texas, is located in the Rio Grande Valley, where they grew up, met, and were married. S.P.I. fulfilled all four of their criteria for a new home: (1) by the water, (2) a warm climate, (3) a casual, laid-back atmosphere, and (4) near people they knew. In other words, living there would be as close to living the *Beachouse* lifestyle as possible.

Building a townhouse proved to be just as frustrating as building a yacht. Buford was cool and calm, while Jerry was a sleep-deprived, emotional wreck.

February 14, 1998. I hardly slept at all last night. I'm beginning to hate that house. Nothing seems to be turning out like I envisioned.

February 15, 1998. I am an emotional mess. I hate the house, the tile, and everything else connected to the house. Hope I get over it.

March 16, 1998. I'm depressed and wish we'd never gotten into this.

All of this sounds familiar.

Buford and Jerry moved into the townhouse on May 13, 1998—five months after the original completion date—and began setting up house all over again. The next day was their forty-ninth wedding anniversary.

Daily life took on a quiet routine. Jerry kept busy by organizing and scheduling social activities on land instead of on boat. Buford was happy not having to fix broken boat parts every day. His daily work consisted of watering plants in the outdoor rock garden. Inside, he watched his beloved Western movies and any football game that happened to be on television. Happy hour was still a daily activity at 5:30 PM, with the two-drink limit still in place.

It took only four months for Buford and Jerry to establish themselves within the social scene on S.P.I. They joined a senior citizens' club.

September 25, 1998. When we walked in, we were taken aback by all the old farts. Unfortunately, we fit right in.

Soon Jerry was having a weekly lunch with the club women—much like the weekly Bonaire lady cruisers lunch. They were now part of a large circle of friends, just as they'd been during the years on *Beachouse*.

Still Traveling

Even though Buford and Jerry were glad to be off *Beachouse*, they were still eager to travel. This time Jerry planned the itineraries. During their road trip through the western United States in the summer of 1997 and the around-the-world trip by air in the fall of 1998, she scheduled visits with former fellow cruisers who'd also moved back on land.

In Prescott, Arizona, Buford and Jerry visited George and Angie Perkins from the yacht *Honeybucket,* whom they'd met in Cumana, Venezuela, in 1987. They relived the cruising life by watching George's videotapes from their time in the Caribbean.

In Tempe, Arizona, they visited Ralph and Ann Hines from the S/V *Pulsar*, a fifty-feet catamaran, whom they'd originally met in Grenada, West Indies, in 1986. In Auckland, New Zealand, Buford and Jerry visited Dave Eliason and Linda Ward from the S/V *Rebecca*, whom they'd met in the Caribbean, sailed with in the Pacific, and lived with on Kanton Island. Dave and Linda had settled in New Zealand after selling their boat.

Every few weeks Jerry called Terry and Laurie Tittle of the S/V *Inshallah,* who still hadn't built on their land in St. John, U.S.V.I. Letters and emails arrived from the yachts *Fiddler, Rainbow, Weluvit, Savant, HoneyII, Nightwatch, Pacific Jade, Lebenho, Savanika, Raffles,* and *Avanziamo*, as well as from Barbara, the wife of the boatyard owner in Cumana, Venezuela.

Bud Smith, the new owner of *Beachouse,* called Buford from the Roques Islands, Venezuela, to report that all was well and that they were thrilled with the boat.

October 13, 1997. He said many, many people have asked about us.

Buford's Ailments

Buford and Jerry completed their around-the-world adventure on February 22, 1999, by flying from New Zealand to Los Angeles. During an overnight layover, Buford suffered deep vein thrombosis (DVT), sometimes called "economy class syndrome," which is caused by being immobilized in airline seats for long flights.

A blood clot in his leg broke off and traveled through his bloodstream to his brain, causing a small stroke.

February 22, 1999. BC lost balance and began to slur. We went to a clinic and on to a hospital. BC has had a mini-stroke.

The result was slight paralysis of Buford's right side, especially his face and neck, and unclear speech. He steadily improved over the next six months, with Jerry as his motivator. By late August 1999, Buford was somewhat self-sufficient but still unsteady on his feet.

Buford's neurologist released him for good at the end of January 2001. Jerry tried to fill the days with anything that would interest Buford.

March 31, 2001. Actually, we lead a very dull life. On the boat we used to say boring was good. I'm not so sure now. It is possible to overdo it.

Jerry's Ailments

For the next year, Jerry experienced pain off and on in her hip and back. She began to tire more easily. After learning that she had a malignant tumor, she completed ten weeks of radiation in June 2002.

August 14, 2002. I told the doctor I'm going to London (to visit Cindy) in October come hell or high water.

And she did.

Through it all, Jerry kept in communication with friends from their *Beachouse* cruising days.

March 12, 2003. We got an email from Terence in Hong Kong. He says there are now four hundred (!) people on Kanton. China has leased it from the Kiribati government. They have a tracking station. He is thinking of setting up a fishing operation.

Doctors found cancer cells in Jerry's bones, spine, and vital organs in May 2003. Jerry spent the summer undergoing radiation treatments at M.D. Anderson Cancer Center in Houston, Texas. Whenever Jerry was depressed, she thought of her favorite lagoon in the Aves to get her through.

She returned home to South Padre Island on August 15, 2003. Coral arrived on September 1 for Labor Day weekend. Realizing that time was precious, she and Jerry cataloged the many artifacts the Beaches had collected from faraway places while cruising on *Beachouse*; Jerry was the only person who knew the origin of each item.

A New Chapter

Jerry made her final journal entry on September 1, 2003. She died at M.D. Anderson Hospital on Thursday, September 4, 2003, at seventy-two years old. A half-page article about her and Buford's twelve years of sailing, entitled "Cruising 'round the World," appeared in *The Valley Morning Star*, along with two large color pictures of *Beachouse*.

Instead of a funeral, a happy hour was held for friends and family at exactly 5:00 PM, overlooking the Gulf of Mexico—this time with a two-drink minimum.

Buford took his own life three weeks later on September 26, 2003, at the age of seventy-nine. He'd accomplished everything he'd wanted to in life and was lost without Jerry, his wife and companion of fifty-four years.

Messages arrived from all over the world, some of which are included in Appendix E, "Reflections from Fellow Cruisers."

Their ashes were spread together at one of their favorite dive sites off the island of Bonaire, Netherlands Antilles, an island that *Beachouse* visited many times.

To some people, their deaths seemed like an ending to a beautiful love story. Others believed it began a new chapter in Buford and Jerry's travels together.

> "Aren't you happy they are together again? They probably have a nice, big, beautiful boat and are so happy together sailing the wide blue heavens."

Mir and Jerry Sweeney

Appendices

Appendix A

Beachouse Layout

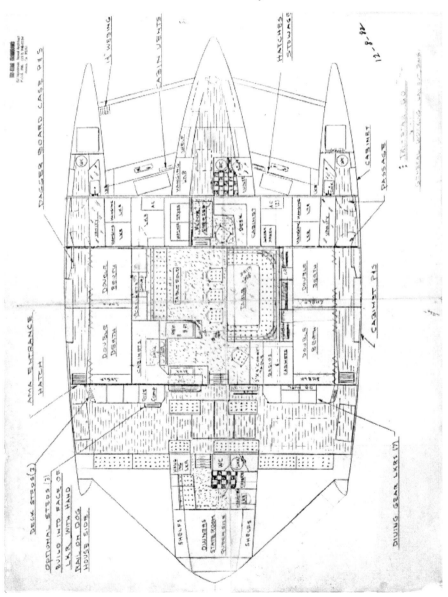

Appendix B

Buford's Equipment List

Our equipment list is long and expensive. We could probably live without a few of these items, but all together they make life a lot more comfortable and safe.

1. Our fuel tanks are built into the boat and carry 650 gallons roped off. We figure it is a six-month supply.

2. Our water tanks hold 650 gallons, but we only carry 200 gallons now because of the water maker.

3. The water maker is the best thing we've added since we left home, but it's very power-hungry. The best approach is to get a big one, engine-driven, to make twenty or so gallons an hour.

4. Water system. We have two complete Paragon Senior pressure systems. A flip of a switch changes one for the other. We quit having any trouble with the water systems after we got the water maker. There's no more mineral buildup.

5. We have two flow-through-type propane water heaters.

6. Refrigeration. We have sixty cubic feet of refrigeration, of which thirty feet is freezer. This is overkill and could be lots smaller, but we like it. It's another power-hungry item, and we run the engine an hour every morning and evening as it is engine-driven. We can run the water maker simultaneously.

7. We have five forty-pound bottles of propane in a compartment in a wing vented at the bottom. Also overkill, as it is a one-year supply.

8. Propane cook stove. It has three burners plus oven and broiler. (A note from the cook: I hate this stove. Be sure you look around and get the one you really want!)

9. Microwave. Little used, but it makes a good backup.

10. Gas grill for cooking outside.

11. Solar panels. We have twelve large Arco panels made for offshore drilling platforms. You can't have too many. No room on a monohull for many of these.

12. Radios. We have VHF and VHF handheld. Also, an HF SSB that can transmit all marine and Ham bands. Most boats maintain contact with cruiser nets on marine frequencies.

13. Weather fax. We get good pictures on a cheap one, $750, which receives through our HF radio.

14. GPS. We have a Trimble Navtrac powered by ships' power and a Garmin handheld that we keep in reserve.

15. We have the two satellite navigation sets we started with. They are no longer necessary, and the system is due to be phased out.

16. Autopilots. Don't skimp on this item even if you have a self-steering system. It is very important, especially when you are sailing shorthanded.

17. Radar.

18. We have a one-hundred-gallon gasoline tank built into the wing, with access underneath for dinghies. Most boats have to carry jerry cans on deck.

19. We have a Bauer 7.2CFM air compressor on board for scuba tanks.

Appendix C

Letter 36
Buford's Words on the Cruising Life

Duke of York Islands, Near Rabaul, Papua New Guinea
April 2, 1993

Dear Joe and Jan,

We're sitting in a beautiful anchorage in a group of islands about twenty miles from Rabaul. We're waiting for our new sail to arrive from New Zealand so we can move on through the Admiralty Islands to the north coast of P.N.G. at Madang. We are in fifteen feet of white sand, surrounded by palm trees and great reefs for snorkeling and diving—also lots of canoes with little boys in them who love to come and watch the white people. We seem like Martians to them, but they love the hard candies we pass out. They call them "lollies" here. Most of them have a working knowledge of English, as their village schools teach both in English and pidgin, the local patois.

Now to answer your questions about the cruising life—including probably more than you want to know. First—"it ain't all beer and skittles" out here for two big reasons. One is that anything that is on, around, or near saltwater immediately begins to rust, rot, corrode, smell, mildew, and rapidly deteriorate. Number two is that the things that must be done for day-to-day living are much more difficult here than at home, where everything is available and convenient. I once made a new burner for our gas grill out of a tuna fish can, and it lasted a year. Jerry does the laundry in a bucket, using her foot for a plunger. You have to improvise a lot.

As to trimaran, bimaran, or unihull, it's a matter of personal preference—they can all be individually good or bad. They have very different motions. We went for a tri because of comfort and safety. We went all out for comfort, since we planned to live on the boat. You live 100 percent of the time, but you only sail a small percentage of the time.

I would not want a tri under forty-six feet, as they don't open up and all space becomes unusable below that length. It's true, a cat is cheaper for the space, but a tri has one big advantage—you can hole any one hull and continue, although deeper in the water. An outer hull can't raise the opposite hull enough to sink far.

Beachouse *is at the opposite end of the scale from most trimarans. It has large amas (outer hulls) with a lot of buoyancy. We are heavy, deep in the water (five feet), and slow for a multihull, but we go to wind with the average monohull and won't sink even if all three hulls are holed. (That's his story, and it'd better be true.)*

A lot of boats are poorly equipped for cruising fulltime. Most unhappy cruisers left home in a boat they enjoyed camping out on for weekends but aren't really set up for long-term living. Jerry asked one couple why they were quitting—the lady said she had bathed on deck for nine years and was ready to go home to a real shower. Sounds reasonable to us. A lot of boats have no refrigeration, but I say living without ice cubes and cold water "ain't really living."

As to health care, we are most fortunate in not having any chronic conditions that require care or medications. Prescription drugs are available everywhere, mostly without a doctor's slip, and at prices usually much lower than in the States. We carry many antibiotics, malaria preventives, bandages, syringes, and painkillers, plus the usual assortment of over-the-counter stuff. We are traveling with another boat that has a husband-and-wife doctor team. He is a gynecologist, and she is a trauma specialist. We expect to travel through Indonesia with them. It's surprising how many doctors are out here. Malpractice insurance has soured them on the profession—or, I should say, the practice of the profession. A lot of them work in these islands on short-term contracts while making their way around.

We feel expenses, excluding the cost of the boat, are less than we would spend ashore. Not owning cars with the insurance and upkeep is a help to the budget. Our entertainment budget is almost nil. We have a TV and VCR on board, so we entertain ourselves. We've seen most of the movies so many times that we can recite the dialogue, even though we have three hundred aboard. When we are anchored with other boats, the problem is sometimes getting a little privacy.

We don't know how long we will continue sailing, but, obviously, we'll go at least long enough to finish our circumnavigation. We are still enjoying it, and the old bodies are hanging in there.

If all of this has scared you and put you off, now for some good news. There are always other boats around, almost everyone is friendly, no matter what the nationality, and all help each other out. We make new friends easily and quickly in the cruising community, and the hard part is saying good-bye to people we know we will never see again.

Beachouse is one of the larger cruising boats around, and many people seem very happy with much less than we have. We met a Danish boat in Cumana, Venezuela, and again in Suva, Fiji. It is under twenty feet long and single-handed by a little old man who was having a great time. Don't let all the negative factors put you off. The good times make it all worth it. Either come see us or take a bareboat cruise in the Virgins to see if you really like the life. It's a big commitment. Most all the boats we know had sailed for years before jumping off the deep end. We are the exception.

We built because it is almost impossible to buy a good trimaran. I don't recommend it, but we have been very happy with our boat. It was a long, dirty, and frustrating process.

Our longest crossing was from the Galapagos to the Marquesas. This is the longest leg to be made on a circumnavigation, three thousand miles. Or, to be exact, 2,980 nautical miles. We took just under twenty-two days for an average speed of 5.7 knots. A little slow, but not bad for on and near the equator, where the winds can be very light. This was a very easy crossing, with good weather all the way. Cindy and Roger were on board, so each of us had only one watch each night. Normally, Jerry and I sail the boat alone, and in eight years I have had to get out of the cockpit only twice. Roller furling is the only way to go.

We have never been in really bad weather. We've seen winds of over fifty knots but in a squally that didn't last long. I call myself a 20-20 sailor. If you stay within twenty degrees of the equator and out of hurricane season, you will almost never be in bad storms.

With GPS, any idiot can navigate. You should learn dead-reckoning techniques. There are short courses available, and it's easy. All you need for navigation now is two GPSs, one a handheld battery-operated for backup. The sextant is now as obsolete as the butter churn, although we still have one on board.

You have to carry a lot of spare parts and do most of your own repair work. *The help that is available in most of these islands is less than expert. A number of cruisers earn their living by working on other boats. We are traveling now with a boat that has two electrical engineers on board, a husband-and-wife team.*

Hope all this information is helpful.

*****

Appendix D

The head of the family is listed in bold.

Bureniti	Police and customs chief, overall guy in charge. BC called him Benny.
Ioanna (Joanna)	Wife
Children	Taai, son, sixteen (Left in January)
	Taake, daughter, fourteen (Left in February)
	Taotai, son, five
	Tekarube, daughter, two
Eruma	Taai's friend, boy, twenty-one
Bakeua	Policeman
Veronika	Wife, schoolteacher of the small children
Children	Eritabeta (Elizabeth), daughter, ten
	Tekimari, daughter, eight
	Randy, son, five
	Lillian, daughter, two
Nakau	Postman, NOAA radio operator, and BC's fishing buddy
Tonga	Wife
Children	Ruthi, daughter, eight
	Sari, daughter, two
Tautika	Tonga's brother, seventeen
Tematang	Tonga's mother and fiancé to Ionnie
Tataaki	Mechanic, nickname Kong
Taati	Wife
Children	Ioane, son, seventeen
	Lisa and Bongiti, twin daughters, four
	Taoua, daughter, one

Betero (Peter)   Schoolteacher   (This family left in February)
Maru   Wife
Children   Beia, daughter, fifteen
   Mari, daughter, three
   Rabwena, daughter, one

Tabora   Nurse
Teakai   Wife
Children   Tiata, son, twenty
   Teweia, son, fifteen
   Bwenaua, daughter, thirty-one
   Reretau, granddaughter, thirteen
   Boata, grandson, four
Tinnau   Bwenaua's girlfriend

Karekennatu   Carpenter, nickname Tata, but BC called him
   "Big Un" because of his size.
Teveve   Wife
Children   Tewenako, daughter, seven
   Bio, son, five
   Naborau, son, three
   Ataia, son, two
Ionnie (Johnnie)   Teveve's father, fiancé to Tematang

Nateri   Schoolteacher
Rakaba   Wife

Luke   Policeman and radio operator
Tewani   Wife
Children   Iaokiri, son, twelve
   Edward, son, five
   Cecilia, daughter, three
   Peter, son, one

Appendix E

Reflections from Fellow Cruisers

There is no reason why someone sails around the world. It is done because it is natural. Just like some people go to school, get a job, buy a house, and get married, others go to sea and sail around! The world is big and round, and to many, it cannot be left alone. It has to be seen. And what better way to do this than on a big, comfortable trimaran (ignoring the storms, annoying officials, and boatyard mishaps). *Beachouse* belonged in its environment. We are happy to have been in the same harbor and that we were able to toast to the same ventures with her wonderful crew, sharing jokes and tall tales. *Beachouse*'s circumnavigation has been a benefit not only for her crew but also for all those who had the privilege of meeting them.

Your parents really knew how to live. That is what we will remember about them. We feel that the best way to honor their memory is to follow their example and try to always live life to the fullest. We still often drink a toast to Jerry and Buford and will never forget them.

Robin & Serge Testa
S/V *Encanto*
Author of *500 Days: Around the World on a Twelve Foot Yacht*

*****

We met Jerry and Buford in 1986 in Puerto La Cruz, Venezuela, and became good friends, meeting numerous times in many of the islands between Venezuela and the Virgins. Probably the last time we were together was in the Virgins when, if I remember correctly, Buford was installing new rigging prior to starting their circumnavigation. I don't know how to put their desire to sail around the world into words, except to say that we had the same desire but were thwarted in our ambition to do so. When we were together with Jerry & Buford in the Virgin Islands the last time, they asked us to join them sometime in the Pacific, and we surely had every intention at that time of doing so. Circumstances in the following years until the later 1990s made it impossible to leave for that long or go that far.

Buford and I also shared an interest in aviation, which he made a career of and I had engaged in as a pilot since 1955, owning numerous airplanes and even having a brief stint in the general aviation business. Our deepest sympathy to you and your family in your loss and the loss of two of the best friends we ever had cruising.

Art & Nicole Becker
S/V *Avanti*

*****

Buford and Jerry were wonderful, kind, and generous people. We first met them in Venezuela, probably in 1987 or 1988. We were in the Cumana Marina, and Jerry stopped by our boat to issue an invitation for cocktails and hors d'oeuvres on *Beachouse*. We were surprised at the invitation because we'd never even met your parents before. Imagine, we thought, they picked us out of all those other boats in the marina. Not until we arrived at *Beachouse* at the designated time did we realize that Jerry had invited the entire marina to their boat that evening. What a blast! They even had ice for our drinks. Now, that was a treat all by itself!

Later, we met up with them again in the South Pacific. We were on the same mooring in American Samoa. That was when I had dengue fever, and Jerry brought me some of her homemade turkey soup. After I became well and we all continued our cruising, we often found ourselves in the same anchorage with your parents. One time, when family was on board *Beachouse*, Buford was admiring the grill we had on the stern of our boat. He thought it might be an easy way to cook for everyone and said he'd been considering having one sent to him.

"Don't do that," my husband said. "Just take ours. We never use it." So Tom and Buford took it off our boat and mounted it onto *Beachouse*.

Shortly after that, Buford learned we were looking for information and charts for New Zealand. He called us on the VHF and said, "Come on over to *Beachouse*. I have something for you." He gave us his New Zealand chart book. (We still have it.)

As to why they chose to go cruising. Well, that's simple.

1) It is the ultimate opportunity to spend close time with your mate.
2) It is the only way to explore parts of the world where hordes of tourists can't get by airplane.
3) It's an opportunity to enjoy one's own company and to reflect on who you are without all the trappings of the fast-paced world around us.
4) It's a time to enjoy the simple things in life and be at peace with yourself.

LaVonne Misner & Tom Olsen
S/V *VonnieT*
Author of *No More Mondays*

*****

It's a rainy day here in sunny Florida, and what better to do than reminisce about *Beachouse* and its exceptional crew. We anchored with *Beachouse* from the Virgin Islands to the out island of Venezuela. It was always a pleasure to enter an anchorage and find *Beachouse* there. On one such occasion we arrived in the B.V.I.s to find the boat empty; what was going on? As you know, Buford and Jerry were avid divers and as such modeled their vessel after the *Lammer Law*—a humongous trimaran that accommodated perhaps twenty or more divers. It seems that Buford was offered a berth on a repositioning of the *Lammer Law* from the B.V.I.s to the west coast of South America—I think the Galapagos. In any event, Jerry and Buford had no easy way to communicate. Basically her "captain" was incognito.

But, and there is always a but, the *Lammer Law* did have a long-range SSB radio and so did the *Honey Too*. Jerry had a marine VHF, a short-range radio at *Beachouse's* shore accommodation. She gave us their SSB schedule, and we relayed "live" to and from Jerry and Buford as follows: Buford would transmit, and we put the mike of our VHF to the speaker of the SSB, which was tuned to Jerry's frequency; she could then hear her husband. When she spoke we put the mike of the SSB to the speaker of the VHF, and Buford was able to speak to his wife. Sometimes Don and I got confused with left-hand, right-hand tasks, but I think they enjoyed the contact nonetheless.

These folks were friends to everyone. On one New Year's Eve, Don was designated as the dinghy parking attendant. *Beachouse* had no less than THIRTY dinghies trailing behind; that translates to no fewer than seventy people aboard *Beachouse*. The best Seven Seas Cruising Association Party, bar none!! Amazing and marvelous.

In Los Aves, an island off of Venezuela, our vessel, the *Honey Too*, had been anchored near *Beachouse*, enjoying the daily sundowners, watermelons from the mainland, and their "video-exchanges" (we were always sure they had more videos than any other cruisers in the whole Caribbean). As we reluctantly sailed away, we were escorted by a glorious sight—four spinner dolphins! They were leaping out of the water, spinning on their tails with the water flying horizontally, as only they are famous for doing, and then just as quickly disappearing. Honey called to Jerry on the VHF, and her response was, "I have been looking for spinners through all our sailing days. I really envy you that extraordinary sight." We will never forget those dolphins and their show and our good friends.

In Cumana, Venezuela, Jerry had the toilet seats painted with first-class paint and suggested that we do the same. When we sold our boat fifteen years later, the paint still looked fresh. Thank you, Jerry. All the best and safe harbors to them both.

Don and Honey Costa
S/V *Honey Too*

*****

We were very fond of both of them, enjoyed their great spirits and joy of life. Their rescue of us in Bonaire when our boat crashed was really sweet, and, because of them, when we got off the boat in Panama, with no place to go, no house in the States, and totally "off center" so to speak, we ended up in Costa Rica and still, twelve years later, maintain a beach house there where we now live half the year.

So, it is hard to say why people end up sailing around the world. I don't think it was ever their intention. Possibly, they were just plain getting bored with the Caribbean and not yet ready to give up the cruising life. *Beachouse* was an incredibly comfortable boat; they had everything they needed and a lot of living left to do. They never seemed nervous about it, ya know like, "What in the hell are we doing?" sort of talk. I guess when it comes right down to it, the reason they sailed around the world was because they just wanted to.

I'm not sure about Buford (since he never said much!), but Jerry sure loved to have people around her. Some of the *Beachouse* parties were great. I remember one in Bonaire, a sunset party, where they invited the whole anchorage, or so it seemed. It was a great evening, lots of yummy food provided by all and a remarkable "green flash" at sunset. Those cruising memories never go away. They are present long after the ugly storms and nasty officials and dragging anchors and all the other shit that goes along with cruising fade into the murk. I think they had a boatload of great memories.

Shar Squier and Jerry O'Donahoe
S/V *Raffles*

*****

Your parents were the most wonderful people, and in all our years of chartering and sailing, we never met anyone else like them. So together and yet so different!! We remember so clearly the time they arrived here on *Beachouse* and the hours Duncan and Buford spent on the deck rearranging things so they could sail the boat without crew, whilst Jerry, Sasha, and I just enjoyed being together on board. Very special times. We have so many memories of your parents, *Beachouse*, and their trips with us that it is impossible to put it all together in time. Jerry always blamed us for her being on a boat for so many years!

Duncan, Annie, and Sasha Muirhead
S/V *Lammer Law* and S/V *Cuan Law*

*****

Jerry and Buf had always been very kind, spontaneous, and considerate friends. They were always out and about, doing amazing things. While in

Chagos, *Beachouse* was very often the relaxing gathering place for fellow yachties. I was with them in Durban after the launching accident of the boat. I learnt a great deal about life from them and consider myself very fortunate to have met them. A few years after our circumnavigations, it was so good of them to look me up in Hong Kong. They are two of those rare people that make a difference to one's life.

Terence Lam
S/V *Cadenza*

*****

It was 1986, and we entered the long, oval harbor in Guadalupe at dusk, tired after a long sail. We dropped our anchor in the only available spot, behind a very large and very wide trimaran. Name? *Beachouse.* Within minutes, we got a call on our VHF radio. A female voice said: "Come on over!" I answered, "Thanks, but our dinghy is still stored on deck, and we're too tired to launch her now." "No problem," said the voice. "We'll be over to get you in fifteen minutes."

And thus we met Buford and Jerry and began a long and deep friendship that lasted as long as they did. We oohed and aahed over their vessel. Jerry said, "Wanna see my root cellar?" I thought she was joshing until she pulled a carpet runner aside, slid the staircase into place, and I was introduced to the vast storage below deck. Amazing. Someday I'll tell you about filling in the shelves with watermelons, but that's another story.

Why they sailed around the world? King of the Mt. Everest theory—because it's there; because they were confident in their *Beachouse* and knew how to maintain it; because they sought adventure in new places with new people, and, perhaps most of all, because they believed in each other and wanted to share more and more experiences. They were such a happy and compatible couple that they drew people to them as magnets, and we all benefited.

Carol and Shel Nemeyer
S/V *Rainbow*

*****

We met Jerry and Buford in Indonesia, where they towed us into an anchorage after we had lost our propeller somewhere in the Banda Sea. Our spare prop had never been trialed, and Don spent a day underwater adjusting it bit by bit and with frequent refills of air from the compressor on your parents' boat. The story is recounted in a chapter of our book, in an incident called "A Tale of Two Props," and Buford will remember it well. We have often quoted your mother, and one quote that always appealed was, "Often wrong but never in doubt." I think we used that somewhere in the book as well.

From that time on we were frequent guests on *Beachouse* for sundowners and remained close friends in spite of taking alternate routes after Thailand. Cruising friendships are enduring. Dealing with adversity bonds people in a way that wouldn't happen in any other life. We felt very privileged to have been considered their friends.

Robyn Boase & Don Gilchrist
S/V *Stylopora* and author of *Here Be Dragons*

*****

Our very fond memories of Buf and Jerry will always stay vivid. Jerry was a gal always with a smile and ready to invite someone aboard the *Beachouse*. We all had fun in the Caribbean as well as with *Beachouse* and the *Rebecca* in the Kiribati Island of the Pacific and elsewhere. We enjoyed the two visiting us in New Zealand, once we settled on land.

I am so pleased to be able to look back on what for me was the "Best of Life"—being on the boat—meeting like-minded people. Cruising with *Beachouse* was the best of all life's rewards.

Linda Ward & David Eliason
S/V *Rebecca*

*****

While Jo and I didn't know Jerry and Buford when they were sailing, I remember Buford remarking once that designing and piloting a boat was similar to designing a plane—only one went on the water. I guess that typified their courage and love for adventure that had no bounds.

What fantastic people they were. Their friendship enriched our

European trip in 1998 so much. Wherever we stopped, it was always a race to see who would buy the wine, the cheese, and whose room we would party in. The funniest time was when Buford kicked over a bottle of red wine on the steps of the Trevi Fountain and we all scrambled to save the last drops as they trickled toward the unsuspecting public sitting in front.

We stayed with them in London before our return to Australia, and then they stayed with us on the Gold Coast on their way home to the States. We are going to dedicate a space in the front yard to our terrific friends. They loved the rainforests behind the Coast, so it will be an Australian native tree that we will plant. We still have the Bacardi and gin we bought before Jerry and Buford visited, so tonight we will drink a toast to a wonderful, wonderful couple who filled our lives with such humor and candor and love.

Carmel Ryan and Jo Acton
Gold Coast
Queensland, Australia

*****

We have many fond memories of Jerry and Buford. Their parties were legendary. But most of all they were really nice, kind, generous, "regular" people.

George and Laura DeSalvo
S/V *Oscarina* and editor of the *Bonaire News*

*****

I will always remember going to "school" every day on *Beachouse* for a couple of weeks in St. Thomas so your dad could teach me how to run the boat. He was usually good for a couple of hours, and then he would tell me that was "enough for the day" and dismiss class. I understood the mechanical stuff because I grew up in a household of mechanics, but I had never sailed a boat in my life, so I was really looking forward to that part of the lesson, where he would teach me how to sail. We spent one day on the AC electrical, one day on the DC electrical, one day on the water maker, two days on the hydraulics, one day on the engine, etc. When it came time to learn about how to sail, he just said, "Oh, hell, you're pretty smart; you'll figure all that stuff out." It took me a couple of days to figure out if he was just tired of teaching, pissed off, or if he really meant it. He really was a great man in my opinion.

Bud, Sharon, and Tiffani Smith
New owners of *Beachouse*

*****

References

Akerholm, Lars. *A Cruising Guide to Panama: Including San Blas and Pacific Islands*. Balboa, Republic of Panama: Lars Akerholm, 1996.

Hart, Jerrems C. and William T. Stone. *A Cruising Guide to the Caribbean and the Bahamas*. New York, New York: Dodd, Mead and Company, 1982.

Kopp, Heather. "Retired US couple enjoy luxury at sea." *East London Daily Dispatch* 1995: 1.

Lucas, Alan. *Cruising the Solomons*. Melbourne, Australia: Castle Books, 1981.

Nemeyer, Carol. "Trimaran Around the World." *Port Call* 3 (1996): 1, 3.

Piprell, Collin. *Sail Thailand: Exploring the Andaman Sea by Sail*. Bangkok, Thailand: Artasia Press and Company Ltd., 1991.

Salvador, Mari Lyn. *The Art of Being Kuna: Layers of meaning among the Kuna of Panama*. Los Angeles, California: University of California, Los Angeles, 1997.

Scott, Shaun. "NSRI rescue yacht caught in fierce gale." *Cape Argus Southern Edition* 1995: 3.

Smith, Bruce Lee. "Cruising 'round the World." *Valley Morning Star* 92.126 (2003): B8.

Stone, Gregory. "Phoenix Islands." *National Geographic* 205 (2004): 48–65.

Street Jr., Donald M. *Street's Cruising Guide to the Eastern Caribbean: Volume IV-Venezuela.* New York, New York: W.W. Norton and Company, 1980.

Suder, Ismail. "Crash goes a yacht—and their dream." *Durban Daily News* 1995: 8.

Sycholt, August and Peter Schirmer. *This is South Africa.* Cape Town, Royal South Africa: Struik Publishers, 1992.

Teste, Serge. *500 Days: Around the World on a Twelve Foot Yacht.* Aspley, Australia: Trident Press, 1988.

Uhlig, Mark A. "Violence Ebbs in Venezuela, but Crisis Burns On." *Multinational Monitor* 9.1 (1988): 8.

LaVergne, TN USA
09 November 2009
163547LV00004B/2/P